BEING
THE
BOSS

THE IMPORTANCE
OF LEADERSHIP
AND POWER

BEING
THE
BOSS

THE IMPORTANCE
OF LEADERSHIP
AND POWER

ABRAHAM L. GITLOW

BeardBooks

Reprinted 2004 by Beard Books, Washington, D.C.
ISBN 1-58798-234-X
Originally published by Business One Irwin

Printed in the United States of America

For Elissa
Whose Present Insights
Bode Well for
Her Future

In memory of my beloved Beatrice

FOREWORD

Here is a compilation of business policies, administrative practices, organizational behavior, and management techniques for the edification and admonition of the next generation of wiser managers and executives.

For the past several years, a select group of students has been assembled at New York University's Stern School of Business to meet with active and retired executives and exchange viewpoints, experiences, and philosophies. These mentors represented a wide spectrum of the business world and during these three-hour sessions they gave the graduate students an analysis of their successes and failures as managers of those two precious articles—talent and capital. Based on these recent seminars and on years of instructing students in the conduct of business affairs, Dr. Gitlow has distilled the essence of leadership in a rapidly changing and complex world of commerce.

A remarkable balance has been achieved in the analysis and treatment of such difficult areas as labor management relations, equal opportunity, and ethical behavior. The viewpoint and operational analysis are those of the chief executive, yet the principles and conduct are applicable to any position in which power has to be exercised with effectiveness and appropriateness. Throughout, there are real-life experiences to illustrate management problems and opportunities, not in a case-study treatment, but in an attention-arresting narrative with actual people and companies.

There is probably no single textbook or course of study that will equip either an experienced and practicing executive or a young business school graduate with the knowledge and background to meet effectively and successfully the complex array of situations and events of the current interrelated international business climate. But this work comes as close as anything to date.

William F. May

PREFACE

The heart of the book is the possession of power. Its pulse is the exercise of that power. Leaders possess power by virtue of status; the power is inherent in their positions. Leadership, however, involves the successful exercise of power. This is a significant distinction, for the possession of power does not automatically insure its successful exercise. It was this significant difference that Chester Barnard wrote about earlier in the twentieth century, when he differentiated authority of position from authority of leadership.

Power is the capacity to command, to influence the behavior of other human beings. It is also the ability to allocate nonhuman resources, to decide priorities, and to order the implementation of those priorities. Leaders initially achieve this ability by virtue of their position at the head of an organization, but they do not concurrently achieve the capacity to exercise it successfully. The exercise of power stands separate and apart, and is the essence of leadership. Indeed, the one who manifests leadership will in time become the *de facto* leader. When leadership capability is coupled with power of position, then the latter is legitimized by the former, and the exercise of power is most likely to be successful. Of course, power may be exercised successfully for ends either magnificent or mean.

The chief executive of an organization has the power of position. The successful exercise of that power over the long run, however, requires also the authority of leadership. In any case, the exercise of power is indivisible, as is the individual responsibility and accountability of the chief executive. This is not to say that a wise CEO eschews the participation and meaningful involvement of managers and other employees in organizational decisions. It is to say that participation is not permissiveness, which easily degenerates into a lack of structure and anarchy. And this is especially true in a period of change and uncertainty, when the time required to achieve consensuality is usually not available. At such times the chief executive's leadership is most truly tested, and the indivisibility of his responsibility, accountability, and exercise of power most surely evident.

Having developed the preceding points, the book goes on to explore leadership and the exercise of power in business organizations, that is, the interactions between the chief executive, the board of directors, and labor. This book goes further and explores the power implications of the CEO's interactions with power centers external to the organization, for example, government and its regulatory agencies, the media, investment analysts, and "stake-holders" (i.e., nonowner groups having a stake in the activities of the corporate entity). Finally, we seek insights into the emerging role of women as their numbers increase among chief executives, and we conclude with an exploration into the characteristics of those who succeed in the climb to the top of the organization, and whether, retrospectively, they think the climb was worth the effort.

The book benefited greatly from the comments of several readers, most notably Samuel Shapiro, past president of the American Society of Association Executives; Richard West, dean of the Leonard N. Stern School of Business, New York University; and Professors Richard J. Thain and Richard G. Newman. Such deficiencies of commission or omission as may remain are entirely the responsibility of the author. And he would be clearly derelict if he failed to express appreciation for the long-suffering patience of Beatrice, who has tolerated spells of silence and trance-like immobility while an inner spirit was forming concepts and creating the sentences with which to articulate them. That she continues to tolerate such behavior after a golden wedding anniversary is remarkable, and happy for me. Finally, I must express great appreciation for the indefatigable help of Maureen George, my secretary and able assistant.

Abraham L. Gitlow

CONTENTS

Author's Note

As this reprint edition is being published, readers might find
Chapter 3 on "Executive Power and the Board of Directors" to be
especially significant and relevant to the recent corporate
accounting scandals. It shows how a corrupt CEO can get away
with malfeasance. All that is necessary is the failure of the
regulatory structure, the board, and other gatekeepers of
shareholder interests to confront the power of greedy CEOs. When
this book was originally published in 1992, I and others thought
that such a failure was unlikely because there were so many
lawsuits and cases that should have been adequate warnings to bad
CEOs and weak, complacent boards. My optimism was a decade
too early. Hopefully, the Sarbanes-Oxley Act, the recent
prosecutions, and the attendant public outrage have gotten the
attention of greedy CEOs, CFOs, CPAs, lawyers, and others.

Abraham L. Gitlow
April 2004

CHAPTER 1

LEADERSHIP, POWER, AND ORGANIZATIONAL STRUCTURES

LEADERSHIP AND POWER[1]

Is leadership an aspect or consequence of status; is it an automatic possession of a leader in an organizational structure, whether business, political, or social? Or, is it an attribute of some people who, entirely apart from organizational position, are able to inspire, energize, and command the willing, even enthusiastic support of other human beings? Leadership is an elusive quality. When it is present, it is widely recognized. When it is absent, its absence is equally known. But one thing seems certain: leadership is the ability of one human being to stir the sentiments and influence the behavior of others. And that influence is an inherent source of power, the power to direct other people toward the achievement of a leader's goals by transmuting those goals into the aims of everyone. But the power to direct other people is also a function of status or position, for example, as in a hierarchical organization.

Decades ago, Chester I. Barnard,[2] a pioneer thinker on organizational theory and practice, explored the relationship between status and power in words reflecting profound insight. In 1938, he wrote:

> Men impute authority to communications from superior positions, provided they are reasonably consistent with advantages of scope and perspective that are credited to those positions. This authority is to a considerable extent independent of the personal ability of the incumbent of the position. It is often

---

[1]A broad review can be found in Bernard M. Bass, *Bass and Stogdill's Handbook of Leadership*, 3rd edition (New York: The Free Press, 1990), pp. 11–20.

[2]C. I. Barnard, *The Function of the Executive* (Boston: Harvard University Press, 1938), pp. 173–75.

recognized that though the incumbent may be of limited personal ability his advice may be superior solely by reason of the advantage of position. This is the authority of position.

But it is obvious that some men have superior ability. Their knowledge and understanding regardless of position command respect. Men impute authority to what they say in an organization for this reason only. This is the authority of leadership. When the authority of leadership is combined with the authority of position, men who have an established connection with an organization generally will grant authority, accepting orders far outside the zone of indifference. The confidence engendered may even make compliance an inducement in itself.

Barnard's "zone of indifference" refers to the acceptability of a superior's orders to his subordinates. Orders that are acceptable fall into the "zone of indifference"; they do not inspire any sense of antipathy or opposition in the subordinates. But there are also orders that are "neutral," as well as those that are clearly unacceptable, and that will therefore inspire opposition and disobedience. The last category is comprised of orders to which subordinates are not indifferent. Yet, when such orders are issued by one who possesses both authority of leadership and of position, they are most likely to be obeyed.

What Barnard calls the authority of leadership, as contrasted with the authority of position, was articulated further by Harry Levinson and Stuart Rosenthal in *CEO-Corporate Leadership in Action*.[3] They wrote:

> Leaders are able to use their power base and implement their strategies because they are thinkers as well as doers. When a program, product, or strategy isn't working, they don't throw up their hands—they figure out what has to be done, confident that their efforts can make the future better than the present. Leaders enjoy conceptualizing, projecting, fantasizing. Where others dread ambiguity, leaders are not afraid to take over a failing unit or company, embark on a risky longterm venture, or face a sea of conflicting pressures: they welcome the challenge. And they know full well that safe ventures quickly go stale and never lead to significant success.

Where does all this leave us? It should leave us with a recognition of the fact that leadership is a function of both position and the ability to lead. Perhaps more important, it should make us realize that position is, in and of itself, insufficient, especially as time passes. Authority of position can command, at least temporarily, the obedience and compliance of subordinates. But such support will prove transitory unless authority of position is accompanied by ability to lead, the ability to win the voluntary support of subordinates. When authority of position and authority of leadership are wedded in a leader, then compliance may not have to be imposed from above through harsh disciplinary punishment that inspires fear. Rather, compliance will arise from the self-discipline of subordinates who want to follow their leader.

IS LEADERSHIP DIVISIBLE?

Some currently popular buzzwords among organizational gurus are decentralization, horizontal structures, consensual decision making, and globalization. Ability in creating and working with such organizational structures is promoted as the touchstone of executive leadership and success in the 90s and the years beyond. Perhaps the best illustration of the point is from an article in *Fortune*:[4]

> Forget your old, tired ideas about leadership. The most successful corporation of the 1990s will be something called a learning organization, a consummately adaptive enterprise with workers freed to think for themselves, to identify problems and opportunities, and to go after them. In such an organization, the leader will ensure that everyone has the resources and power to make swift day-to-day decisions. Faced with challenges we can only guess at now, he or she will set the overall direction for the enterprise, *after listening to a thousand voices from within the company and without.* In this sense, the leader will have to be the best learner of them all. You'd better begin practicing now—only six months until the 1990s are upon us. [Italics added.]

The foregoing paragraph is remarkable, especially the italicized words about "listening to a thousand voices." One senses that the reporter's rhetoric outran reason, for it almost sounds as though this new-style leader is one who best knows how to follow a multitude. And what is the marvelous, osmosis-like process that transmutes the "thousand voices" into the leader's vision? Further, how does the multitude—the "thousand

---

[4]Brian Dumaine, "What Leaders of Tomorrow See," *Fortune*, July 3, 1989, pp. 48, 50.

voices"—recognize that the leader's vision, as announced by him, is their own?

An opposite view was expressed by Robert N. McMurry in a *Harvard Business Review* article late in 1973.[5]

> The most important and unyielding necessity of organizational life is not better communications, human relations, or employee participation, but power. I define power as the capacity to modify the conduct of other employees in a desired manner, together with the capacity to avoid having one's own behavior modified in undesired ways by other employees. Executives must have power because, unfortunately, many employees resent discipline; to these employees, work is something to be avoided. In their value systems, "happiness" is the ultimate goal. For the organization to be made productive, such persons must be subjected to discipline.
>
> Without power there can be no authority; without authority, there can be no discipline; without discipline, there can be difficulty in maintaining order, system, and productivity. An executive without power is, therefore, all too often a figurehead—or worse, headless. The higher an executive is in his management hierarchy, the greater his need for power. This is because power tends to weaken as it is disseminated downward.

McMurry's language is extreme, even rigid. He was clearly aware that this was the case, because he went on to list eight "strategies for chief executives . . . who possess little or no equity in a business . . . ,"[6] thereby assuming that substantial equity in the hands of the chief executive automatically conferred power and authority. For those lacking the power and authority of ownership, however, he proposed (1) taking "all steps he can to ensure that he is personally compatible with superiors"; (2) obtaining "an employment contract"; (3) obtaining from superiors "a clear, concise, and unambiguous statement in writing of his duties, responsibilities, reporting relationships, and scope of authority"; (4) taking "exceptional care to find subordinates who combine technical competence with reliability, dependability and loyalty"; (5) as a useful defensive device, selecting "a compliant board of directors"; (6) establishing "alliances," with superiors, peers, and subordinates; (7) recognizing "the power of the purse," as a lever controlling subordinates; and (8) understanding "the critical impor-

---

[5]Robert N. McMurry, "Power and the Ambitious Executive," *Harvard Business Review*, November–December, 1973, no. 73610, p. 7.

[6]Ibid., p. 8.

tance of clear and credible channels of communication upward from all levels of his personnel and downward from him to them." He amplified his eight points by suggesting, in addition to formal channels of communication, direct contact with the work force and periodic reports to it, solicitation of anonymous questions and expressions of dissatisfaction, work councils, opinion polls, interviews, and community surveys. Yet he seemed not to perceive any inherent conflict between the rigidity of his initial statement of view and his eighth point.[7] And his fifth point about selecting a compliant board of directors, while long descriptive of the relationships between chief executives and boards, is out of touch with reality in recent years, especially as directors have become increasingly exposed to personal liability for failures to fulfill their "duty of care" to shareholders.

Dumaine and McMurry are poles apart. The former sees leadership as diffuse, as a function of some sort of organizational osmosis through which the chief executive (the leader) discovers and articulates the mission and culture of the organization. Presumably, the consequence will be profitability and success in the marketplace. McMurry has a rather Machiavellian view of the organization and the leader's role in it. He sees a traditional hierarchical, authoritarian, top-down structure, led by a leader who, in the language of the street, is always conscious of covering his rear.

These opposed views are "straw men." In my view, neither is correct, for the truth lies somewhere in between. If leaders are to be successful, then they must be able to lead. But free, effective communication with and among subordinates in the organization is a key to successful leadership. Effective communication yields understanding, which encourages agreement with and acceptance of even unpleasant decisions. And I think that is the acid test of leadership: that subordinates are willing to support unpleasant and even painful decisions.

Lee Iacocca made some succinct and pertinent remarks in *Talking Straight*. In his words:[8]

> The big fuss about consensus management is another issue that boils down to a lot of noise about not much. The consensus advocates are great admirers of the Japanese management style. Consensus is what Japan is famous for. Well, I know the Japanese fairly well: They still remember Douglas MacArthur with respect and they still bow down to the Emperor. In my deal-

---

[7]Ibid. Quoted phrases are from pp. 8–11.

[8]Lee Iacocca with Sonny Kleinfield, *Talking Straight* (New York: Bantam Books, 1988), pp. 78–79.

ings with them they talk a lot about consensus, but there's always one guy behind the scenes who ends up making the tough decisions. . . .

Another thing that a lot of management experts advocate importing from the Far East is that the boss should be one of the boys. Democratic as that philosophy may sound, I don't think it's very practical. If the boss lets his hair down too much, he ends up like Rodney Dangerfield. No respect. . . .

And yet, the boss can't be aloof either. A lot of the guys in the Fortune 500 seem to feel it's beneath their station even to talk to their own work force. . . .

Leadership resides in and emanates from the individual. Effective communication and wise decisions, proved by subsequent experience, buttress and validate authority born originally from position. If a committee is successful, it is most likely because a member of the group became its leader by virtue of ability to persuade, to convince, and hence to lead the others in the group. The notion is unproven that organizational structures that diffuse the role of the leader by creating multiple committees to seek organizational goals and consensus, are inherently and necessarily more effective than other ones.

LEADERSHIP, CHANGES IN THE ECONOMIC ENVIRONMENT, AND THE EXERCISE OF EXECUTIVE POWER

The point becomes clearer when one considers changes in the economic environment. In the context of change, a chief executive's leadership quality is most sorely tested, because then difficult decisions must be made. And the choice is difficult between sitting still, hoping a satisfactory prior status quo will reassert itself, or opting for painful actions. It is also true that painful decisions do not generally emerge from committee deliberations, because some committee members may be the unhappy victims who suffer pain. Alternatively, a committee may be made up of members who will not be personally affected by a painful decision that it makes. In fact, that may be the raison d'être underlying the composition of the committee. When that is the case, it may also be true that the chief executive is using the committee as a stalking horse, a screen to cover his own decision. If that is the intent, I suspect the organization will not be fooled. Attempts to diffuse responsibility and make it a group matter are ultimately unsuccessful when confronted with the harsh realities of an adverse economic environment.

Under conditions of prosperity and good profitability, the hard, unpleasant decisions associated with economic adversity, such as layoffs and organizational restructuring can be avoided and ignored. The chief executive can choose, given satisfactory profits, not to press for maximum profitability. In a prosperous economic climate, large staffs and committees seeking consensus are affordable and coexist easily with organizational diffusion of decision making and responsibility. It is then easy to conclude that profitability is the result of such an organizational structure and method of governance, rather than the reverse.

Under adverse economic conditions, when the survival of the organization is in doubt, hard, painful decisions must be made. But such decisions are typically evaded under consensual governmental structures. They are generally made by and under executive authority and are not consensual. The *New York Times* printed a relevant story by Edwin McDowell.[9]

> Just as the normally clubby book publishing industry was wondering last week why Robert L. Bernstein was departing as chairman of Random House, the news came that Robert G. Diforio, the chief executive of New American Library, had been informed that his contract would not be renewed.
>
> "What is going on in our industry?" said one dismayed senior executive at Random House. "Publishing companies depend on morale. These are not cement companies."
>
> Perhaps not. But throughout the industry, which had its toughest summer in many a year, concerns about mounting costs and sagging profits have enhanced the anxiety about the bottom line, moving morale to a distant second place in priorities.
>
> Book publishing is hardly the only industry to conduct periodic purges and wholesale dismissals, nor is it the only industry in which morale is important. But publishing prides itself on promoting and protecting the written word and, by extension, exemplifying the values that are implied in so sacred a trust. When change is deemed necessary, however, those ideals are often brushed aside.

A follow-up story in the *New York Times* announced that S. I. Newhouse, Jr., had hired Alberto Vitale, chief executive of Bantam, Doubleday Dell, to replace Robert L. Bernstein as chief executive of Random House. The story described the qualities of Mr. Vitale that apparently made him attractive to Mr. Newhouse:[10]

---

[9]*New York Times*, November 6, 1989, Business Section, p. 30.
[10]*New York Times*, November 9, 1989, p. D21.

Alberto Vitale's eight lieutenants at Bantam Doubleday Dell refer to the 55-year-old chief executive as "The General" for his leadership in bringing financial discipline to the publishing company where he has served as a senior officer for 14 years.

The nickname might have appealed to S. I. Newhouse Jr., who hired Mr. Vitale away from Bantam to become the chief executive of Random House, the publishing house owned by the Newhouse family. Even insiders at Random House say the company has more hands than jobs and that it may take a battlefield commander's tactical skill to make the company more profitable without sacrificing too many of the infantry. . . .

"Every one of the 1,400 employees here has plenty of work to do." Mr. Vitale said yesterday of Bantam which is part of Bertelsmann A.G. of West Germany. "If that isn't true at Random House now, I won't tolerate it for very long."

Another illustration involves Donald E. Petersen's retirement as CEO of Ford and his replacement by Harold "Red" Poling. That succession was described in the *Wall Street Journal*.[11]

After a decade of leadership by a corporate philosopher, Ford Motor Co. is about to turn the wheel over to a bulldog with a balance sheet. . . .

Mr. Poling is well-suited to face tough times. Within a week of taking over as head of Ford's North American automotive operations in 1980, when Ford was incurring record losses in the U.S. Mr. Poling canceled an important engine program. He then cut white-collar employment and permanently closed an assembly plant.

"We really threw him into the furnace," recalls Phillip Caldwell, Ford's chairman at the time and now a Ford director and senior managing director at Shearson Lehman Hutton. "He was the strong hand to get [the operations] under control." By the time Mr. Poling left five years later, the unit had record profits.

Mr. Poling had similar turnaround success as head of Ford's European operations in the late 1970s. "There was no single heroic act," says Robert A. Lutz, now president. "It was just blocking and tackling, done with energy and drive and dynamism—and not being overly concerned if some people didn't like your decisions."

---

[11]Melinda G. Guiles, and Bradley A. Stertz, *The Wall Street Journal*, November 13, 1989. See also Alex Taylor III, "The Odd Eclipse of a Star CEO," *Fortune*, February 11, 1991, pp. 87–96. This article suggests that Donald E. Petersen was pushed into retirement.

A further illustration is provided by the early retirement of R. Gordon McGovern as chief executive of the Campbell Soup Company. In the *New York Times,* Claudia H. Deutsch reported:[12]

> The chief executive of the Campbell Soup Company said yesterday that he would take early retirement. His responsibilities were quickly divided between two top executives of the company, and its stock jumped on the news.
>
> . . . , the stock is rising on hopes that the new regime will do something about Campbell's weak returns and about the company's unwillingness to use more debt. "This company has to be more aggressively managed," said Pavlos M. Alexandrakis, an analyst at Argus Research.
>
> Mr. McGovern's would-be heirs clearly agree. "What you are going to see right out of the box is a much tighter bottom-line orientation and more focused, tighter business strategies," Mr. Baum said in an interview yesterday afternoon. Mr. Harper added, "Our immediate priorities are to keep our momentum going in the U.S. while achieving overall profitability worldwide."
>
> Mr. McGovern has always stated those as his priorities, too. Many who know him, however, say he simply did not have the stomach to pursue that profitability, and that his job had, in fact, become an ordeal for him. "I know that many people think the Dorrance family forced Gordon to resign but it didn't," said a person who spends a good deal of time with the Dorrances. "The truth is, he was really burned out. . . ."
>
> . . . Campbell insiders said he was strong-armed by the board into agreeing to a restructuring last summer that will involve closing four plants domestically and five overseas.
>
> "His demeanor has certainly not been wonderful since August," said one longtime associate, who requested anonymity. "He used to be a feisty guy who enjoyed jousting with the press and colleagues. Toward the end he didn't seem to enjoy anything very much."
>
> People on Wall Street had the same impression. "McGovern was being forced to do things he just did not want to do," said John M. McMillin, an analyst with Prudential-Bache Securities Inc. "Laying off people and closing plants just isn't as much fun as growing the top line."

Subsequent events have confirmed the opinions expressed. McGovern was succeeded by David W. Johnson as CEO of Campbell. By February 15, 1991, *The Wall Street Journal* reported that Johnson had "overturned the

---

[12]*New York Times,* November 2, 1989, pages D1–5.

company's paternalistic culture."[13] Two back-to-back quarters of record earnings resulted, and the company's stock rose dramatically to a year-long high of $68.125—a higher level than when it was a takeover target. Alix M. Freedman, author of the *Journal* report, summed up the situation by noting that Campbell Soup had been transformed "into a downsized outfit that is run strictly for the bottom line."[14]

A final illustration should suffice. It involves the McDonnell Douglas Corporation, a major producer of military and commercial craft. Despite a booming business for commercial airliners and a major position as a supplier of military aircraft, the company has been only sporadically profitable in the 24 years since the merger of McDonnell Aircraft and Douglas (in 1967).[15] Yet Boeing, the leading manufacturer of commercial aircraft and also a major producer of military aircraft, has been consistently profitable.

According to a *New York Times* report, the major reasons for McDonnell Douglas's poor results is a lack of leadership. A sweeping internal reorganization of the Douglas division in 1989 required "most executives to change jobs and sought to improve quality and productivity by pushing more responsibility and authority down to production workers. . . ." Its major effect seems to have been to confuse, demoralize, and divide all levels of the division's employees. The *Times* report continued:[16]

> Industry executives, analysts and some Douglas employees say the problem is a longstanding inability on the part of the division's management and its corporate headquarters in St. Louis to keep sufficiently tight control over costs, to meet schedules and to motivate a work force that has long had a reputation for being undisciplined. The problems became especially severe over the past several years as orders for commercial jets poured in at twice the pace the company could produce the planes and the work force nearly doubled in size.
>
> "The lack of leadership, which includes the failure to recognize the difference between participative and permissive management, is the biggest problem facing Douglas Aircraft," said Col. Kenneth Tollefson, the top United States Air Force representative at Douglas, in an unusually frank interview published several months ago in Douglas's employee newspaper.

---

[13]*The Wall Street Journal*, February 15, 1991, p. B1.
[14]Ibid., p. B1.
[15]*New York Times*, July 22, 1990, section 3, pp. 1 and 6.
[16]Ibid., p. 6.

CONSENSUS AND THE EXERCISE OF EXECUTIVE POWER

Howard S. Gitlow, in *Planning for Quality, Productivity and Competitive Position,* discusses the implications of consensus decision making. While his discussion has particular reference to quality-control teams, his observations have much wider applicability. He notes:[17]

> Consensus decision-making requires that: (1) all team members have a chance to voice their point of view with respect to the problem discussed, (2) the team must find a solution to the problem that meets the needs of all team members and is acceptable to all team members, (3) enough time is allocated to discussion of the problem so team members have a chance to buy in to a decision, (4) team members commit to follow through with the decision in a consistent manner outside of the meeting, (5) all data relevant to the problem have been made available to all team members, (6) voting is not done in an attempt to resolve the problem, and (7) the problem is important enough to require the support of all team members. A team that does not consider these seven issues will not be able to use consensus decision-making to solve a problem.

Although a single vote in which a majority opinion becomes ruling is not done, multivoting is one method used to achieve consensus. In multivoting a series of votes is taken successively, with the proposal or action receiving the least votes being dropped from consideration.

The time-consuming nature of this procedure, plus the possibility of deadlock and indecision, cause it to collapse in a context of change and crisis. At such times, the inherent need for decisiveness is most likely to bring about leadership that manifests itself through the exercise of executive power. It would be wrong to assume or to conclude that the exercise of such power will be obvious. It will not necessarily manifest itself in an overt and naked display of authoritarian decision making or implementation by unilateral executive fiat with the threat of punishment in the case of noncompliance. Organizational life is not so simple. As suggested earlier, the exercise of power may be cloaked and subtle. It may operate through organizational structures and processes having a surface semblance to participatory decision making and consensus building. But one must look care-

---

[17]Howard S. Gitlow, and Process Management International, Inc., *Planning for Quality, Productivity and Competitive Position* (Homewood, Ill.: Dow-Jones-Irwin, 1990), p. 76.

fully beneath the surface of style and form to grasp the fundamental forces at work. And, to repeat, these forces are often those reflecting power and its exercise.

EXECUTIVE POWER AND ORGANIZATIONAL STRUCTURES

Chester I. Barnard's insight into and articulation of *authority of position* revealed a significant relationship between authority, that is, executive power, and organizational structure, because position, as he uses the term, refers to status in an organizational structure. In that context, it is logical to conclude that the traditional hierarchical, pyramidal, authoritarian military model, in which power flows vertically top-down and obedience bottom-up, is uniquely the one in which authority of position is crucial, meaning that any undermining of authority of position compromises the strength and integrity of the structure itself. There is certainly a body of evidence to sustain that view. In the military, any breach of obedience to a superior office or rank is viewed as a serious offense, and more serious breaches, for instance, an enlisted man striking an officer, are treated severely. Punishment and fear of it are central sources of discipline in such structures. Of course, obedience up is associated with authority down for all holders of position in the hierarchy except those at the very bottom, so that in such organizational structures many find the onerousness of obedience up sweetened and offset by the psychological satisfaction of authority down.

I think it is no accident that the hierarchical model is probably the oldest paradigm of a large-scale organization. Indeed, the concept of scale or size is a key, for military campaigns may well represent the oldest organized human activity requiring the movement and disposition of large numbers of men, equipment, and supplies in an organized way and in accordance with some overall strategy and body of tactics. Alexander the Great conquered his immediate and even remote neighbors by his brilliant use of the phalanx. So the hierarchical, pyramidal, authority-of-position organizational structure is a potent instrument, with a long history of effectiveness in harnessing and directing large-scale human activities.

The military model identification is not the only one. The world of religion offers powerful examples of the very same hierarchical model. A case in point is the Roman Catholic Church. Indeed the church's structure is referred to as the hierarchy, proceeding upward from parishioners to parish priest, monsignor, bishop, archbishop, cardinal and pope. The central authority resides in the Vatican, which is, literally, the pope's seat, along with the Curia, the College of Cardinals, and the Church Councils. The sisterhoods and monastic orders are also organized hierarchically, and authority of position is very great. But it is not absolute in the Church, for the doctrine of papal infallibility is rarely invoked, and then only when the pope speaks on a matter of faith. Nor is authority of position in the religious sphere a characteristic only of the Roman Catholic Church. It is also found in the position and authority of a chief rabbi in Judaism, of an Imam in Mohammedism, of a Dalai Lama in Tibetan Buddhism, or of high priests in ancient times. However, chief rabbis and Imams have typically not had organizational structures of the scale and strength of those of the Roman Catholic Church to undergird their authority of position. Indeed, in Barnard's terms, the title Imam is one more associative of authority of leadership than it is of authority of position. But the Dalai Lama in Tibetan Buddhism sits atop an elaborate organizational structure, and his authority of position is viewed by his followers as bordering on the divine, if not in fact divine.

A fascinating example of an ancient hierarchical organizational structure is found in the Old Testament, Exodus, Chapter 18, verses 13–27.[18] The passages describe Moses sitting as a magistrate interpreting God's law for the people of Israel and settling disputes among them. His father-in-law, Jethro, observes Moses and criticizes him, saying,

> The thing you are doing is not right; you will surely wear yourself out; you cannot do it alone. Now listen to me. I will give you counsel, and God be with you! You represent the people before God: You bring the disputes before God, and enjoin upon them the laws and teachings, and make known to them the way they are to go and the practices they are to follow. You shall also seek out from among all the people capable men who fear God, trustworthy men who spurn ill-gotten gain; and set these over them as chiefs of thousands, hundreds, fifties, and tens. Let them exercise authority over the people at all times; let them bring every major dispute to you, but decide every minor dispute themselves. Make it easier for yourself, and let them share the burden with you. If you do this—and God so commands you—you will be able to bear up; and all these people will go home content.

The *Torah* continues:

---

[18]*The Torah, The Five Books of Moses* (Philadelphia, Pa.: Jewish Publication Society of America, 1962), pp. 131–32.

Moses heeded his father-in-law and did just as he had said. Moses chose capable men out of All Israel, and appointed them heads over the people—chiefs of thousands, hundreds, fifties, and tens. And they exercised authority over the people at all times: the difficult matters they would bring to Moses, and all the minor matters they would decide themselves. Then Moses bade his father-in-law farewell, and he went his way to his own land.

Douglas McGregor categorized hierarchical, authoritarian organizations as Theory X structures, and contrasted them with a newer, presumably superior type that he labeled Theory Y structures. Instead of being pyramidal and vertical, Theory Y structures are flatter, more decentralized, and horizontal. They are characterized by a diffusion of authority in decision making, by a heavy emphasis on consultation and consensus. Their superiority, it is claimed, resides in their greater tolerance of and ability to use the knowledge and skills of all the people in an organization. And this capacity is seen as critical in societies that are affluent and in which education is widely spread. McGregor believed poor societies, struggling to eke out an existence of bare necessities, would have neither time, inclination, nor energy to question or challenge the exercise of authority of position. But richer societies, like our own, require appeals to a higher order of needs than those of mere physical existence. We have become a knowledge-based society, one in which obedience and discipline are more responsive to ability and leadership than to position. But authority (executive power) still exists, even though it is not based solely on position.

No one seems to have put the matter better than Barnard, who said:[19] "It is too generally assumed that a man filling a leading position is for that very reason a leader . . . many leading positions are not filled by leaders." He continued: "The creative function as a whole is the essence of leadership. It is the highest test of executive responsibility because it requires for successful accomplishment that element of 'conviction' that means identification of personal codes and organization codes in the view of the leader. This is the coalescence that carries 'conviction' to the personnel of the organization, to that informal organization underlying all formal organization that senses nothing more quickly than insincerity."

The central point being made is that authority—power—exists and is necessary in all organization structures and forms. But the form and style

---

[19]W. B. Wolf and H. Iino, *Philosophy for Managers: Selected Papers of Chester I. Barnard* (Tokyo: Bunshindo Publishing Co., 1986), p. 157.

of its use may vary greatly in accordance with variations in such personal characteristics of executives as (1) integrity; (2) initiative; (3) intellectual capacity and ability to conceptualize; (4) desire to lead; (5) perceptiveness; (6) vision, or foresight; (7) curiosity and receptivity; (8) articulateness—the ability to communicate, to persuade; and (9) psychological maturity, or a sense of emotional security. Marvin Bower, former managing Director of McKinsey and Co., noted the first eight characteristics. I have added the ninth to draw attention to those individuals who are placed in positions of authority, but who diminish their ability to lead because they are excessively arbitrary, abrasive, and aggressive, all in an often unrecognized effort to overcome a deep-seated sense of emotional insecurity. We shall explore this point further in the next chapter.

CHAPTER 2

PSYCHOLOGICAL MATURITY, LEADERSHIP, AND CORPORATE GOVERNANCE

PSYCHOLOGICAL MATURITY

People who suffer from a sense of insecurity find uncertainty unsettling, even traumatic. They hate to delegate responsibility and authority and are inclined to seek sycophants as subordinates. But people who feel secure are comfortable with competent colleagues and readier to delegate responsibility and authority to them. Secure people do not feel threatened by competent associates, but insecure people do.

Perhaps a personal experience that turned out tragically will help illustrate and make my point. In 1955, I was elected a member of the board of education in a newly formed central school district in Rockland County, New York. The district was entering a period of very rapid growth as the area's population burgeoned, following the opening of the Tappan Zee bridge and the New York State Thruway, along with the Garden State Parkway and the Palisades Interstate Parkway. All these arterial highways made the school district's area attractive as an accessible suburb in the New York Metropolitan area. Consequently, school building programs, rapid staff expansions, and exploding budgets became pressing issues facing the board and the school management team (i.e., the superintendent of schools and his immediate staff).

After a couple of board meetings, I realized that tension existed between the board members and the superintendent. The tension manifested itself in some exchanges between the board members and superintendent during meetings, when the latter and his immediate staff did not provide pertinent information in response to board questions. In most such instances, the failure to provide information was due to the staff's lack of understanding and competence, rather than deliberate stonewalling. The tension also manifested itself in connection with occasional behavioral hints that the superintendent had been drinking. Finally, the tension manifested itself in the unwillingness of the board to grant a multiyear contract to the superintendent, a refusal that had already occurred twice before my election.

After several months on the board, I asked for an executive meeting of the board and superintendent. At that meeting, I aired my perception of the tension, making it an open issue of discussion. I felt the issue was too important to dodge, while its existence was real and reflected board dissatisfaction with the management of the school district. I suggested to the superintendent that his problem might reside in the incompetence of his immediate staff. He resisted and I pressed the point, drawing support from other board members. Finally, in frustration, the superintendent exploded, saying, "I'll be damned if I'm going to have staff who are smarter than I am!" His remarks shocked the board. It also ended the discussion.

But the issue could not be buried, surfacing a couple of months later when renewal of the superintendent's contract came up. Privately, I argued with the other board members that we should not renew the contract. Most of them had difficulty with the severity of that position, feeling sorry for the superintendent and his family. They preferred to continue temporizing, offering an additional one-year renewal. They agreed, however, that a candid discussion with the superintendent was needed, in which their concerns would be made clear to him, and he would be told that this was a final one-year renewal. If things changed for the better, then he would receive a multiyear contract next year. If not, then he would be out.

The meeting took place and the board members made their respective comments. The superintendent argued the issue of competence, but did not do so by defending his past record of performance. Rather, he sought to explain that poor record as being the result of his sense of insecurity, which he, in turn, laid at the feet of the board, saying it was a result of their failure to give him a multiyear contract. Such a contract, he maintained, would be a sign of board *love* (his word) and support. Given that sign, his sense of insecurity would be replaced by one of security and confidence, permitting him to go forward with confidence and decisiveness in hiring competent assistants and managing the affairs of the district.

When the superintendent used the word *love,* I reacted strongly and negatively. I said, "I don't understand you. What do you mean by love? I don't want to love you. I love my wife, my children, my family. I love some dear old friends. I want to respect and admire you because you are doing a competent job. You have the cart before the horse. A multiyear contract and such security as it offers come after a demonstration of competent performance, not prior to and as a prerequisite condition. If you prove your competence and we find ourselves colleagues over a period of years, we may become close friends and may develop a stronger feeling, perhaps bordering on love. But, for now, talk of love is irrelevant and out of place."

Perhaps a step back is needed to provide some family background about the superintendent. His father was a prominent, successful educator, who had recently served as associate commissioner of education of New York State. When I discovered that fact, I thought it more than a passing possibility that that connection may have been a major factor in his having been hired by the board. I also thought it likely that the powerful figure of his father was a possible source of psychological problems, a thought given credence in my mind by the occasional borderline inebriation of the superintendent. With these considerations in mind, I asked for another executive session of the board. With the superintendent out of the room, I reminded the board of our earlier tentative understanding that we renew his contract for a final year, but hold out the possibility of a future multiyear contract if the superintendent (1) sought professional psychiatric counseling for alcoholism and other problems, for which the board would pay and (2) demonstrated competence in the period prior to the next consideration of his contract. The superintendent returned, and the board president presented the board's suggestion and decision. The former was clearly not happy, but, having no alternative, accepted.

In the months following, things did not improve, although the superintendent was seeing a psychiatrist and receiving certain medications. One day, the situation ended, tragically. While I was teaching class at the university, a departmental secretary called me out of the room to take an emergency phone call. The caller was the board president, who wanted to inform me that the superintendent had closed himself in his car in his garage with the engine running and committed suicide.

No discussion could undo the finality of the superintendent's action. I admit to retrospective reviews of my own conduct. Had I been harsh? Had I pushed the poor man over the psychological edge? I knew he felt I was pressing the board to resolve the tension and had pushed for a decision deadline a year hence. He had said as much to the board president, who had repeated it to me. The superintendent had put the matter as a question to the board president asking, "Why does Dr. Gitlow dislike me?"

And that is truly how he saw the matter. He did not believe that I, or others, might be focused on competence, and that competence could stand by itself and apart from personal feelings of a subjective kind. I concluded, happily for myself, that I was not guilty. But I have never forgotten that his mental state, in particular his sense of insecurity, was reflected in his selection of staff, his management style, his performance, and the organizational structure he preferred.

PSYCHOLOGICAL MATURITY, LEADERSHIP (DECISION-MAKING STYLE), AND THE EXERCISE OF POWER

The Conference Board, in the report *Chief Executives View Their Jobs*, noted four unique characteristics of the CEO's position: (1) ultimate accountability for the organization's success; (2) the power to make or take final decisions; (3) the power to define his own job and role, and, given that power, the importance of his own character; and (4) loneliness.[1]

The third characteristic is the key one because character influences how the CEO exercises "the power to make or take final decisions," and because the exercise of that power, in turn, determines how he meets and discharges the responsibility for painful decision making.

While observing that ultimate accountability is to the board of directors and to shareholders, The Conference Board report notes that in the contemporary industrialized world there are other so-called stakeholders, most notably employees, the community (as represented by government and, oftentimes, by private special interest groups claiming a public role and responsibility), and consumers.[2] One could easily add even posterity, which represents the future well-being of society.

Returning to characteristics other than ultimate accountability, The Conference Board report observes that, although "humility is not a characteristic often associated with CEOs,"[3] they feel it when faced with serious, large decisions that may determine the fate of their organizations. Such decisions, the report maintains, are beyond the capability of the lone CEO. So many CEOs turn to participative decision making, thereby

---

[1]Harold Stieglitz, *Chief Executives View Their Jobs* (New York: The Conference Board, 1985), p. 7.

[2]Ibid., p. 8.

[3]Ibid., p. 18.

reducing the loneliness of their position. But the report notes that "loneliness *is felt most forcibly when participative decision making has not made the right answer evident—and the CEO must decide.*"[4]

Despite the obeisance to participative decision making, it is significant to an understanding of the CEO's psychological maturity that "most CEOs, when asked to categorize their general approach to decision making at the top, check off: '*I* listen to recommendations and arguments, then *I* decide'; or '*I* develop a consensus with which *I* can agree.' Rarely do the CEOs go with a decision 'even if *I* personally disagree' or, 'bow to the most competent person.' " (See Figure 1-1.)

The key to the exercise of executive power and leadership in a context of participative decision making and consensuality is the *process*, not the surrender of ultimate executive authority. It is the *involvement* of other people with the CEO as he works his way to a decision. Thus, the CEO's emphasis on having the *agreement* of others to make decisions operative is understandable. Indeed, any display of naked executive power is probably unnecessary. Generally, constant questioning and discussion in a group of intelligent people working with the CEO enables him to wind up verbalizing the sense of the group, with which he happens to be in agreement.

The Conference Board report concludes:[5]

> The significance of the CEO's personal agreement is revealed by several CEOs who, though committed to consensus or collegial decision making, can think of no decision reached during their tenure with which they have not agreed. The very few who acknowledge going with a consensus while still privately demurring react, as does Harvey-Jones—on matters "I feel desperately about." Edwardes, for example, in restructuring British Leyland in order to revive its Jaguar, Austin, and other Brand-name units, commented: "For the only time in my business career, I imposed a decision on senior colleagues against an overwhelming majority view.

RELATIONSHIP TO STRUCTURAL PREFERENCES

It is implicit in our foregoing discussion that leadership and executive power can be effectively exercised through a variety of organizational structures, although the individual CEO's mind-set, character, and personal style may

---

[4]Ibid.
[5]Ibid., p. 19.

FIGURE 1-1

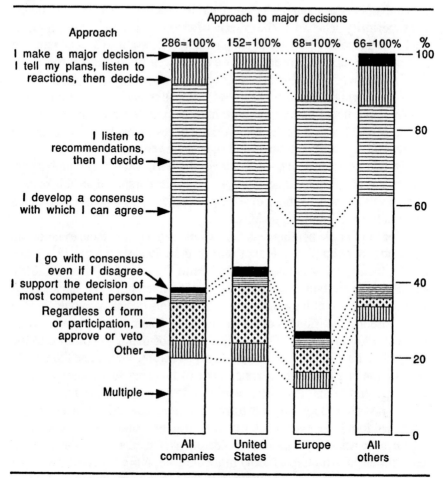

Source: Harold Stieglitz, *Chief Executives View Their Jobs* (New York: The Conference Board, 1985), p. 19.

lead to a preference for one as against another. A CEO suffering from some degree of psychological insecurity will probably favor the more traditional hierarchical, pyramidal, top-down structure, with its inherent emphasis on authority of position. Another CEO, emotionally secure and mature, will lean more toward the horizontal, diffused, participative paradigm.

Is one structure inherently superior or more successful than another? The answer is not as clear to me as it appears to be to others, who would quickly approve the presently popular horizontal model. Personally, I like that model better. And it is the one I have used myself in my own career as a university dean and business executive. But it seems to me that inherent superiority depends on the criteria of success that one applies. Significant criteria include (1) speed in implementing decisions; (2) accumulation and concentration of power (to those executives finding this important); (3) financial considerations (is the organization facing a financial crisis, or is it enjoying prosperity?); and (4) ethical considerations (is one organizational model inherently more humane and hence morally superior to another?). These considerations do not necessarily drive one to decide in favor of the horizontal model and against the vertical one. But the weight of my own experience leads me to favor the horizontal, participative paradigm, especially since it need not, under the leadership of an able executive, result in the surrender of executive power and the ability to make and implement painful decisions.

Speed in implementing decisions would seem prima facie to favor the pyramidal paradigm. If the authority of the CEO is supported by those below, then speed in implementation seems assured. But if his authority of position is not buttressed by authority of leadership, then those below may sabotage, or at least delay and obscure, his decision, in which case the apparent conclusion becomes questionable. There is no argument about concentration of power. If power is a matter of major importance to the CEO, then he will opt for the pyramidal structure, which has the weight of tradition and the obvious appearance of favoring such concentration. In a financial crisis, the exercise of top-down authority is likely to triumph, favoring the pyramidal form. But since executive power can be exercised top-down even in a horizontal structure, one cannot be categorical in his conclusion. In ethical considerations, the case favors the horizontal, consensual structure as being more humane, more concerned with the intrinsic value of all the individuals making up the organization. Consequently, given the arguments on both sides, one cannot conclusively say that under *all* conditions one structural model is inherently superior.

THE EXERCISE OF EXECUTIVE POWER, MOTIVATION, AND THE STRENGTH OF THE MANAGEMENT TEAM

A CEO of my acquaintance once said to my seminar at the graduate school that "sound discipline becomes self-discipline." The remark is pregnant with meaning, for it implies that executive power, exercised intelligently and reasonably by a person possessed of authority of leadership as well as authority of position, inspires self-discipline in associates and workers. And self-discipline generates voluntary self-actuation, so that the urge to perform at the peak of one's ability is aroused from within (self-motivation) rather than imposed from without. Seen in this light, the exercise of power (authority) and voluntary self-actuation (cooperation) are completely compatible.

But we know that traditionally, and oftentimes today, the exercise of executive power reflects only authority of position. In that case, power aims at obedience, which reflects fear, rather than cooperation, which reflects voluntary self-actuation. Of course, this brings us to the use of fear as a motivational lever. Fear is a powerful motivating force, but its use by those with authority of position is today widely and passionately debated.

Perhaps the most notable collision of views on this matter is that between W. Edwards Deming and Joseph M. Juran, America's two leading gurus of quality control. Both men had a major impact on Japanese business-men and manufacturing practice after World War II, when the Japanese invited them to explain their theories of quality control. What is relevant now is that Deming's philosophy, which features 14 points, includes prominently among them one that mandates that management "drive out fear." Howard S. Gitlow, Professor of Management Science at the University of Miami, articulated the Deming view in *Planning for Quality, Productivity, and Competitive Position:*[6]

> Fear in organizations has a profound impact on those working in the organization and on the functioning of the organization. On an individual level, fear can cause physical and physiological disorders, such as a rise in blood pressure or an increase in heart rate. Behavior changes, emotional problems, and physical ailments are often the result of fear and stress generated in work situations, as are drug and alcohol abuse, absenteeism, and burnout. These maladies affect any organization. An employee working in a climate of fear experiences poor morale, poor productivity, stifling of creativity, reluctance to take risks, poor interpersonal relationships, and reduced motivation to work for the best interest of the company. The economic loss to the company is immeasurable.

---

[6]Howard S. Gitlow, and Process Management International, *Planning for Quality, Productivity, and Competitive Position* (Homewood, Ill.: Dow Jones-Irwin, 1990), pp. 34–35.

Management is obliged to ensure the physical and emotional health of its employees for their well being and that of the organization. Many managers use their power to create fear because they believe the way to motivate employees is through coercive power. Workers believe they will be punished if they do not perform. This generates fear, which impedes their performance and is counterproductive.

On the other hand, Juran thinks Deming's views about fear are platitudes. Juran sees fear as a motivation that "can bring out the best in people."[7] Pursuing Juran's position, one could paraphrase the quote cited above claiming at least some of the negatives are actually positives. For example, an increase of adrenaline flow, rise in blood pressure, and increase in heart rate, all of which are primordial physiological reactions of the body to external danger, make possible, at least short term, the expenditure of enlarged energy, strength, and more intense concentration. But the consequences of fear over the longer term are likely, as claimed, to be harmful. The conclusion may be to rely on voluntary self-actuation and cooperation, with fear held in reserve for moments of crisis.

Perhaps an old joke, long talked about in management circles, is relevant. It tells about a worker with many years in his job who would not observe newly established safety rules requiring the wearing of protective eye glasses. One day, while walking through the plant, the company's chief executive noted the worker's noncompliance. Observing protocol, he mentioned it to the plant superintendent, who in turn pointed out the nonconformance to the worker's foreman, with instructions to make sure compliance was obtained.

A few weeks later, again on a plant walkaround, the CEO found the worker still failing to wear safety goggles. The failure was again brought to the attention of the plant superintendent, this time with somewhat sharper language. The latter, understandably annoyed, called in the worker. He asked the worker if the foreman had spoken to him about the safety rule. Receiving an affirmative response, he asked if the worker understood the hazard that underlay the establishment of the rule. Again, the worker responded affirmatively. To make sure the matter was clear, the plant superintendent reviewed both hazard and rule, emphasizing the importance of following safe procedures.

---

[7]*Fortune*, August 18, 1986, p. 32.

Some weeks passed, and once again the CEO walked around the plant. He was annoyed and angered to discover the worker still working without protective eye gear. This time, he discarded protocol and ordered the worker to come to his office. With the misbehaver before him, he asked, bluntly and curtly, whether the foreman and plant superintendent had spoken about the safety rule requiring the wearing of protective eye goggles. The worker said they had. The CEO exploded and, interlacing his words with a considerable variety of strong expletives, told the worker that if he failed to comply with the rule immediately, he would be fired for cause, cutting off unemployment compensation. Further, he would receive no recommendations for other jobs.

On the CEO's next walkaround, he observed the worker in complete compliance with the regulation. Mollified, he called the worker to his office and asked why the latter had not complied with the foreman's and the plant superintendent's instructions. The worker replied, "They didn't explain it to me as clearly as you did!"

Several aspects of the story have interest. First, the hierarchical protocol was ineffective. Second, the worker did not respond to gentle, or even somewhat less than gentle, prodding. Finally, a naked exercise of authoritarian power produced the desired response. By implication, the third aspect is the most significant. Presumably, an authoritarian manner by the foreman or the plant superintendent would have produced the compliance sought. But then we have to face the further implication that the worker's stubbornness made him nonresponsive to nonauthoritarian approaches. The implication is that the exercise of power, unadorned by any gentle cloaking of raw authority, is ultimately the most effective way to achieve compliance. While that is a proposition hotly contested by many management experts, it is one which cannot simply be dismissed. There are cases in which naked authority and fear can bring desired results.

Do the CEO's personality and management style affect the strength of the management team, upon which he depends for information, support, and implementation of decisions? I believe the answer is yes! An insecure, immature CEO is unable to deal with strong colleagues who pose challenging questions. The odds are overwhelming that such a CEO will surround himself with people of similar weakness, who will be "yes" men. Lacking competent colleagues, who offer different views and alternative approaches to solving problems, the insecure CEO has to rely on his own limited abilities. One result is that the danger of a misjudgment or a bad decision is magnified, as are the consequences. Once taken, a bad judgment or decision is likely to be pushed to the point of endangering the future viability of the entire organization. Another result is that the management group finds it almost impossible to function truly as a team. Individual members are usually worried about their standing with the boss and inclined to destructive behavior patterns (e.g. politicking), as they seek to improve individual position by jockeying to reduce the position of another. The reverse is true when a management group is led by a secure, mature CEO.

DOES AUTHORITY OF POSITION AFFECT THE CEO'S PERSONALITY?[8]

To this point, we have been exploring the nature and impact of the CEO's personality, or psychological maturity, on the exercise of executive power. But what about the reverse? Can authority of position alter the CEO's personality and behavior? Can it convert a genial, collegial personality into an authoritarian one? Years ago, Lord Acton made the pertinent observation that "all power corrupts, but absolute power corrupts absolutely." I think that observation is as true today as it was in the early years of the twentieth century. Power does have a tendency to corrupt its possessor. No matter how gentle the hand holding power in the beginning, its possession influences those around the holder. They know they depend for job and compensation on the opinion of the CEO, and they do not easily or readily act to upset that opinion and possibly endanger their position. Typically, they will be open and responsive only under the active encouragement of the CEO. But agreement is often sweeter to his ears than is opposition. And so, as time passes, even a mature, secure CEO may manifest increasing sureness in his rightness of view and impatience with those arguing against it. This fact enlarges the importance of preventing possession of absolute power, of having other centers of power in the organization, such as a board of directors representing shareholders, a union or other organizational spokesman for employees; or external centers of power, such as government, free media (press, TV, radio), and so on.

---

[8]A relevant feature article appeared after this section was written. It contains pertinent illustrations of the point made. See "CEO Disease," *Business Week,* April 1, 1991, pp. 52–60.

Much of a CEO's time is spent dealing with relationships with other sources of power. Internally, he must deal with the board of directors, who represent the shareholders; top management, on whom he relies for information, consultation, and implementation of decisions; and employees, who may be represented by a union or some other organizational entity. Externally, he must deal with the government and its agencies, which have huge importance through their legislative and regulatory activities, including legal actions; with the media, which have a huge impact on public perceptions of a firm and which affect stock values; and with special action groups which have become a scourge to some and a concern to other CEOs. In the chapters that follow, we will discuss the impact of these other centers of power on the CEO's exercise of executive power. We should note now, however, that in all the CEO's relationships and dealings with these other centers of power, none is as powerful as the board of directors. Even when the board is quiescent, it is like a sleeping lion. It can awaken, and, in a display of power, fire the CEO. Further, it is a body on which other centers of power can focus and through which they can seek to exercise power over the CEO and management. While the board, in strict terms, is the representative of the shareholders and is responsible to them, it can, and increasingly seems willing to, give serious weight to the interests and preferences of "stakeholders." This board inclination is most sharply curbed when a company is for sale, "in play," in the language of Wall Street. In that case, the board's sole and exclusive responsibility may be to maximize shareholder value. I say "may be," because some recently enacted state laws (e.g., Pennsylvania) have been admitting stakeholders' interests as a valid concern even when a company was in play.

CHAPTER 3

EXECUTIVE POWER AND THE BOARD OF DIRECTORS

CONTROL IN THE MODERN PUBLIC CORPORATION[1]

The modern public corporation is a creation of the state, a disembodied legal entity with the economic attributes of a person: it can buy, own, and sell property; it can hire and fire; it can enter into contracts; it can sue and be sued, and so on. But, being disembodied, it is not mortal; hence, it affords continuity of life long after its human founders die. It has other significant attributes, but perhaps the most immediately relevant one is the relationship between ownership and operational control: that is, management.

In the corporation's beginnings, its ownership and operational control were usually united in the figures of one or a few founders, who used the corporate form as a convenient, practical way to raise capital and limit personal liability, while pursuing a dream involving the production of some good and/or service for society. The dream was theirs; hence, the operational control of the enterprise was also usually theirs. Even if capital was provided by other holders of equity, the founders had substantial holdings as stockholders. Ownership and operational control were not divided.

As time passed, this situation changed. The founders died. Within two or three successor generations, ownership became diffused, due to

---

[1] An excellent discussion of this topic is found in Jay W. Lorsch, with Elizabeth MacIver, *Pawns or Potentates, The Reality of America's Corporate Boards* (Boston, Mass: Harvard Business School Press, 1989). An older discussion is in Courtney C. Brown, *Beyond the Bottom Line* (N.Y.: Macmillan, 1979), especially, Chapter Five. Additional discussions are found in *Harvard Business Review*, reprint series: (1) Boards of Directors: Part I; and (2) Boards of Directors: Part II. These compendia of *Review* articles are available from *Harvard Business Review* (Boston, Mass.: Harvard University's Business School).

estate taxes and numbers of heirs among whom ownership was divided and then subdivided. In other instances, heirs had no interest in running the businesses created by their fathers or mothers. Professional managers entered as controllers of operations. Alternatively, heirs lacked the ability to exercise operational control of the corporation. Although there are some famous examples of ownership and operational control surviving two or more generations, they are unusual, and more rare than common.

As ownership became diffused and passed into the hands of a multitude of stockholders, it became separated from operational control of the corporation. Control passed to management, now separate from ownership. The locus of the transfer of power is in the board of directors. Originally, the board was a creature of the owner-operators (i.e., managers) of the enterprise. The owner-operators, as owners, selected and controlled the board, which was dominated by themselves and their appointees. But, as ownership became diffused among a multitude of stockholders, management became able to nominate directors, while stockholders had only power to ratify the nominations. The entire process of nominating and electing directors, which became costly and complicated to challenge, placed power in the hands of management and removed it from the stockholders, except in those rare instances where some individual stockholders possessed the wealth and persistence of spirit to resist successfully. While outside, public directors on boards so selected were theoretically independent of management, and were even under a legal and moral obligation to act in behalf of the stockholders' interests, they were in fact compliant to management's wishes. Being a director of a large corporation was prestigious and pleasant. The compensation was agreeable, the perks attractive, and personal liability was, for many years, practically nonexistent.

This description of the shift of operational control from ownership to management is too broad. Management really meant top management: specifically, the chief executive officer, who usually doubled as chairman of the board. In that capacity, he occupied the key position, enabling him to control nominations to the board; number, type, and composition of board committees; agendas for board meetings; and type and amount of information flowing to board members. Under these conditions, boards were almost always compliant. And the CEO-manager could and did command key power in the corporation. The idea that stockholders continued to command power because they elected (voted into office) the directors was an illusion. It was also an illusion that they exercised power over management because they could sell their stock, thereby withdrawing their support for the value of the corporation's securities and weakening management's continued control. The business scene would be littered with corporate cadavers, an unlikely picture, before this alleged power might mean anything in practical terms. The transformation described here was well advanced by World War II, and was depicted by Adolph Berle and Gardiner Means in their famous book *The Modern Corporation and Private Property,* published in 1932.

The long-accepted picture of the board of directors as a compliant body, typically responsive to the wishes of the chief executive, was well captured by Ralph Windle, a management consultant. A poem he penned on the subject was published in *The Bottom Line,* and republished in *Fortune.*[2] Titled "The Directors," it said:

> Directors are the firm's elite;
> They fall, but mainly on their feet;
> For once they have their Board regalia
> Most seem impervious to failure;
> And changes, when the critics frown,
> Are mainly somewhat lower down.
>
> They come in two quite separate blends,
> Professionals, and Chairman's friends;
> The former tested by survival,
> The latter non-executival;
> The first have offices and functions,
> The second don't, except for luncheons.
>
> We love our board, and hold them dear,
> So long as they don't interfere.

THE EMERGING IMPORTANCE OF INSTITUTIONAL SHAREHOLDERS

Management control (executive power) has been significantly circumscribed during the decade of the eighties by at least three major developments: (1) lawsuits against directors, which have enlarged their personal liability; (2) new legislation (e.g., Foreign Corrupt Practices Act) and intensi-

---

[2]*Fortune,* February 25, 1991, p. 100. "See also: Bertie Ramsbottom (Ralph Windle), *The Bottom Line, A Book of Business Ballads* (London: Century Publishing, 1985), p. 18.

fied regulatory activity (e.g., Securities and Exchange Commission), which increase the burden on directors to be independent and active; and (3) the growth of institutional shareholders. The last development is the focus of our interest at the moment.

Specifically, institutional investor asset holdings in 1988 exceeded $5 trillion and represented some 45 percent of all equities. In 1988, ranked by stock market value, the top 50 U.S. corporations showed 52 percent of their outstanding stock being held by institutional investors. For the top 100 companies, the percentage was 53 percent, while 47 percent of the outstanding stock of the top 1,000 companies was held by institutional investors. Almost one half of the total institutional assets in 1988 were held in public and private pension funds (over $2.3 trillion). This huge sum accounted for one quarter of the equity market and 15 percent of the bond market activity. This growth is in large measure a result of the passage of the Employee Retirement Income Security Act (ERISA). While intended mainly to prevent abuse in the administration of pension fund assets, it encouraged a large flow of funds into private pension funds.[3]

Looking at the assets of private pension funds, we find a growth of 108 percent from 1982 to 1989 (from $655 billion to $1,362 billion). Other trends show an increase in the proportion of these assets invested in equity between 1982 and 1989 (from 36 percent to 41 percent), while the proportion invested in bonds declined from 20 percent to 16 percent.[4]

If we narrow our focus even more and examine the growth in the top 20 pension funds between 1985 and 1989 (as of September 30), and the equity held by those funds in the top five U.S. companies, we find the results shown in Table 3–1.

The major point of the foregoing data is that enormous equity power is now concentrated, and growing, in the hands of institutional investors. These "stockholders" are not the diffused multitude of largely powerless individuals who so long characterized corporate ownership. Including public as well as private institutions (pension funds, as well as other funds), they possess latent power that is increasingly being flexed and exercised relative to management.

In fact, as the decade of the 90s opened, institutional investors showed an increasingly strong disposition to challenge management control through

---

[3]*Deloitte and Touche Review,* February 26, 1990, pp. 3–4.
[4]*Deloitte and Touche Review,* June 18, 1990, p. 2.

TABLE 3-1

Top 20 Pension Funds Jump in Size . . .
(In millions of dollars)

	1985*	1989*	Percent Change
TIAA-CREF	$40,000	$81,000	103%
California Public Employees	29,166	54,000	85
General Motors	26,300	40,900	56
N.Y. State/Local	25,997	44,238	70
N.Y. City Employees	25,063	45,422	81
AT&T	24,887	42,700	72
General Electric	15,812	28,912	83
N.Y. State Teachers	15,303	28,130	84
California Teachers	15,100	30,335	101
IBM	13,939	25,775	85
N.J. Investment Div.	12,494	24,526	96
Texas Teachers	11,188	23,500	110
Ford Motor	11,000	22,800	107
Wisconsin Investment	10,800	20,033	85
Ohio Public Employees	10,760	19,305	79
Michigan Public Employees	10,516	17,948	71
Ohio Teachers	10,178	18,059	77
DuPont	9,665	18,681	93
Nynext	9,447	16,062	70
Florida State Board	8,911	18,700	110

*As of Sept. 30
†Replaced in 1989 by North Carolina State Fund

. . . And Raise Their Stakes in Big Firms
Stock held by top 20 funds in top five companies*

	1985	1989	Percent Change
IBM	8.1%	9.1%	12%
Exxon	5.0	7.4	48
General Electric	6.9	8.5	23
General Motors†	6.5	10.6	63
AT&T	4.5	6.1	36
Average	6.2	8.3	34

*Dec. 31, 1989, market capitalization
†Replaced in 1989 top five by Philip Morris
  Sources: Columbia University Law School Institutional Investor Project, Pensions & Investments

Source: *The Wall Street Journal*, June 28, 1990.

proxy fights. The central issue in these proxy contests is a demand by institutional investors for direct representation of their views and interests in the board of directors; they are seeking seats on the board. This is a significant step beyond earlier attempts to influence management through submission of policy demands, which were generally rebuffed by existing boards of directors. Such complaisance that continues to characterize the behavior of boards of directors is likely to be shaken by the pressures generated by proxy fights initiated by institutional investors.

It would be premature to argue that a transfer of power from management to institutional shareholders has already occurred. For one thing, to the degree fund assets are in private corporate pension funds (invested in the corporations themselves), management may exercise influence over the fund trustees. For another thing, the institutional shareholders are not united, while an individual corporation's chief executive and his immediate management team usually have the enormous advantages of unity, namely, immediacy of urgent self-interest and hands-on operational control of the corporation. *But the trend is of major importance, and corporate managements will ignore it at their own peril.*

In passing, it may be in order to note these other aspects of the emergence of institutional shareholders. These shareholders are not individuals. They are themselves corporate entities (institutions) managed by professional managers who may reflect interests other than maximizing the narrow financial interests of the funds' participants (corporate employees, retired and present). This observation may have special significance in the case of public funds, which are exposed to political pressures. For example, special interest groups may press for these funds to invest assets in risky, low-yielding "public projects," maintaining that there is a social obligation more important than the fiduciary obligation to the funds' participants, whose pensions and security in retirement are dependent on how fund assets are deployed. Even private funds are subject to pressures: for example, to avoid investment in the equities of firms doing business in South Africa. But the potential pressure on the public funds seems greater. Years ago, Peter Drucker observed that the growth of institutional shareholders represented a socialization of the ownership of American business, an enlarged diffusion of ownership. Of course, in one sense, this is true. But in terms of control and the exercise of power, the "fund managers" hold the reins!

A highly significant aspect of the power and role of fund managers involves their own narrow interest to show an earnings performance level that is better than market averages. In pursuit of this interest, they are powerfully inclined to demand *high short-term earnings* results from the firms whose stock is held in their fund portfolios. This short-term orientation puts pressure on corporate managements to concentrate on quarterly earnings and to take actions that enhance short-term results. The unfortunate consequence of such "short-termism" is avoidance of critical steps that will enhance the long-term health and vitality of the enterprise, but which are costly in up-front financial terms and so depress quarterly earnings in the near future. Examples are research and development expenditures, pursuing projects that offer a near-term earnings return less than that demanded by the insatiable appetites of the fund managers, capital investment and maintenance expenditures with a long-term effect on quality of plant and equipment, and so on. Emphasis on the short term seriously damages the competitive capacity of U.S. business vis-à-vis Japan and Germany, for firms in those countries typically focus on the long run.[5]

It is one thing to observe trends that tend to weaken executive power. It is quite another thing to conclude that such power has become so weak that it is no longer dominant, at least under normal circumstances. Note in this connection comments made in Korn/Ferry International's *Sixteenth Annual Study, 1989, of Board of Directors.* The world's leading executive search firm, Korn/Ferry wrote: "Directors' performance should be scrutinized carefully and . . . *CEOs should have authority to ask for the resignation of a director who does not measure up.* CEOs and directors believe such resignations should be requested in cases of poor attendance at board meetings, insufficient interest or commitment to the company, and inadequate contributions to board meetings. . . ."[6] [Italics added] Note also that the prevailing opinion places authority for asking for a director's resignation in the hands of the CEO. Of course, the authority is just to ask for resignation, to request rather than to order it. But the location of the power to ask, to originate the action, is significant. It would be more appropriate if placed in a nominating committee of the board, which should be aware of the deficiencies noted. Significantly, a year later, the

---

[5]An important discussion of relevant issues is in Peter F. Drucker, "Reckoning With the Pension Fund Revolution," *Harvard Business Review*, March–April 1991, pp. 106–14.

[6]Korn/Ferry International, *Sixteenth Annual Study, 1989, of Board of Directors* (New York, 1989), p. 2.

Korn/Ferry International *Seventeenth Annual Study of Board of Directors,* *1990,* observed:[7]

> Clearly, the balance of power between the CEO and the board has shifted. The CEO no longer reigns as an absolute monarch, expecting corporate policy to be rubber-stamped. Rather, directors have become stronger and more independent partners in corporate leadership.

But nominating committees, which were reported for 59.2 percent of the boards surveyed in 1985 and which increased to 60.4 percent of the boards surveyed in 1988, declined to 57.3 percent of the boards in 1989.[8]

THE FUNCTIONS OF THE BOARD; THE DATA REQUIRED AND THE ISSUES FACED

The traditional view sees the board of directors as representatives of the shareholders, as charged with the moral and legal obligation to protect and further the interests of the "owners." More recently, a broad constructionist view has emerged. It sees the board of directors as having a far broader responsibility, one which embraces the interests of the "stakeholders" as well as those of the shareholders. But which set of interests is primary? The answer depends today in large part on whether the corporation is for sale—"at auction." In that case, the predominant view is that shareholder interests are primary, and directors who fail to maximize shareholder value will certainly be sued, and may be found personally liable. As of mid-1991, however, some 30 state statutes (e.g., Pennsylvania) and court decisions *(Time Warner v. Paramount)* have modified the absoluteness of that view, so it is increasingly likely that stakeholder interests will receive heavy weight.

Whether looking after shareholder or stakeholder interests, or, more likely both, directors discharge these functions: (1) selection of corporate officers (i.e., management), in particular the chief executive and the chief operating officer; (2) evaluation of management performance and determination of compensation; (3) setting corporate strategy and policies; and

---

[7]Korn/Ferry International, *Board of Directors, Seventeenth Annual Study, 1990* (New York, 1990), p. 1.

[8]Ibid., p. 17.

(4) consultation, providing independent external judgment and advice to management.

To properly discharge its functions, the board requires certain types of information. At a minimum, I note:

1. Financial data for the most recent quarter and year to date, with comparisons to prior years' quarters, year to date, and to budget (in this connection I think careful attention must be given to receivables, inventories, and debt to equity ratios).
2. Significant corporate commitments and expenditures, in product and research areas as well as otherwise.
3. Significant operational developments, such as strikes, environmental issues, ethical issues.
4. Any CEO contacts involving mergers, acquisitions, leveraged buyouts, etc.
5. Any significant acquisitions of the company's stock.
6. Any insider transactions involving management or directors, such as business dealings between the corporation and outside entities with which management or directors have significant relationships.

No less important, the board requires that information in a timely way, so that board discussions occur *after* the directors have had an opportunity to study and absorb the significance of the data that comes to them. Thus, I think it is important for directors to receive copies of the agenda of board meetings in advance of the meetings, along with relevant supporting data. Otherwise, the board is unprepared for substantive discussion, and is, in effect, weakened in its ability to engage management in meaningful discussion of issues.

Relevant data enable the board to contribute optimally to deliberations relating to the major issues that it is likely to confront. According to a 1989 survey of CEO opinions by Heidrick and Struggles, the executive search firm, the most important issues facing their boards were (1) strategic planning, (2) enhancing shareholder value, (3) management succession, and (4) changing government policies and regulations (Table 3-2). Korn/Ferry's 1990 survey agreed that the first two issues are dominant, but in reverse order, with management succession a close third.[9]

---

[9]Ibid., pp. 12–13.

TABLE 3-2
Most Important Issues Facing Boards

Issue	Percentage of CEOs Naming Issue
Strategic planning and long-term positioning	83.3
Enhancing shareholder value	78.2
Management succession	45.9
Changing government policies and regulations	32.3
Unsolicited hostile takeover attempts	12.8
Corporate debt	11.3
Financial survival of the firm	10.5
Liability	3.9

Source: Heidrick and Struggles, *The Changing Board* (Chicago, Ill., October 1990), p. 11.

THE POWER OF THE BOARD

In reality, the board's degree of power and its exercise of that power depend on several factors, some of which operate positively, some negatively. Jay Lorsch, Louis E. Kirstein Professor of Human Relations at Harvard Business School, and Elizabeth MacIver summarized these factors succinctly in *Pawns or Potentates*.[10] Enhancing factors that operate to elevate board power are (1) the legal authority invested in the board, which is fundamental; (2) the degree of solidarity in the board as a group; and (3) the openness and receptivity of the CEO to board involvement and activism. Of course, legal authority ultimately overshadows all other factors, for it places the legal power to finally decide and dispose issues in the hands of the board. The fact that this power is not exercised nakedly and frequently should not blind one to its reality, even though boards tend to be quiescent except under crisis conditions. Solidarity or lack of it is always a major determinant of the ability of a group to arrive at a consensus, and then to act upon it. A divided board is a fractious and weak board that may make it less difficult for a CEO who is under pressure

---

[10]Lorsch, with MacIver, *Pawns or Potentates*, p. 170. Note Table 8-1.

to maintain his position, at least temporarily; but it is inherently unstable and, eventually destructive to the morale and effectiveness of the organization. A CEO whose style is open and receptive will likely have a stronger and more useful board than a CEO whose style is opposite.

Factors that inhibit board power, according to Lorsch, are:

1. The limited time that directors give to their directorial duties.
2. The limited knowledge and expertise in the detailed affairs of the organization.
3. Lack of solidarity, when it exists.
4. Accepted social usages, such as avoiding criticism of the CEO or open discussion of accountability, avoidance of sensitive issues generally, and/or contacts with sources of information external to the board (which might be viewed as a breach of loyalty, or of confidentiality).
5. The CEO's power (especially as it is manifested through his ability to select directors; control the agenda, the number of meetings and the flow of information to the board; and, finally, superior knowledge and expertise with respect to the detailed operations of the organization).

THE IMPORTANCE OF BOARD COMMITTEES

Board committees assume special importance to board power and ability to meaningfully discharge board functions because they (1) increase the time directors spend on organizational business; (2) increase the information in the hands of directors, and, consequently, their knowledge and expertise; (3) increase a sense of intimacy, social interaction, and readiness to openly discuss sensitive issues; and (4) encourage the growth of solidarity, first in committee, and then in the board. Of course, the committees are thus an instrument for reducing the strength of the factors that inhibit board power vis-à-vis the chief executive.

The most frequently found and most important board committees are audit, compensation/personnel, executive, and nominating. Korn/Ferry International reported in 1990 that, of the corporation boards surveyed, 96.6 percent had an audit committee, 91.1 percent had a compensation/personnel committee, 73.5 percent had an executive committee, and 57.3 percent had a nominating committee.[11]

The audit committee is most common because the thrust of legislation and government regulation (e.g., SEC) practically requires it. If not most important in terms of power, it is certainly equal in power to any other committee because its specific responsibility embraces reviews of financial statements and the auditing process.[12] In short, the basic focus of the audit committee involves nominating the external auditor; meeting periodically with both external and internal auditors; meeting with internal and external auditors privately (apart from management); monitoring compliance with the Foreign Corrupt Practices Act; reviewing quarterly financial statements; monitoring conflict of interest policies, codes of ethics or behavior, and compliance with laws or regulations in general. In connection with all these activities, the audit committee can initiate investigations and ferret out information that might otherwise not come to the board. While not all audit committees engage in all these activities, the trend is for them to be increasingly active in discharging their responsibilities. Plainly, these activities enlarge board power as they lessen the weakening effect of Lorsch's inhibiting factors.

The executive committee is empowered to make decisions and to take action in behalf of the entire board between meetings of the full body. Therefore, the executive committee becomes an instrument for increasing the board's ability to be informed and to spend time as an active decision-making entity. Since board meetings typically number fewer than 10 per year (73.4 percent of the boards reported by Korn/Ferry International in 1990),[13] the meetings of this committee and other committees are important. Fifty point two percent of the boards met less than seven times per year.

The compensation/personnel committee reviews and recommends to the entire board the compensation packages for top management. Nominally, therefore, it has the persuasive power of the purse. In reality, this power is limited by the CEO's ability to bring in outside compensation

---

[11]Korn/Ferry International, *Seventeenth Annual Study, 1990*, p. 17. For further information on compensation of outside directors, see pp. 18–19. Also see Hewitt Associates, *On Compensation* (February 1991), pp. 3–5.

[12]Deloitte, Haskins, and Sells, *Review*, February 27, 1989, p. 3.

[13]Korn/Ferry International, *Seventeenth Annual Study, 1990*, p. 21.

consultants who usually provide data palatable to management—supporting higher salaries, bonuses, and benefits. In fact, an inherently inflationary bias is built into the process, for the consultants provide comparative data that almost invariably results in CEOs leap-frogging one another. But, while that is the usual situation, the latent power to curb management's compensation exists. Like a sleeping lion, the board can awaken and devour the unsuspecting chief executive.

The importance of nominating committees resides in their ability to assert more actively the board's power to select its own membership. To the degree they do so, the CEO's power is curbed, and the independence of the board is enlarged. Other board committees include finance, benefits, public affairs, corporate ethics, and science/technology. It should be noted that the Korn/Ferry International survey now combines compensation and benefits in one committee. As such, their presence increased from 82.2 percent to 91.1 percent between 1985 and 1989.[14]

Finally, it should be noted that board committees are typically comprised mostly of outside directors, and audit committees have no inside directors as members.[15]

ARE BOARD DIRECTORSHIPS DESIRABLE?

The 80s was a decade marked by massive corporate restructuring, resulting from enormous increases in the use of leverage (debt), which was facilitated by the great growth in the marketability of high-yield ("junk") bonds. It was a decade of huge leveraged buy-outs, "greenmail," and "go-go" financing. It seemed that every day some new, sophisticated financial instrument appeared. The use of debt mushroomed, supplanting equity as the major source of capital. Of course, such easy financing encouraged an increase in executive and corporate megalomania, so that a number of sound corporations were made unsound by being loaded with mountains of debt.

Raids, mergers, acquisitions, defensive restructurings, and conversions of public corporations into private ones became common. And corporate boards were thrust into the midst of this financial and organizational

---

[14]Ibid., p. 17.
[15]Ibid.

cauldron. The things that directors could most surely count on in this climate were lawsuits and enormously increased demands on their time as directors. The earlier picture of the director's job as cushy and pleasant was destroyed. And, by the middle of the decade, a common view emerged that directors were fleeing the field. Indeed, the September 8, 1986, issue of *Business Week* (page 56) featured a cover story article titled "The Job Nobody Wants; Outside Directors Find That the Risks and Hassles Just Aren't Worth It."

The actual picture is not quite so grim. For one thing, the availability of directors' liability insurance has become much easier since 1986, and the cost has come down. In that year, 82.1 percent of the boards surveyed by Korn/Ferry International reported increases in such insurance premiums.[16] And some found liability insurance coverage almost impossible to obtain. Where it was obtainable, in addition to sharp increases in premiums, deductible levels rose sharply and the range of coverage was circumscribed. Many directors became frightened and cut back on their directorships. But, by 1989, only 18.9 percent of the boards surveyed reported increases in premiums, and 81.1 percent reported no increases.[17] Also, where decreases in dollar coverage amounted to 50.3 percent of the boards reporting in 1986, that percentage had dropped to 12.5 by 1988.

Seventy-seven and seven-tenths percent of prospective directors accepted invitations to serve in 1985 and 75.1 percent accepted in 1989. In both years, the overwhelming majority of invitees (some three quarters) *accepted.* Declinations did rise from 20.4 percent to 24.9 percent in the five-year period (there were 1.9 percent "no" responses in the survey in 1985), but this cannot be described as a mass exodus.[18] Interestingly, only 5.2 percent of those declining appointments as directors in 1989 cited increasing legal liability as their main reason (while this percentage was up from 3.7 in 1984, it was down from 8.3 percent in 1988). Time commitment was the primary reason given for declining (67.0 percent in 1989, up from 60.2 percent in 1985); membership on too many boards next (up to 37.1 percent in 1989 as against 28.8 percent in 1985); and conflicts of interest third (24.7 percent in 1989 as compared with 21.2 percent in

---

[16]Korn/Ferry International, *Sixteenth Annual Study, 1989,* p. 21.

[17]Korn/Ferry International, *Seventeenth Annual Study, 1990,* p. 21.

[18]Korn/Ferry International, *Sixteenth Annual Study, 1989,* p. 23.

1985).[19] Time is clearly a major concern. And it should be observed that membership on too many boards may be another way of expressing the time constraint; that is, as time required on each board expands, one must cut back on the number of boards one can serve on properly. I believe an indeterminate number of prospective directors found it more convenient to allege time constraint than to admit to fear of legal liability.

In short, board directorships remain attractive and desirable to many qualified people. But the responsibility and time demands are greater, and prospective directors are more selective and less likely to involve themselves in too many boards.

COMPOSITION OF THE BOARD: THE TRAITS DESIRED

The 426 companies surveyed by Korn/Ferry International in 1989 revealed a variation in average board size between 10 and 18 members.[20] The number of inside directors (management) varied little, averaging 3 or 4, while the number of outside directors averaged between 7 and 14. Consequently, outside directors outnumbered inside ones. Indeed, in 1978, Harold Williams, then chairman of the Securities and Exchange Commission (SEC), asserted that the ideal board would be limited to only one inside member.[21]

The foregoing paragraph emphasizes numbers of inside directors versus outside ones, implying that a preponderance of outside directors is inherently a superior arrangement. From the standpoint of the power relationship between board and chief executive, we have already observed that a majority of outside directors encourages board independence, because it weights the numerical balance of power on the side of the board.

Richard R. West, dean of New York University's Leonard N. Stern School of Business, discussed the insider-outsider composition of the board most perceptively, focusing on the qualities insiders bring rather than on the issue of relative numbers.[22] In those terms, there is no inherent reason

---

[19]Korn/Ferry International, *Seventeenth Annual Study, 1990*, p. 23.

[20]Ibid., p. 14.

[21]Richard R. West, "Inside Directors and Former Corporate Officers as Board Members," in Edward Mattar, and Michael Ball, *Handbook for Corporate Directors* (New York: McGraw-Hill Book Co., 1985), 25.3.

[22]Ibid. pp. 25.5–25.10.

to view insiders as less desirable than outsiders with respect to such qualities as integrity, an inquiring mind, vision, ability to work with others, and broad experience. However, when it comes to independence of the chief executive, West notes there is strong opinion that members of management are unlikely to stand up against the CEO before the board, even though some commentators think otherwise. Other observers point to an inherent conflict of interest facing insider board members when issues such as hostile tender offers come up. After all, as West notes, "Their jobs may be on the line." An interesting and novel view sees insiders as focusing too narrowly on the bottom line and the short-term interests of shareholders, while outsiders are more inclined to be sensitive to other stakeholders (the public interest) and the longer term. Probably the strongest argument favoring insiders as board members is the fact that their knowledge and expertise relative to the company are great, so that their presence increases the board's knowledge base. Of course, this point assumes that insiders will be sufficiently independent to share their knowledge with outside directors, especially when it may be critical of the CEO.

The actual board composition picture revealed by the Korn/Ferry International survey seems to reflect the considerations discussed. The presence of a minority of insiders is justifiable, while overall board independence in pursuit of broad objectives and the long-term health of the enterprise is enhanced by a majority of outsiders.

Harold Williams, in addition to questioning the presence of insiders on boards of directors, challenged the arrangement whereby the chairman of the board is also the chief executive officer. The overwhelmingly predominant arrangement is presently one in which the board chairman and the CEO are one and the same person. Korn/Ferry International reported that in 1989 almost 79 percent (78.6) of the 426 companies surveyed had that arrangement.[23]

What is the desirable arrangement? The answer is colored by the bias of the respondent! At one end of the opinion spectrum, to one who is exclusively concerned with board independence, the answer is clear: the CEO should not also serve as board chairman. In the opinion of one who sees authority of position as critical to the CEO's ability to lead the organization, the CEO absolutely should have the chairman's place. For those who fall between these poles, the answer is not so clear. Since I have already

[23]Korn/Ferry International, *Seventeenth Annual Study, 1990*, p. 14.

expressed myself with respect to authority of leadership, as against authority of position, I do not think the CEO's ability to lead is compromised if he is not also board chairman, nor do I think board independence is compromised if the CEO is also the board chairman. Either arrangement can work. But I do believe the CEO should be a member of the board, able to participate in its deliberations as a matter of position and right, rather than as a guest and by invitation. I think the CEO's knowledge and expertise is critical and should be brought to the board, but not in a structural arrangement that can invite separation, suspicion, and an adversarial climate.

What about former corporate officers as board members, especially the CEO? On the surface, it would seem they would be most desirable. Their knowledge and expertise should be great. And their removal from day-to-day operations should give them a degree of detachment and objectivity. Unfortunately, the opposite is too frequently the case. Rather than detachment, they may be wedded to the policies and programs they instituted when active executives. If so, they become a hindrance and danger to present management, which may have to respond to rapidly changing conditions requiring new programs and policies, oftentimes at variance with those that existed earlier. In this case, it is wiser for retirement from the executive position to be coupled with retirement from the board.

Allen Neuharth, former CEO of Gannett and founder of *USA Today*, expressed himself forcefully on this subject in his autobiography *Confessions of an S.O.B.*[24]

> Under Gannett's bylaws, directors are elected to three-year terms. I was re-elected in 1988 to a term expiring in 1991. And Gannett bylaws then set seventy as the retirement age for directors who have served as CEO. So everyone expected me to stand for re-election in 1991 and serve until 1994.
>
> On March 22, 1989, the day of my sixty-fifth birthday, I conducted my last board meeting as chairman in a normal and usual way. When we came to the last agenda item, "Other Business," I distributed a letter to the board members, each personalized with handwritten special thanks.
>
> It was my letter of resignation from the board. I had discussed it with only two board members in advance—with Curley a few days before and with McCorkindale a few hours before. I pledged each to secrecy.
>
> The letter read, in part:

---

[24]Al Neuharth, *Confessions of an S.O.B.* (New York: Doubleday, 1989), p. 351.

"My own experiences and observations convince me that when a retired former CEO remains on the board of directors of a corporation, his/her mere presence is often an inhibiting factor. I do not wish to risk bridling either my successor or the board in any way. Therefore, this is my resignation as a Gannett director."

I moved the resolution to accept my resignation. Several directors raised their hands. Several spoke simultaneously. I cut off all discussion and called for the question, then quickly declared the motion passed and adjourned the meeting.

What traits should board members have? West, cited earlier, noted a number. Joseph F. Alibrandi, president of the Whittaker Corporation, listed these:[25]

1. Integrity.
2. Acumen.
3. Mature business judgment.
4. Vision and imagination.
5. Independence.
6. Cooperation.
7. Achievement.

Some traits support and reinforce others. For example, substantial achievement in other fields provides an aura of authority of leadership from outside the board and enhances independence within the board. Cooperation, it must be noted, does not mean subservience and surrender of independence. It does mean that after debate is over and a decision is reached, one gives his best efforts to successful implementation of the decision. Obviously, directors possessing the foregoing roster of traits will not be lackeys or compliant tools of any chief executive.

Alibrandi's judgment is supported by the results of the Heidrick and Struggles 1989 survey of CEOs. Table 3–3 shows the personality characteristics deemed to be valuable by the respondent CEOs.

What backgrounds characterize the members comprising the board of directors? Korn/Ferry International's 1989 survey reported the results shown in Table 3–4.

---

[25]Edward Mattar, and Michael Ball, *Handbook for Corporate Directors*, p. 23.2.

TABLE 3–3
Most Valuable Traits of Directors

Trait	Percentage of Respondent CEOs Naming Trait
Objectivity	71.3
Intelligence	64.2
Honesty	48.3
Management know-how	41.7
Leadership qualities	22.1
Credibility	20.8
Board knowledge	8.8
Loyalty	7.1
Supportiveness	7.1
Team player abilities	5.8
Assertiveness	2.9
Hardworker	1.3

Source: Heidrick and Struggles, *The Changing Board,* p. 10.

The percentages shown in Table 3–4 are nonadditive; a single individual may have more than one characteristic (e.g., be an ethnic minority member, an academic, and a woman). Nonetheless, executives, present or retired, inside or outside, clearly predominate as board members. Women, academicians, and ethnic minority members are more recent arrivals, at least in the proportions now shown. But attorneys and bankers are probably somewhat less prominent than they were in earlier decades. To the degree attorneys provide paid services for the corporation, their independence seems to be reduced by an inherent conflict-of-interest. The same observation would apply to bankers, whether commercial or investment, where the corporation is a depositor and/or borrower of the financial institution. Former government officials may be tainted, especially if they were in government agencies having substantial business dealings with the firm they now serve as directors. In fact, all relationships might be tainted by incestuous business dealings, past or present. The key point is that such relationships are best avoided if one wants an independent board.

The general order of importance in the backgrounds of board members reported by the Korn/Ferry survey is confirmed by the 1989 survey of board chairmen (CEOs) by Heidrick and Struggles. The latter's results are shown in Table 3–5.

TABLE 3-4
Backgrounds of Board Members, 1989

Background	Percentage
CEO/COO of other companies	79.5
Retired executive (other companies)	64.1
Woman	59.1
Academician	55.4
Retired corporate officer	47.0
Senior executive (other companies)	39.5
Attorney (not providing legal services for the company)	33.5
Ethnic minority member	31.6
Former government official	27.7
Major shareholder (not officer of company)	24.1
Commercial banker	22.7
"Professional" director	27.0
Investment banker	22.9
Attorney (providing legal services for the company)	25.8
Non-U.S. citizen	12.0
International executive (U.S. citizen)	6.7

Source: Korn/Ferry International, *Seventeenth Annual Study, 1990,* p. 15.

LITIGATION AND DIRECTORIAL INDEPENDENCE

It requires no stretch of the imagination to grasp the point that litigation, which is expensive and time consuming as well as threatening in terms of personal liability, has an impact on directors. One impact is to encourage a flight from board membership, about which we commented earlier. Another impact is to stiffen the spines of those directors who remain, making them less compliant to the leadership of the chief executive and more prone to question and challenge his dominance.

What are the issues that tend to stimulate litigation against directors? Bayless Manning, former dean of the Stanford Law School, was quoted in the *DH&S Review* as suggesting three sorts of issues: (1) enterprise decisions of the board (e.g., authorizing plant closures); (2) government regulations and related litigation (e.g., product liability cases and environmental impact situations); and (3) shareholder suits, usually by shareholders

TABLE 3–5
Occupations of Outside Directors, 1989

Occupation	Percentage of Chairmen Having Directors with the Listed Occupation
CEO or COO of another company	93.6
Retired executive of another company	80.0
Academician	61.9
Retired corporate officer	51.3
Senior executive of another company	49.8
Attorney who Doesn't provide Company legal services	31.3
Former government official	28.7
Commercial banker	21.5
Major shareholder (not company officer)	20.8
Investment banker	18.9
Attorney who provides company legal services	16.6
"Professional" director	13.2

Source: Heldrick and Struggles, *The Changing Board*, p. 9.

who believe the board has failed to maximize the value of their ownership of corporate stock.[26] The third set of issues is the one most commonly thought of in connection with litigation against directors. But the second set of issues is important and will probably become increasingly so. The first set, enterprise issues involving basic business decisions, are not commonly the basis for litigation aimed at the board, but that may change as unions seek to insulate their members against decisions to close plants.

Personal liability of directors for board decisions is a relatively new phenomenon. Traditionally, the directors of a corporation enjoyed substantial protection against litigation due to the "business judgment rule," a principle that reflected "judicial recognition that actions taken by directors in good faith and in the exercise of business judgment should not be second guessed by the courts."[27]

---

[26]*DH&S Review*, Deloitte, Haskins, and Sells, New York, February 2, 1987, pp. 1–2.

[27]Scott V. Simpson, "The Emerging Role of the Special Committee—Ensuring Business Judgment Rule Protection in the Context of Management Leveraged Buyouts and Other Corporate Transactions Involving Conflicts of Interest," *The Business Lawyer* 43 no. 2, February, 1988, pp. 669–70.

The rationale underlying the business judgment rule rests on several principles of corporate law: (1) directors have the primary responsibility for overseeing corporate affairs; (2) directors are in the best position to bring together information as a basis for an informed decision on complex business matters; and (3) being under a fiduciary obligation to stockholders to act in the corporation's best interests, directors should be allowed broad discretion in conducting corporate affairs. It follows that holding directors liable for honest mistakes in business judgment would overburden the courts, make directors insurers against corporate losses, and frighten qualified people away from serving as directors.

Of course, the business judgment rule is a protection for directors only if they satisfy their fiduciary obligations—the duty of care and the duty of loyalty—in making business decisions. To satisfy the duty of care, a director must carry out his duties "with such care as an ordinarily prudent person in a like position would use under similar circumstances."[28] Generally, the statement means that directors must have sufficient knowledge of a proposed transaction, independently examine the information available, and take sufficient time to insure proper consideration of the transaction. The duty of loyalty involves conflicts of interest. "The business judgment rule does not protect directors who stand on both sides of a challenged transaction unless steps are taken to insulate the decision making process from actual or potential conflicts of interest.[29] Perhaps the most significant cases involving duty of care are *Smith v. Von Gorkom* and *Hanson Trust PLC v. ML SCM Acquisition*. In both cases, the boards of directors were presented with faits accomplis and did not have an opportunity to analyze or negotiate the transaction at arm's length. Perhaps the most significant early cases involving duty of loyalty were *Unocal Corp. v. Mesa Petroleum Co.*, and *Revlon, Inc. v. MacAndrews and Forbes Holdings*.

A major protective device is found in board appointment of a special committee of outside directors, whose charge is to gather information about and independently evaluate a proposed transaction (e.g., merger, acquisition, leveraged buyout). The special committee was not discussed in this chapter's section on committees because it is not a standing committee of the board and because its existence and nature is most relevant here. A key feature of the special committee's role is its authorization by the board

---

[28]Ibid., pp. 671–78.
[29]Ibid., p. 674.

to retain independent advisors (attorneys and investment counselors). Lawyers are necessary to insure that the special committee satisfies all requirements of *process* with respect to organization, meetings, agendas, minutes, review of relevant agreements and documents, and obligations under applicable federal and state law. Investment counselors are needed to advise the special committee as to the fairness of value in a proposed transaction, to insure that the interest of the stockholders is upheld. It is important that the committee meet with its advisors independently of management, and that its advisors be separate from and independent of those advising management. Finally, the special committee's deliberations must be independent of management.

It was noted earlier, using Korn/Ferry International's 1988 survey data, that the inclination of directors to leave the board seems to have peaked around 1986, with signs of abatement since. The major reasons for the easing seem to be (1) the return of reasonably available directors and officers liability insurance; (2) the enactment of new state laws (perhaps most notably in Delaware and Pennsylvania); and (3) recent court decisions (e.g., *Time Warner v. Paramount*). Korn/Ferry International data indicated the improved availability of D and O (Directors and Officers) insurance. The relevant Delaware statute went into effect on July 1, 1986. It allowed companies chartered in Delaware to excuse directors from liability for money damages for negligent injury to their companies and stockholders, if the shareholders voted approval of the arrangement. However, the protection does not apply to a director in cases of bad faith, disloyalty, or intentional misconduct.[30] The Pennsylvania law, enacted at the end of the decade of the 80s, explicitly recognized the right and responsibility of directors to weigh stakeholder interests along with those of stockholders. Interestingly, some major corporations are not availing themselves of the law's protection, presumably out of concern that so doing might adversely affect the market value of their stock. Indeed, there were reports that some major pension fund trustees had threatened to unload the shares of companies chartered in Pennsylvania that did use the protection of the law.

The *Time Warner v. Paramount* case involved the issue of the primacy of stockholder interest, at least when that interest was measured by

---

[30]Leo Herzel, Richard W. Shepro, and Leo Katz, "Next-to-Last Word on Endangered Directors," *Harvard Business Review*, January–February 1987, pp. 38–43.

maximizing immediate, short-term stock value. L. Gordon Crovitz discussed the *Time Warner* decision, saying:[31]

> *Paramount* v. *Time* shows how far the law has moved from the notion that corporate boards exist to serve stockholders. Delaware corporate law risks losing touch with one reason corporations were created as a way of doing business in the first place. This is that people will offer their capital to strangers only if they know that their agents—corporate directors—are legally bound to maximize share prices.
>
> Courts have a rule, the "business judgment rule," that they won't second-guess decisions by corporate boards such as mergers; stockholders select corporate directors, not judges, to make decisions for the corporation. But there is an exception. Judges are supposed to intervene when directors in some way violate their fiduciary duty to stockholders. The markets and common sense suggest that a failure to maximize share price is a pretty good indication that a board has let its stockholders down.
>
> The law, naturally, is not so simple. The justices said Time's plan to merge with Warner didn't mean that Time had put itself up for sale, so it was free to reject bids, even Paramount's all-cash bid for all shares. "Absent a limited set of circumstances," they wrote, "a board of directors, while always required to act in an informed manner, is not under any *per se* duty to maximize shareholder value in the short term, even in the context of a takeover." It left unclear what duty directors owe to whom over what time period.
>
> Instead, the justices noted that Time directors, "expressed their concern that their stockholders would not comprehend the long-term benefits of the Warner merger" and that Paramount's "cash premium would be a tempting prospect." So tempting that Time changed the structure of its merger with Warner to avoid New York Stock Exchange rules that would have required stockholder approval.

A key point in judging the responsibility of directors to shareholders as against stakeholders is whether a company is being sold, whether there is a change of control! The court was careful to observe that in the *Time Warner v. Paramount* case it did not see a change of control. Consequently, it upheld the right of the Time board to reject an all-cash offer from Paramount, which followed an announcement that Time Warner would merge in a cash-free, tax-free exchange of stock. That deal would have left the

---

[31]L. Gordon Crovitz, "Can Takeover Targets Just Say No to Stockholders?" *The Wall Street Journal*, March 7, 1990, p. A 19.

stockholders of both companies with stock in the new merged entity, rather than with the $200 per share cash ultimately offered by Paramount. Time's board didn't just turn down the Paramount offer (originally $175 per share). It agreed to change the original plan and have Time buy Warner, without putting the decision to a shareholder vote. The judge, William T. Allen, ruled that the revised transaction did not involve a change of control (the shareholders remained as owners) so there was no sale, and, consequently, the directors had the right to make their decision without putting it to a stockholder vote. However, when there is a change of control and a sale is involved, the directors' overriding responsibility is to maximize shareholder value.[32]

IS LONG-RUN CORPORATE HEALTH ENHANCED BY CEO-BOARD COOPERATION?

As stated, the question is rhetorical. One is compelled to answer affirmatively, for the opposite of cooperation is conflict. And conflict involves division and internal battling that is destructive of morale and undermines the effectiveness and efficiency of the organization. Conflict between CEO and board spills over from the boardroom, infects and poisons the corporate body, and endangers the organization. Yet the American Law Institute, the most prestigious private sector legal institution in the country with some 3,000 members, including about 70 law professors and 400 judges, has been involved in a huge decade-long project to state the legal principles applicable to the governance of U.S. corporations, which seems to be producing a "litigation model" of corporate governance.[33]

Donald V. Seibert, former chairman of J.C. Penney Company, believes this model would limit the role and powers of directors, encourage lawsuits against directors and officers, and undermine the trend toward stronger and more effective boards of directors. Even if the adverse effects were less, Seibert believes they would discourage highly qualified people from serving as directors and reduce the incentives for corporations to seek the best candidates.

---

[32]See also Lorsch, with MacIver, *Pawns or Potentates*, pp. 49–53 and Courtney C. Brown., pp. 7–10.

[33]Donald V. Seibert, "The ALI and its 'Litigation Model' of Corporate Governance," a National Legal Center for the Public Interest, White Paper 1, no. 2, April 1, 1989.

Having served on half a dozen boards of public corporations, as well as on the boards of public (government) bodies and private corporations, I am convinced that the litigation model would be a disaster. It would clog the courts, even beyond their present condition, would cause a resurgence of the flight of qualified directors, and would discourage their replacement by other qualified people. Without overstating the matter, it seems fair to observe that derivative litigation; that is, lawsuits brought on behalf of a corporation by any shareholder, no matter how small his holdings, provide a pleasant, lucrative market niche for the legal profession, because a successful shareholder suit involves payment of the stockholder's attorney's fees by the corporation. And such fees are far from inconsequential. In fact, such lawsuits are known as strike suits, and there are attorneys specializing in such suits who have built what is much more than a "cottage industry" in the field. Seibert charges that "in most cases, the real moving force behind such litigation is a lawyer who is interested only in a settlement which will maximize his fee.[34] As chairman of the special committee of the board in one public corporation involved in a management-inspired leveraged buyout, I was deposed in a strike suit. The deposition came many months after the successful completion of the leveraged buyout (LBO), and following a settlement reached with the plaintiff shareholders in the strike suit. The sole purpose of the deposition, as far as I could see, was to justify the fees paid to the shareholders' lawyers, although that purpose was not evident to any casual observer.

Boards need to be independent, and their independence is good for chief executives and their organizations. But independence should involve helpful advice and cooperation, not conflict. It is a grave error to think that conflict between board and CEO will avoid compliant, subservient boards. In fact, the effort to stimulate an adversarial climate by such devices as the "litigation model" of corporate governance could bring out the very opposite result from the one intended, for only weak, indecisive, and inexperienced people would agree to serve as directors.

---

[34]Ibid., p. 9.

CHAPTER 4

EXECUTIVE POWER AND LABOR

IS LABOR SUBSERVIENT?

Does executive power rule, while labor is subordinate? Idealized competitive price theory answers in the negative, for it sees employers bidding for workers in competitive labor markets where both employers and workers are knowledgeable about market conditions and able to move freely in pursuit of their respective best interests. The interaction of demand and supply rules employment and labor's price. But the real world's labor markets are not perfectly competitive, and power resides essentially in the hands of the party controlling access to employment: the one with power to hire and fire.

In private business enterprises, this power resides in those possessing ownership. In fact, this is the source of the ultimate power of the board of directors over the chief executive in public corporations. As the agents of the shareholders (owners), the board has the power to hire and fire management, including the CEO. In closely held corporations, where the CEO is also the major stockholder, he is his own boss, and the dichotomy between ownership and management doesn't exist. But in the public corporation, it does. It is simply an extension to view management's power over labor as resting on the same base of control over access to employment. In this case, management's power is an extension of the power of ownership, with management acting as an agent of ownership.

Karl Marx, almost a century and a half ago, focused on private ownership of capital, and its inherent power over the employment relationship, as the basis of capitalism's alleged ability to exploit labor and extract what he called surplus value. He thought, mistakenly, that socialism, which would socialize the ownership of capital, would also destroy the employer's (management's) power over labor. But we have seen in the 20th century that state-controlled management has even greater power.

Power over access to employment has both material and nonmaterial aspects. The material aspects relate to wages, benefits, and other conditions of the employment relationship. The nonmaterial aspects relate to social status, to a person's position in society. An employed person possesses status, he or she can say who he or she is and what he or she does in the community. An unemployed person carries a sense of social stigma, of being an outcast, a failure.

Labor's overwhelming concern over the employment relationship underlies its efforts to build countervailing power to that of ownership. These efforts are most dramatically reflected in unionization and the efforts of workers to enlarge their own power through concerted action (e.g., the strike). But labor can and does engage in joint action in the absence of unions. It does so through a variety of informal understandings on the "shop floor," relative to output norms and work practices. Also, the employer's power over the employment relationship is today circumscribed by an extensive web of governmental regulations relating to wages, hours, and working conditions.

Still, in the overall interplay of power between management (the executive) and labor, the balance is on the side of the employer. And this is more true today than it was four decades ago, when organized labor in the United States reached its zenith as a percentage of the organizable labor force, and as a power equal to that of management in major industrial sectors of the economy (e.g., steel, automobiles, trucking, coal mining, tires, etc.). Between 1973 and 1989, the percentage of civilian wage and salary workers, ages 14 and over, who were union members declined from 23.6 to 16.3.[1] The decline was even greater if one goes back to the 1950s.

John Kenneth Galbraith forecast the decline of U.S. trade unionism in *The New Industrial State,* published in 1967.[2] But he did not envisage unionism's demise, seeing for it useful purposes in the emerging indus-

---

[1]Michael A. Curme, Barry T. Hirsch, and David A. Macpherson, "Union Membership and Contract Coverage in the United States, 1983–1988," *Industrial and Labor Relations Review,* 44, no. 1, October 1990, p. 9.

[2]John Kenneth Galbraith, *The New Industrial State* (Boston: Houghton Mifflin Co., 1967), Chapters 23 and 24.

trial system that would be dominated by professionally managed giant corporate organizations. Of course, his view of the power of these mega corporations did not anticipate the effect on them of foreign competition in the late seventies and the decade of the eighties. He did, however, describe a partnership of power between corporate management and organized labor, in which, unchallenged by effective competition in the marketplace, they would negotiate cost-increasing agreements and pass the increased costs onto consumers. This partnership allowed a period of industrial relations harmony, which was ended by fierce competition from abroad in the 80s, a harsh reminder of the power of market forces. Indeed, "the new industrial state" did not survive in accordance with Galbraith's analysis.

POINTS OF CONFLICT BETWEEN
EXECUTIVE POWER AND LABOR

I set aside here any element of ideological class conflict and restrict my remarks to the major issues that have marked labor-management relations in the pragmatic context of U.S. unionism. Not that ideology was absent from the historical development of U.S. unionism, for it was not absent. There were socialists, communists, and anarchists aplenty—men and women wedded to violent action as well as those peacefully inclined. But the eventual character of our trade union movement was never expressed better than it was by Samuel Gompers early in the 20th century. Asked by a U.S. Senator about labor goals, he replied simply, "More." Not the overthrow of the capitalistic system! Not its replacement by socialism! Just, "More!"

In that context, management and labor have concentrated on (1) wages and benefits; (2) productivity (i.e., output/man hour); (3) production costs (i.e., the relationship between (1) and (2)); (4) quality of output; and (5) job security. There is no order of importance intended or implied by this listing; all topics are major, although their primacy will shift with time and changes in the economic environment. Order of importance will also vary among industries, as they are variously affected by economic conditions particular to each.

Generally, when the economy is flourishing, wages and benefits will tend to rise, with productivity rising less rapidly. Consequently, production costs are driven upwards. But labor markets will be tight in a booming economy, so that industrial discipline will probably slip and output quality drop. That combination of conditions emerged in the U.S. economy as it evolved during the long post-war boom of the 50s and 60s. But, as we have noted before, the emergence of powerful economies in Germany and Japan, as well as elsewhere in the Pacific Rim and Europe, brought strong, competitive challengers to confront a U.S. economy grown slack and sloppy in its management and quality of product.

The competitive challenge to the U.S. industrial heartland industries, most notably autos, rubber, steel, and so forth, changed the climate dramatically. Jobs were lost by the thousands. Once proud, powerful firms succumbed to the adverse economic pressures of severely competitive markets and were threatened with liquidation or absorption. Productivity improvement and better output quality became goals essential to survival. Once powerful unions lost members and market power. U.S. management rediscovered W. Edwards Deming, the elderly guru of quality improvement, whose ideas had been so influential in Japan's postwar revival. They also discovered other voices spreading the doctrine of quality improvement. And a mutuality of interest in quality, productivity, and competitive costs and prices was perceived by both management and labor. Leading unions negotiated wage, benefit, and working condition "give-backs." Both sides began efforts to improve quality. These efforts have had significant results, although they are still a distance from where they need to be.

In particular, job security has emerged as labor's major, if not overriding, concern. Give-backs in wages and such have been traded for job security guarantees of one sort or another. Where jobs cannot be secured at prior aggregate levels of employment, labor has settled for a variety of early retirement arrangements. The central economic issue between management and labor in this connection is that the former desires labor to be treated as a variable cost, while labor would like itself to be a fixed factor of production (to have some form of guaranteed employment). Of course, labor's desire is not compatible with fluctuations in market conditions, although the human, social, and political costs of substantial unemployment are heavy. A humane society provides cushions to aid the unemployed as they adjust to cyclical and structural unemployment (e.g., unemployment compensation, retraining programs). But blanket governmental guarantees of jobs are ill advised, and, in the long run, disastrous. Recent revelations of experience in the Soviet Union and Eastern Europe have made this abundantly clear. And we learn more every day of the underemployment (idleness on the job) and grotesque inefficiency that characterized those economies. Military might could not in the end obscure these things, and, indeed, military might finally collapsed under their burden.

THE INSTRUMENTS OF EXECUTIVE POWER

In the give and take of industrial relations, the instruments or means of exercising executive power are both pleasant (the "carrot") and punitive (the "stick"). The pleasant ones involve rewards (positive incentives) to encourage labor to the type of behavior desired by the executive and his managerial agents. Among them are (1) wage increases that can be tied to output or other incentive plans; (2) bonuses (i.e., direct money payments for meeting specific goals); (3) awards and prizes (e.g., cruises, cars, TVs, VCRs, other electronic appliances, and so on); (4) promotion (i.e., advances in status, as indicated by a higher title, which may or may not be associated with an improvement in pay or other direct material reward); and (5) nonwage benefits (e.g., perks, such as credit cards, company housing, meals, and travel allowances).

Alongside the "carrot" of rewards lies the "stick" of punitive and painful executive actions. The arsenal of unpleasant instruments includes (1) discharge, (2) suspension without pay, (3) fines, (4) demotion, (5) warnings, (6) harassment, and (7) litigation, where an employee is charged with wilfully destructive actions (sabotage). The foregoing list is self-explanatory and understood as to its nature, with the possible exception of harassment. Harassment, as a means of punishing uncompromising and disobedient workers, is nastier in nature than the others because it is oftentimes cloaked and devious. It includes techniques such as deliberate assignment to inconvenient work schedules, made to appear as being necessary to the needs of the organization's operations. Harassment can also include riding, which is uncalled for criticism of worker performance, appearance, and mannerisms. The range of possibilities is limited only by the creativity of the manager's imagination.

Whether pleasant or punitive, all the above actions are instruments of power, and they are exercised for the purpose of enforcing the executive's ability to channel labor's behavior in directions desired by him or her.

THE INSTRUMENTS OF LABOR'S POWER

But labor is not defenseless. It has some instruments of power on its side, although their number and strength vary with the absence or presence of unionization, the degree of cohesiveness in the worker group, and market conditions.

In an unorganized environment, labor will typically rely on informal or customary work rules regarding the pace of work and acceptable output levels. These rules usually reflect a notion or belief common to labor, known as the "fixed lump of work." Its central idea is that there is a fixed amount of work to be done, and anything that speeds up its completion results in unemployment. The idea is attractive, because it seems self-evident in the microcosm of the individual shop, in the short-run time period. Indeed, in that context, the immediate impact of an increase in productivity may be the discharge of some employees. But in the longer run, as increased productivity makes possible lower prices of output, more can be sold (depending on demand elasticity), and, especially when demand is elastic, a vast increase in output and employment can be experienced. In any event, labor can and does oppose managerial efforts to step up the pace of work, usually through peer pressure. If peer pressure in its more subtle forms fails, then physical force can be and is exercised. Labor will oppose not only a management-inspired "speed-up," but may also oppose the introduction of new technology, once again fearing unemployment as its outcome.

Beyond informal, customary work rules, labor may engage in a concerted slowdown, in which case output is deliberately held below the customary or normal level. Of course, a concerted action such as this one is likely to elicit the exercise of countervailing power from management's side. The outcome of such a struggle will depend on the relative staying power on each side.

Known but relatively uncommon in the United States is the use of sabotage: the willful, deliberate destruction of the employer's plant, equipment, and/or inventories. Sabotage is inherently violent in nature, and is illegal. But desperate workers do have recourse to it as a tactic intended to bring an employer to terms. The 1990 strike of the Greyhound Bus Company's drivers provided instances of sabotage. Indeed, press reports indicated it went beyond the destruction or damaging of equipment, to low-level guerrilla warfare when strikers fired guns at Greyhound buses.

In an organized trade union context, the spectrum of instruments of power available to labor is much greater. First and foremost is the collective bargaining agreement, a legally binding contract which recognizes the union as labor's exclusive agent, and which sets forth an elaborate web of rules bearing on (1) wages; (2) benefits (e.g., pensions, health and welfare); (3) work rules and practices (e.g., "manning" tables, output norms, incentive plans); (4) limitations on executive power to punish alleged worker infractions of work rules bearing on such matters as output quality, output amount, absenteeism, tardiness, insubordination, drug use, alcoholism; and (5) dispute settlement arrangements (e.g., grievance procedures and arbitration). This list is indicative, but not exhaustive.

In the absence of a collective bargaining agreement, or when one has broken down in the face of an intractable dispute, trade unions have an arsenal of weapons available. These weapons include the organized, concerted withdrawal of labor power—the strike. Its aim is to bring the employer's business to a halt, shutting off operational revenues while fixed business costs continue. Its effectiveness depends on the relative staying power of the two sides. On the employer's side, staying power will reflect financial strength, anticipated loss of market position, public relations, possible government intervention, and the intangible, emotional element known as stubbornness. On labor's side, staying power will also reflect financial strength, in this case of the union and its members (possibly buttressed by unemployment compensation in some states after a certain waiting period), concern over the possible destruction of the company and a consequent loss of jobs, reaction of the public and other trade unions, and, again, stubbornness. For many years after World War II, the typical employer reaction to a strike was to shut down. But, since the Federal government broke the PATCO (air traffic controllers) strike in 1981, employers have become more combative, and frequently strive to maintain operations by hiring strike-breakers.

Other instruments of union power are the slowdown, more effective when orchestrated by a union than by a nonunion work force, the boycott (a concerted refusal to buy the employer's product), and litigation, usually alleging unfair labor practices, discrimination, unsafe working conditions, violations of environmental regulations, and so on. Even without litigation by the union, efforts can be made to involve regulatory agencies by alleging company infractions of the regulations noted. Of course, secondary boycotts are illegal; that is, boycotts of firms not directly involved in the dispute but doing business with the employer who is a primary participant in the dispute.

In general, union power is limited by market conditions: that is, competition, both foreign and domestic; and unemployment, whether cyclical or structural. There was a time after World War II when it was popular in certain quarters to believe that U.S. trade unions had overcome market restraints. I am reminded here of the influential article published in the *American Economic Review* of September 1947 entitled "The Trade Union as a Wage-Fixing Institution," by the late Professor Arthur M. Ross.[3] In that article, he expressed the view that the American trade union movement could set wages without significant regard for the employment effect. The article was widely quoted and had a large impact on academicians and others. Of course, the immediate post-war period was one in which U.S. industry dominated a war-devastated world, and effective competition was nonexistent. In short, what appeared to be trade union power and market control really reflected a lack of effective competition in a market starved for goods.

The world has changed. It is rebuilt and vigorous. Competition is real. And the brilliant insight of four decades ago is fallen before the spectacle of a U.S. trade union movement in retreat and even disarray. The auto workers, the steel workers, the teamsters, and the coal miners are all reduced in number and have made major concessions, even in so basic a matter as standard industrywide wages and conditions. The problems of *individual* firms are being recognized and allowances made for them. Essentially, ground has been given on the wage, work rule, and benefit front to achieve greater security on the employment front. And, as these changes have occurred, employer resistance has undoubtedly strengthened. A tacit understanding between big business and big labor, which characterized less competitive times, appears to have broken down. Cushy, costly collective bargaining contracts, with their costs readily passed on to consumers, are no longer viable. And this situation confronts both U.S. management and labor with a major challenge, for their mutuality of interest has never been greater. Will they recognize that mutuality, and, having recognized it, will they find significant ways of implementing their recognition?

---

[3]See Abraham L. Gitlow, and Howard S. Gitlow, "Labor-Management Relations: A Vital Piece of the Quality Puzzle," *Rivista Internationale di Scienze Economiche e Commerciali*, Anno XXXIII, n. 6–7, pp. 546–47.

THE EMERGING MUTUALITY OF INTEREST

Quality is the litmus test for competitive power in today's economic environment.[4] Seller success in the marketplace depends greatly on buyer perceptions of the quality of the product or service offered. Yet, often due to shoddiness, inefficiency, high costs, inertia and/or incompetence, both management and labor seek protection from competitors and their high-quality output. Indeed, it is probably no overstatement to say that one of the greatest dangers of the present day is the danger of protectionism unleashed and running rampant in the Western world. The restrictive trade wars thereby unleashed would surely impoverish all, and, too terrible to contemplate, revive and exacerbate nationalistic rivalries, threatening the onset of a severe depression.

The proper response to competition is to become competitive by building up one's own efficiency and reputation for quality. The root problem is that this sort of response requires a readiness to accept changes in technology, methods of work, and, obviously, jobs and job territories. In short, the pursuit of quality founders when it encounters rock-like resistance from traditional work methods and the rules that reflect them. But labor, driven by its deep desire for job security, seeks to uphold the very restrictions which, under competitive market conditions, will inevitably lead to collapse of the employer's business and its jobs.

On management's side of the matter, a guarantee of employment (not job, but employment) security seems a road to bankruptcy and economic collapse. Yet some guarantee of employment security, perhaps not absolute for 100 percent of a firm's labor force, may well be the necessary precondition for winning labor's cooperation in achieving quality—giving up restrictive work procedures and rules, cooperating in accepting changes, and pursuing jointly with management quality of output.

For labor and management's underlying mutuality of interest to triumph over a history of push-and-shove negotiation, with periods of marked militancy and outright conflict, it will be necessary for both sides to surrender some treasured ideas.

On labor's side, the hoary concept of the fixed lump of work will have to give way to a recognition that job security and employment security are not the same. Indeed, guarantees of job security may eventually mean the loss of employment. A job refers to a particular task or set of tasks

---

[4]Ibid., pp. 548–49.

in the frame of a particular industry, company, and technology. To secure the job, therefore, implies protecting and preserving the particular industry, company and/or technology. It implies, further, resistance to change and the building up of a web of work rules designed to insulate the job from external pressures. Employment security, on the other hand, can welcome change, for it allows workers to shift technologies, tasks, companies, while they continue to work. The distinction strikes me as important, for much union activity has been designed to protect particular jobs rather than employment. And that effort dearly costs unions, their members, and society at large. As noted already, flexibility will have to replace rigid work rules, job classifications, and other restrictive job-related practices.

No less fundamental, and possibly even more basic, is the need for labor to reorient its loyalty, from the industry or craft to the firm. That is the Japanese orientation, and it is important to a degree of labor-management cooperation in each firm that will enable it to achieve quality (the bellwether of competitive position). Of course, such a shift is profoundly counter to the traditions of the U.S. trade union movement, with its powerful historical urge to seek standardization of wages, benefits, and work practices across entire industries and crafts. Variations in technology and regional conditions, which result in variations in the economic conditions of individual firms across industries and crafts, will now have to be more readily and meaningfully recognized. This will not be an easy pill to swallow, and many will fail to see any reason for swallowing it.

The foregoing observations lead me to management's side of the matter, and to the significance of executive power in achieving a solution. I believe the ball is on management's side of the court, and the CEO is the key figure who must call the play. In accepting that mantle of responsibility, the CEO must withstand a great temptation: namely, to use the union movement's present relative weakness to seek its destruction. It is better by far, I think, to seek labor's cooperation. But winning that cooperation will require tangible actions by the CEO and his management team that will demonstrate to labor honesty of intent and integrity of purpose in implementation of cooperative policies. Perhaps most significant will be some form of employment guarantee, coupled with humane and meaningful measures for work-force attrition and retraining in place of sudden, drastic discharges. Labor can suggest, accept, or helpfully modify these measures, but it cannot initiate them unilaterally. And while management can initiate unilaterally, it cannot achieve successful implementation minus labor's cooperation.

The challenge is clear, but the ultimate outcome remains yet unclear.

CHAPTER 5

GOVERNMENT REGULATION
AND EXECUTIVE POWER

TYPES OF REGULATION

The United States is seen worldwide as the quintessential capitalistic, free market economy, with laissez-faire its central cultural characteristic. But we know that this stereotype is far from the truth, for, while it is predominantly free market, it is also significantly stamped by omnipresent, though not yet overwhelming, government regulation.

Richard Rosenthal, retired board chairman and CEO of Citizens Utilities, presented a useful classification of the types of government regulation.[1] He spoke of regulation of (1) persons, (2) property, (3) process, and (4) markets and prices.

Regulation of persons, in its simplest and most obvious form, involves rules for individual or group behavior. It establishes by law the limits or boundaries of what is permissible. Fundamentally, it reflects the Judeo-Christian biblical proscriptions of the Ten Commandments: "Thou shalt not steal"; "Thou shalt not murder"; "Thou shalt not bear false witness." Contemporary laws regulating behavior cover an enormous range of conduct, from prohibitions against spitting in subway cars and exceeding specified speed limits, to the ancient prohibition against murder. Of course, behavioral proscriptions involving persons often involve property, process, prices, and markets, because all of them are affected by people who seek to disobey, cheat, and/or otherwise get around the proscriptions.

---

[1] Richard Rosenthal, "The Chief Executive: Views from the Top of the Organization." (Discussion with my seminar, Leonard N. Stern School of Business, New York University, Graduate Division, November 19, 1986.)

Regulation of property involves the location and use of physical resources (land, buildings, etc.). Its most obvious form is seen in zoning regulations, which relate to land and cover the residential, commercial, and industrial uses of land. *Regulation of process* involves the production of goods and services, and reflects society's concerns relative to their impact on its health and welfare. It is a type of regulation that has expanded enormously in recent decades, embracing health and safety in the workplace, the use and disposal of hazardous materials, and the racial and sexual composition of the work force (antidiscrimination policies and their implementation).

Regulation of markets and prices, the antithesis of laissez-faire, free market capitalism, has been omnipresent during wartime national crises. In normal times, regulation is generally focused on the prevention of monopolistic practices (antitrust activity) and the regulation of industries regarded as "natural monopolies" (utilities). But it also embraces the regulatory activities of agencies such as the Food and Drug Administration (FDA), which oversees the marketing of drugs and foodstuffs. And one should also mention the impact of government on the marketing of cigarettes and alcoholic beverages, as well as basic agricultural commodities. These activities hugely affect the availability of many goods, and cost Americans many billions of dollars a year as taxpayers and consumers. Much of the regulatory activity is desirable and desired, growing out of past abuses of the freedom of a free market. But not all, as we will see later.

REGULATION, LITIGATION, AND EXECUTIVE POWER

If war is an extension of diplomacy, then in a parallel sense, litigation is an extension of regulation. Both resort to a form of force. But force has both defensive and aggressive aspects, depending on one's viewpoint. Thus, a preemptive first strike will be seen as an aggressive act by the target, while it will be seen as a preventive (defensive) act by the attacker. Without overdoing the parallelism, we know that there are preemptive lawsuits. In any case, regulation and its handmaiden, litigation, circumscribe and inhibit the exercise of executive power: they set limits to the CEO's ability to order certain policies and actions. If the CEO breaches those limits, the regulatory authorities can resort to legal proceedings and compel conformity to the regulations.

Of course, litigation is a two-edged blade that can cut against regulators as well as for them. Regulation that is arbitrary, capricious, and a violation of due process can produce counterlitigation against the regulators and their agencies. And, in a free society governed by rules of law, the regulators do not always win. But, in general, power is on their side, even against the most powerful private corporations, because the costs of litigation are huge and create great pressure to settle. These costs are not only financial. Equal or even greater costs may be encountered in time, energy, and attention diverted from business to litigation.

Although the greater power is usually on the government's (the regulators) side, private parties can and do win victories in litigation. A significant case in late summer 1990 involved the savings and loan industry, which had witnessed numerous government takeovers of failed and failing savings institutions. In February 1990, the Franklin Savings Association of Ottawa, Kansas, America's 19th largest savings and loan with $9.2 billion in assets, was seized by government regulators who alleged it had used improper accounting standards to avoid reporting losses. The owners of Franklin Savings sued the government and won the first round of litigation, when a Federal judge in Topeka, Kansas, ordered the regulators to return Franklin to its owners and managers.[2] The decision was overturned on appeal,[3] but for a time, it might have checked regulators. Further appeals are in prospect.

After the announcement of the decision, regulators reiterated their confidence in the correctness of their original action in taking over Franklin. They alleged that Franklin's accounting procedures had been improper and had enabled the savings institution to recognize gains and defer losses "while distributing more than $45 million of the institution's funds in dividends to the shareholders." Deloitte and Touche, Franklin's accountants, disputed the regulators, maintaining that Franklin had employed proper practices, and the alleged losses did not have to be recognized. Federal District Judge Dale E. Saffels sided with Franklin and, as noted above, ordered the regulators to return Franklin to its owners. Of course, the regulatory agency, the Office of Thrift Supervision, appealed. But, in the meantime, litigation served to check the power of the regulatory agency.

The case of the Long Island Lighting Company (LILCO) and its Shoreham nuclear power plant is informative. After World War II, there was a

---

[2] The *New York Times*, September 6, 1990, pp. D1 and 6.
[3] *The Wall Street Journal*, May 29, 1991, page A-2.

period of years during which nuclear power plants were seen as a major long-run source of energy, which would reduce our dependence on fossil fuels such as oil and coal. But, as the years passed, powerful antinuclear sentiment developed, accompanied by well-organized, militant groups. After the accident at the Three Mile Island plant in Pennsylvania, which, incidentally, claimed no lives, the efforts of these groups achieved success. In this, they were greatly aided by a policy announced by the federal agency responsible for nuclear power. That policy required the development of emergency evacuation plans, to be implemented in the event of a nuclear accident. In the Shoreham case, a plant that had already encountered serious problems with large-cost overruns and technical delays could not be put into operation when finally completed because local antinuclear groups, with the support of local politicians and Governor Mario Cuomo, refused to cooperate in developing an emergency evacuation plan. Other opposition measures were also used, involving legislation and litigation. Finally, a deal was worked out that was financially viable for LILCO, and which involved the purchase by New York State of the plant, which, although completed and ready to run, is either to be dismantled or converted to fossil fuel. The dollar cost to taxpayers and consumers of LILCO power will be large, but a powerful utility company led by an astute, capable CEO, Dr. William Catacosinos, was compelled to bow before the combined pressures of regulation and litigation.

Of course, there are hazards in the use of nuclear energy, as we have seen in the case of Chernobyl. But the free societies of the West, subject to scrutiny by a free press and a variety of organized groups, have not experienced a single incident like it, although we are discovering that in the more secretive years following World War II, government-owned nuclear installations did behave in a number of instances in a cavalier and irresponsible way. It should be noted finally that there may now be a rethinking of the nuclear power issue. The fact is that the generation of nuclear energy has ground to a standstill in the United States, in contrast with other nations like France and Japan, where it has grown greatly. Yet concerns over pollution and a possible Greenhouse effect,[4] not to mention the considerable and well-known hazards to life, limb, and the environment associated with the production and movement of coal and oil, have been mounting. To these hazards must be added the political,

---

[4] A hotly debated belief that the burning of fossil fuels depletes the atmosphere's ozone layer, causing a gradual warming of the earth, which could have disastrous effects on sea levels and life.

diplomatic, and military dangers associated with reliance on Middle East oil.

A more immediate and smaller-scale illustration of the possible impact of regulation and litigation on the CEO's exercise of power is afforded by "whistle blowers," people working inside an organization who report regulatory violations to the authorities. Whistle blowing is viewed variously as a noble, public-spirited action, or as a base act of disloyalty (a "ratting" on one's colleagues). Or, depending on the circumstances, it may involve some midway mixture of motivations. But it is a fact that authoritarian executives have been brought down by "whistle blowers." Only an executive blinded by his own arrogance would fail to think about and order his conduct so as to give no ground to possible informers in his organization. It is no coincidence that the sad story of Leona Helmsley comes to mind. Married to the billionaire octogenarian real estate tycoon Harry Helmsley, and a principal executive in his realty and hotel empire, she has been buried in litigation. Charged with allegedly using corporate resources for private purposes, she was confronted with testimony by people who had worked for her organization. Having paraded herself for years in paid advertisements as the "Queen" of the Helmsley Palace hotel in New York, as well as other Helmsley hostelries, she alienated many people. Now, prosecution by arms of government have ensnared her in years of expensive litigation and cost her the self-granted "royalty" she loved.

The New York Telephone Company, a regulated utility, provides an interesting case of the interaction we are examining.[5] New York Telephone is a regulated subsidiary of NYNEX, which also owns nonregulated companies. One of its nonregulated companies, NYNEX Material Enterprises Company, received rebates from a temporary help firm that hired temporary workers for New York Telephone. The temporary help company, Tad Technical Services Corporation, had a contractual relationship with New York Telephone to provide temporary help for a fee equal to 37.5 percent of the temporary employees' wages. While it is not unusual for a temporary help firm (Tad Technical Services) to rebate part of the fee *to the customer* (New York Telephone), it is unusual for the rebate to go to a third party (NYNEX Material Enterprises Company, an unregulated subsidiary of NYNEX). The rebates amounted to 7.5 to 8 per-

---

[5] *New York Times*, September 6, 1990, p. D-2.

cent of the temporary employees wages (20 percent of the basic 37.5 percent fee). The significance of the arrangement is that the rebate never showed in New York Telephone's financial data as a reduction in the cost of hiring temporary help. Consequently, when New York Telephone requested an increase of $1.4 billion in phone rates from the New York State Public Service Commission, opponents argued that New York Telephone's cost basis justifying the rate increase was artificially inflated (to the degree that rebates were not shown). Yet New York Telephone's parent, NYNEX, was getting the benefit of them through NYNEX Material Enterprises Company. The understatement of New York Telephone's earnings existed from 1985 through early 1990. *And it was reported by Scott J. Rafferty, a former NYNEX executive, who is suing the company for wrongful dismissal.* According to Charlie Donaldson, a New York State assistant attorney general who is overseeing one of several state inquiries into transactions between NYNEX's affiliates, the arrangement for payments by temporary help companies to NYNEX Material "is something we have never seen before." Of course, the New York State Public Service Commission is also investigating to see if any of the rebates to NYNEX Material might partly account for New York Telephone's increased costs. If there is such a finding, then part of New York Telephone's rate increase would probably be denied. In the meantime, the rate increase application becomes clouded by suspicion and is delayed, and the public's perception of the integrity of New York Telephone and its parent is damaged.

Litigation can be useful in an aggressive way by an executive who sees it as a means of forestalling competition. Perhaps the most obvious case is found in the pharmaceutical industry, where the CEO of a firm seeking to extend the exclusive market position of a brand drug could litigate to preserve patent rights. Thus, litigation accompanied the introduction of Zantac and Losec, successor competitive drugs to Tagamet. While Tagamet was hailed as a wonder drug against stomach ulcers, Zantac and Losec seemed even more successful. Further, when a patent does run out, efforts can be made to market the original brand-name drug as superior to the generics that enter the market as lower-priced competitors. Indeed, in 1990, we saw a scandal involving a number of generic drugs that were "discovered" to be qualitatively inferior to what they had been represented to the FDA to be.

Of course, patents apply to many products other than pharmaceutical ones, and litigation can be a handy tool for a CEO to use in combatting competition.[6] It is used, not infrequently, against ex-employees who leave a company and take a position with a competitor, in which case breaches of obligations to preserve a firm's production, process, and formula secrets may be alleged. Copyrights, the legal handmaiden of patents, are intended to protect the brainchild of a creative mind but can be also used to fend off competition beyond the original intentions of the law. In fact, any government activity that seeks to regulate markets can provide a fruitful field for imaginative litigation, which seeks to protect exclusivity and combat competition, beyond the original intent of the law. Thus, the introduction to the market of a product, process, or service that is genuinely new, in some respect, may be delayed, perhaps fatally, by time-consuming, expensive litigation. And usually, in such cases, the entrenched party is better suited financially to pursue litigation.

REGULATION, LITIGATION, AND OUTSIDE DIRECTORS, REVISITED

Chapter Three explored the impact of litigation on the independence of outside directors and the freedom of the chief executive to exercise his power. The Emerson Radio Corporation provides a good illustration of this impact. Emerson Radio had a six-member board of directors, of whom three were inside (the Lane brothers, who were chairman and president, and the vice chairman). Three members were outsiders, but one of them was a lawyer who was also a paid consultant to the corporation. Consequently, since only two of the six directors could be thought of as completely independent, management had control over the board.[7]

In 1989, the Emerson Board approved a $5.3 million buy-out of the deferred pay claims of five top executives, three of whom were the chairman, president, and vice chairman, representing one-half the board. The

---

[6] An article in *The Wall Street Journal*, December 31, 1990, p. 9, noted: "In-house lawyers say businesses have come to think of litigation as a management strategy. 'If you couldn't negotiate, you can sue,' says Carl Liggio, general counsel for the accounting firm of Ernst and Young."

[7] It should be noted that the two complete outsiders were Walter F. Mondale, former U.S. Vice President and now a practicing lawyer, and Lyle Gramley, chief economist of the Mortgage Bankers Association and a former Federal Reserve Board governor. *The New York Times*, section 3, August 26, 1990, p. 17.

chairman and president each received $1.27 million, and the vice chairman got $926,000. The corporation's 1990 proxy statement called the arrangement "fair and reasonable under the circumstances," since the board believed the firm's share price, then about $5.50, would rise. And a rise in share value would have increased the value of the deferred pay the involved executives could have claimed upon termination. Based on their expectation of an increase in share price, the board also voted to repurchase $4.5 million of the company's shares, and redeemed certain executive stock options at prices ranging from $5.50 to $6.63 per share. The redemptions cost an additional $6.9 million, of which $5.9 million went to the five-member top management group. Finally, these executives received substantial increases in their base salaries and bonuses. The chairman and president each got just over $1 million, and the vice chairman received a smaller but still large sum.

But the judgment of the directors was abysmally wrong as to the movement of the share price. Instead of rising, it fell by more than 50 percent between September 1989 and August 1990, after unsold inventory accumulated in warehouses, margins dropped, and profits failed to advance. Concurrently, the company's balance sheet deteriorated sharply, with the ratio of current assets to current liabilities declining from 2.4 at the end of fiscal 1989 to 1.6 by March 1990. That development placed the company in default of the terms of a $33 million note issue that required a minimum current ratio of 1.8.

The sharp 1990 downturn in the company's fortunes, which ran so completely against the board's expectations as expressed in the 1990 proxy statement, evidently gave the three outside directors (including the attorney-consultant to the company) second thoughts. In addition, shareholders had instituted a lawsuit against the officers in fall 1989. The three outside directors met with the five executives in the top management group and negotiated a change in the previously approved deferred-pay buy-out arrangement. The shareholders were asked to ratify the 1989 $5.3 million buy-out of deferred pay claims. If the shareholders approved the board's 1989 decision, then the five executives would return $1.6 million to the company in the form of future salary cuts (remember they received salary and bonus increases in 1989). If the shareholders disapproved, then the executives would *repay* the $5.3 million they received, with interest, and retrieve their original rights to the deferred pay.

Significantly, Bruce Coleman, the attorney who represented the shareholders said, "If I were an Emerson shareholder, I would be outraged. *What the situation really needs is a stiff dose of regulatory intervention, and soon.*"[8] [Italics added]

But there is more to the story. In September 1990, it was disclosed that Stephen L. Lane, CEO of Emerson Radio, was suing Drexel, Burnham, Lambert to receive money he lost in commodities trading in the 1987 market crash. Mr. Lane's account with Drexel was managed by a Drexel broker, who, Lane alleged, was unqualified and poorly supervised. The broker was his wife. The consequences of her alleged lack of qualification were aggravated, Lane further argued, by severe illnesses he suffered at the time (brain tumors and major surgery), which impaired his own ability to monitor his affairs. *Yet, at that very time, Lane was presumably the active, functioning CEO of Emerson Radio, receiving major salary, bonus, stock option, and other benefits.*[9]

At this juncture, the power of the press and the publicity it brings to a situation become evident. The *New York Times* of September 19, 1990, suddenly announced that Stephen L. Lane resigned, effective immediately, as president and CEO of Emerson Radio.[10] When it had become known that Lane was receiving payment for his services as an active, functioning CEO at the same time he was claiming inability to manage his affairs because of grave illness, the incongruity of the situation couldn't bear the weight of the publicity directed at it.

The story presumably ended on October 15, 1990, when an arbitration panel ordered Stephen L. Lane and his wife to pay more than $6 million to Drexel Burnham Lambert to settle the dispute between them.[11] The American Arbitration Association panel rejected Lane's contention that Drexel failed to properly supervise the management of his account by his wife.

IS REGULATION A DETERRENT TO MISBEHAVIOR?

There is no conclusive and clear-cut answer to the question, because:

1. While we might get data on successful prosecutions of miscreants who violated regulations, we do not know how

---

[8] Ibid., p. 17.

[9] *New York Times*, September 13, 1990, pp. D 1, 7.

[10] *New York Times*, September 29, 1990, pp. 17–18.

[11] *New York Times*, October 16, 1990, p. c20.

many nonviolators refrained from violation due to fear of punishment.

2. We do not know how many violators were never discovered and prosecuted.

3. We do not know the degree to which those regulated were successful in influencing the regulations and the regulators, so that activities that ought to be regulated are not, or activities that should be regulated more strictly than they are fail to be so regulated.

4. We do not know the degree to which those regulated skirt the edges of regulation, acting in gray areas on the border of the regulations.

It is also probably true that the number of those regulated and the activities subject to regulation vastly exceed the number of regulators and the resources available to them to enforce the regulations. We know, for example, that in centrally planned, highly regulated, and authoritarian economies violations exist widely, as they do in capitalistic, free-market economies during the economic controls characteristic of wartime emergencies.

So regulation can be and is violated. But that is no reason to give up the practice, because, and, I think, correctly, society accepts the idea that misbehavior would be far greater in the absence of regulation. While the judgment is subjective, it no doubt reflects our own individual perception that there are things we might do in the absence of regulation that we refrain from doing in its presence. One need only look at the history of advertising and labelling practices by the cigarette and liquor industries. And we shall shortly look at the record in the pharmaceutical industry. In any case, we have regulation because we believe that it is a deterrent. Certainly, Bruce Coleman reflects that belief when he calls for a dose of regulatory intervention in the case of the Emerson Radio Corporation.

There are other behavioral facets to regulation, having to do with the behavior of the regulators. One facet involves overzealousness by regulators, who may be driven by a desire to use their position and power to press the thrust and coverage of regulations beyond the intentions of the legislators who enacted them. So, in environmental, occupational health and safety, antidiscrimination, and other regulatory areas, regulators may seek societal and environmental perfection based on personal ideological commitments when such a goal goes far beyond legislative intentions. And these efforts may have enormous costs, while the expected benefits from them may be nonexistent or too small to warrant the expenditures. We have already referred to the record in connection with nuclear energy. Perhaps the most famous case was the U.S. attempt to regulate the production and sale of alcoholic beverages. This fiasco, which undermined the nation's law enforcement agencies in the decade of the "roaring 20s," was finally repealed in the first administration of Franklin Delano Roosevelt.

A second facet of regulatory behavior involves the development of a too sympathetic relationship between regulators and those regulated. Consumer advocates have often charged public utility commissions with being too sympathetic to rate raising applications. And, especially during the Reagan Administration, environmental and other advocacy groups charged agencies having those regulatory responsibilities with failure to enforce vigorously.

Another facet of regulatory behavior involves the career moves of regulators who, after a period as regulators, leave the government and go to work for the industry they earlier regulated. In their new jobs, they usually concentrate on testing the scope and depth of the regulations they formerly enforced and/or work in lobbying efforts to influence changes in the regulations or in their interpretation.

Are overzealousness and changing sides forms of misbehavior by present or former regulators? If so, aren't they made possible only by the existence of regulation, and wouldn't they and their negative consequences be avoided by complete reliance on market mechanisms and avoidance of regulation? Possibly, but not probably. And so we will continue to have regulation, since we know that all human beings cannot be counted on to behave ideally. Some will always behave well or almost always. Some will misbehave sometimes, and a small minority will probably misbehave all the time. But all will benefit by the knowledge that society sets regulatory rules, and their violation involves the risk of detection and punishment. The threat and possibility of punishment induces fear, and fear is a deterrent.

CASE OF THE PHARMACEUTICAL INDUSTRY[12]

Benefits of Regulation

Throughout human history, mankind has sought cures for illness and relief from pain. But along with the healers who followed the dictates of the famed Hippocratic oath, there were fakers who offered nostrums,

---

[12] Considerable material in this section is drawn from FDA Consumer Special Report, *New Drug Development in the United States*, January 1988.

elixirs, and placebos. Among these so-called medications were those that harmed rather than healed, even flagrantly. In the United States the 19th and early 20th centuries were periods well populated by patent medicines claiming all sorts of miraculous powers to effect cures or to ease pain. While many were harmless, some contained narcotic and other powerful substances. In any case, lavish claims were made for them. Further, product labeling was frequently misleading or even false and fraudulent. Responding to these conditions, the Congress enacted the Food and Drug Act of 1906, which required that drugs meet official standards of strength and purity. But the Food and Drug Administration (FDA) had the burden of proof to show that a drug's labeling was false and fraudulent before the drug could be removed from the market.

Next, U.S. regulation in this field moved significantly with the passage of the Federal Food, Drug, and Cosmetic Act of 1938. This law was enacted after a drug known as Elixir Sulfanilimide went on sale in September 1937. The term *elixir* implied that the product was an alcohol solution, while it was actually a diethylene glycol solution. It had not been tested to determine its safety, turned out to be poisonous, and killed 107 people within a short time. Because it was labeled an elixir rather than a solution, the FDA charged the manufacturer with mislabeling, under the 1906 law, and was able to force the removal of the product from the market. If the product had been labeled a solution, there would have been no mislabeling and the FDA would have been powerless to proceed.

The 1938 law, for the first time, made it mandatory for a manufacturer to prove the safety of a drug before it could be marketed. It also authorized factory inspections by FDA and added the remedy of court injunctions to the previous remedies of seizure and prosecution. The next major developments were in 1951 and 1962. The Durham-Humphrey Amendment to the 1938 law, enacted in 1951, required that drugs unsafe for self-medication be labeled for sale by prescription only. The 1962 changes resulted from the sale in Western Europe of the drug thalidomide, which was associated with the birth of thousands of malformed babies. The drug was prescribed to relieve the symptoms of "morning sickness" (nausea) in pregnant women. Since the drug had not been tested for safety, its sale in the United States was prohibited. Yet some pregnant women obtained it from abroad, either by the advice of their physicians or others who had heard of it. Fortunately, FDA medical officer Frances O. Kelsey, M.D., succeeded in keeping the drug off the U.S. market, so that its consequences in the United States were small. But the publicity associated with the drug led Congress to enact the 1962 amendments to the 1938 law. Most importantly, drug manufacturers now had to prove a new product's effectiveness in its intended use. Drug manufacturers were also required to send adverse reaction reports to FDA, and drug advertising in medical journals was required to provide complete information to doctors, revealing the risks as well as the benefits of a medication.

To sum up, we can say that the benefits of regulating the pharmaceutical industry are:

1. To protect against inadequate research.
2. To protect against false and misleading reporting of research results.
3. To protect against premature and hazardous distribution of medication to the public.
4. To protect against false and misleading advertising.
5. To establish high standards of research and safety.

Costs of Regulation

Life rarely, if ever, presents us with unmixed blessings. Almost always, benefits are associated with costs, and so it is with regulation. In the pharmaceutical industry, the benefits sought from regulation are associated with several significant costs. Perhaps the most serious of those costs are:

1. The emergence of costly and sometimes tragic delays in the availability of medications to the sufferers of disease.
2. The emergence of bureaucratic rigidity, which makes research excessively expensive and which reduces breakthroughs.
3. The existence of so-called orphan drugs.

These problems and others led the well-known publication *The Economist* to observe: "Overburdened, understaffed, corrupt, and gullible: this is America's Food and Drug Administration, once one of the world's most respected regulators."[13]

Figure 5-1 below indicates the stages and times involved in winning FDA approval to market a new drug. The preclinical, clinical, and new drug application (NDA) reviews can consume anywhere from three years and two months to 20 years, at the outermost extreme, while the average

---

[13] *The Economist*, "Prescription for Drugs," February 2-8, 1991, p. 14.

FIGURE 5-1
New Drug Development

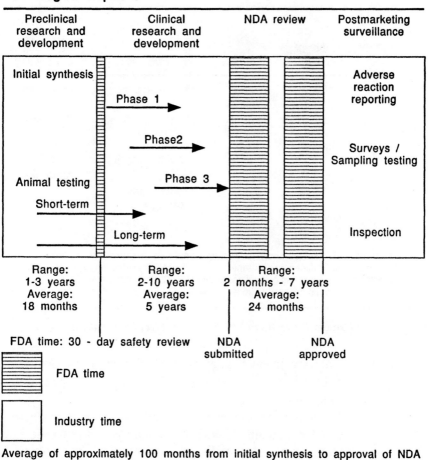

Preclinical research and development	Clinical research and development	NDA review	Postmarketing surveillance
Initial synthesis	Phase 1		Adverse reaction reporting
	Phase2		Surveys / Sampling testing
Animal testing	Phase 3		
Short-term			
	Long-term		Inspection

| Range: 1-3 years Average: 18 months | Range: 2-10 years Average: 5 years | Range: 2 months - 7 years Average: 24 months | |

FDA time: 30 - day safety review   NDA submitted   NDA approved

▤ FDA time

☐ Industry time

Average of approximately 100 months from initial synthesis to approval of NDA

Source: FDA Consumer Special Report *New Drug Development in the United States*, January 1988, p. 5.

is 8 ½ years. According to a survey by the Pharmaceutical Manufacturing Association, this had increased to an average of 12 years by 1990.[14]

Short-term animal testing begins about midway during preclinical research and development, while phase 1 testing in human beings begins only after the 30-day safety review by FDA. Figure 5-2 shows how

---

[14] *New York Times,* January 19, 1991, p. Y21.

FIGURE 5-2
How Experimental Drugs Are Tested in Humans

	Number of Patients	Length	Purpose	Percent of Drugs Successfully Completing*
Phase 1	20–100	Several months	Mainly safety	70 percent
Phase 2	Up to several hundred	Several months to 2 years	Some short-term safety, but mainly effectiveness	33 percent
Phase 3	Several hundred to several thousand	1–4	Safety, effectiveness, dosage	25–30 percent

*For example, of 100 drugs for which investigational new drug applications are submitted to FDA, about 70 will successfully complete phase one trials and go on to phase two; about 33 will complete phase two and go to phase 3; 25 to 30 will clear phase three (and, on average, about 20 of the original 100 will ultimately be approved for marketing).

Source: FDA Consumer Special Report *New Drug Development in the United States*, p. 14.

human testing of experimental drugs proceeds during phases one, two, and three, as well as the time periods involved and the percentage of drugs successfully completing each phase.

Plainly, the approval process is lengthy and expensive. Both Figures 5-1 and 5-2 provide a picture of the time dimension. The expense side was estimated by economist Steven Wiggins of Texas A & M University, in a study done under the sponsorship of the Pharmaceutical Manufacturers Association, to amount to $65 million, on average. However, if we include the opportunity costs (the cost of investing money in long-term research with payoff years away rather than in a more immediate money-making project), the real average cost of bringing a new drug to market increases to $125 million.[15] According to Gerald Massinghoff, president of the Pharmaceutical Manufacturers Association, the cost of discovering and developing a new drug had risen to $231 million by 1990.[16]

---

[15] FDA Consumer Special Report, *New Drug Development in the United States*, p. 9.
[16] *New York Times*, January 19, 1991, p. Y21.

Particular note should be taken of the additional safety resulting from phase three testing. The gain over phase 2 testing is relatively small, as compared with the large gain between phase one and phase two. The relatively small gain in phase three has become a source of considerable controversy between FDA and others deeply concerned with safety and effectiveness, on the one hand, and sufferers of serious diseases who want quick access to new drugs showing some promise of alleviation of a disease's symptoms, or of its cure.

The phase three controversy became especially heated in the mid- and late 80s because of the ravages of AIDS (acquired immune deficiency syndrome), especially when it was realized that azidothymidine (AZT), now known as zidovudine (or Retrovir commercially), had significant success in lengthening the lives of AIDS sufferers. AZT had been developed in the early 60s as a potential cancer treatment, but proved to be ineffective against that scourge. But in October 1984, preclinical tests began to examine AZT's effectiveness against AIDS. During phase two testing, it was discovered that only one AIDS patient died while being treated with Zidovudine (AZT), while 19 died while being given a placebo. As a consequence, phase three trials were not conducted, and the drug received investigational new drug approval in October 1986, and new drug approval in March 1987.

Another drug, lovostatin, which is used against cholesterol buildups, was put into preclinical studies in 1979, but did not get to phase three clinical testing in humans until April 1985. An additional 16 months passed before FDA granted new drug application approval for marketing lovostatin. Significantly, such clinical studies of the drug began abroad in April 1980. Note is taken of this fact because a number of critics of the expensiveness of safety and effectiveness testing in the United States are charging that clinical testing in humans is being driven overseas, with the benefits of that research more rapidly available there than here. Thus, Dr. Anthony De Maria, past president of the American College of Cardiology, said that U.S. cardiologists had largely abandoned work on thrombolytic medicines (which break up clots in coronary arteries to abort heart attacks), because they could not keep pace with European researchers who do not face the bureaucratic procedures required in the United States.[17] In addition to bureaucratic problems, these critics allege that U.S. clinical research is hindered by (1) an overzealous attitude by some about patient

---

[17] *New York Times*, August 7, 1990. p. C2.

rights, which they feel has led patients to regard trials with unnecessary suspicion and made it difficult to recruit volunteers and (2) a lack of incentives in the U.S. health-care system for doctors to refer patients to clinical trials.

In any case, the foregoing controversies did encourage a spate of changes in U.S. drug regulations in the mid- and late 80s:

1. The Drug Price Competition and Patent Term Restoration Act of 1984, which expanded the number of drugs suitable for an abbreviated new drug application (to make it speedier and less costly for generic drugs to reach the market).

2. The 1985 revision of the new drug application regulations and the 1987 revision of the investigational new drug application regulations, both of which made possible more rapid FDA action on new drugs approvals.

3. The 1987 change in the treatment use of investigational new drugs. The last change permitted patients with serious or immediately life-threatening illnesses (e.g., AIDS), to get treatment with experimental drugs that show reasonable evidence of potential benefit, provided no satisfactory approved therapy exists. However, the change applied only to drugs already being studied in controlled clinical trials, where those drugs could not expose patients to unreasonable risk. See Figure 5-3 below.

The arrows in Figure 5-3 indicate when a promising experimental drug can be made available to additional desperately ill patients. With drugs for immediately life-threatening conditions, expanded availability can begin near the end of phase two human testing, after the drug's initial safety testing has been done and the proper dose determined (phase one), and after some evidence of therapeutic benefit has been obtained (phase two). For serious but not immediately life-threatening illnesses, approval for expanded treatment availability can occur only sometime during phase three testing.

The Economist argues that FDA's problems would be substantially reduced by:

1. Leaving proof of efficacy to the drug companies, as well as to doctors and patients (presumably, truth in advertising laws would deter fraudulent claims and punish the firms making them).

2. Requiring drug companies to monitor their drugs *after* approval.

3. Clarifying the FDA's standards, most importantly by acknowledging publicly that there is no such thing as a completely risk-free drug

FIGURE 5-3
New Drug Process: Treatment Use

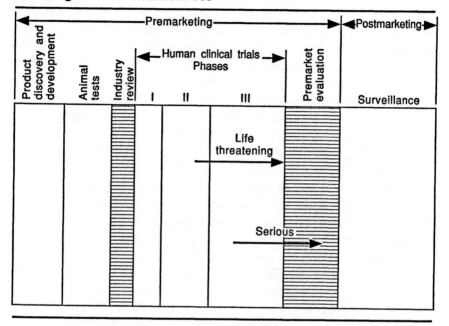

Source: FDA Consumer Special Report; *New Drug Development in the United States,* p. 25.

and indicating some level of acceptable risk for a life-saving drug (perhaps one death in 1,000 patients, as an example).

4. Giving more information to the patient than is now commonly done, particularly with respect to side effects.

5. Requiring physicians to inform patients about the medications they prescribe, both the probable benefits and the possible side effects.[18]

Litigation

Litigation, actual or threatened, has an effect on the market availability of drugs. The case of the antidepressant drug prozac is illustrative.[19] The drug, produced by Eli Lilly and Company, underwent laboratory testing in 1976. More than 11,000 people participated in clinical trials before it

---

[18] *The Economist,* February 2-8, 1991, pp. 14-15.

[19] *New York Times,* August 16, 1990, p. B13.

was put on the market in 1987. An immediate medical and market success, annual sales were projected to top $1 billion in 1991.[20] Its common side effects include anxiety, insomnia, fatigue, tremor, sweating, gastrointestinal complaints, and dizziness, all of which are included on the list of warnings that accompany the drug's packaging. FDA approved it. By mid-1990, more than two million patients worldwide had been treated with prozac, and the manufacturer believed its safety record was well established. However, in February 1990, Dr. Martin H. Teicher and his colleagues at Harvard Medical School and McClean Hospital reported in the *American Journal of Psychiatry* that six patients who were free of suicidal tendencies prior to taking prozac developed such symptoms after ingesting the drug. Based on that, Dr. Teicher predicted that from 1.9 to 7.7 percent of prozac users might be at risk for mania, obsession with suicide, and other dangerous violent behavior. Dr. Teicher noted that these effects would be experienced only in a small percentage of cases, that he heard mostly the bad news about the drug, and that most people are "doing tremendously well on the medication."

Yet, reports like Dr. Teicher's inspired a rash of lawsuits against Eli Lilly and Company, with only six of them seeking a total of $300 million in punitive and compensatory damages. A number of other lawsuits are planned, and the eventual exposure of the manufacturer will probably exceed that sum by a substantial amount. Significantly, Dr. Paul Leber, FDA's director of neuropharmacological drug products, pointed out that the vast majority of the common side effects are relatively mild. He noted further that depressed patients are inherently subject to suicidal tendencies and violent behavior, and that 10 percent of those with a lifelong depressive illness will probably commit suicide. Finally, he said that he and his colleagues at FDA saw no evidence of an *increased* risk of violence or suicidal tendencies.[21]

The foregoing review does not reveal the full range of Eli Lilly's legal problems with prozac. The drug has become the focus of attention by defense attorneys in murder trials where the alleged murderer was on prozac.[22] Despite FDA disclaimers of any evidence of a cause-and-effect relationship between prozac and suicidal or homicidal behavior, defense attorneys are pressing what is now called the prozac defense. And Eli Lilly

---

[20] *The Wall Street Journal,* February 7, 1991, p. B1.
[21] *The Wall Street Journal,* February 7, 1991, p. B1.
[22] Ibid.

must sit on the sidelines in these cases, unable to defend its drug because it is not a party to the criminal litigation. There is also an economic dimension to the litigation: namely, the lawsuits appear to have had a significant impact on the market value of Lilly's stock. From July 1990 to January 1991, the value of a share fell from $90.375 to $69, rising thereafter to $76.125 by early February 1991.[23]

While Eli Lilly said in mid-1990 that it had no intention of removing prozac from the market, that was the action taken by Merrill-Dow in the case of its drug Benedectin. Benedectin, used to treat nausea associated with pregnancy, was effective. But several lawsuits brought against Merrill-Dow in the early 80s proved to be expensive, and the company took the drug off the market.

A final example of the effect of litigation involved a patent infringement suit brought by Schering-Plough against Interferon Sciences, Inc.[24] Schering-Plough sued Interferon Sciences in March 1989, alleging that the latter firm had infringed on its patent for recombinant interferon alpha 2–b, a substance used in treating cancers and viral diseases. As a result of the suit, Interferon Sciences discontinued its use of alpha 2–b to avoid the costly litigation that would be involved. It was able to substitute alpha 2–a as an alternative in its product, a topical gel called Alferon. But Alferon, which was undergoing clinical trials precedent to receiving FDA approval, will now have to conduct more extensive tests (due to the substitution of alpha 2–a for alpha 2–b). Plainly, Schering-Plough's litigation succeeded in delaying the approval of Alferon by FDA, and its eventual appearance on the market.

Orphan Drugs

The term orphan drugs was first used in a 1968 editorial in the *American Journal of Hospital Pharmacy*.[25] It is an apt term and refers to drugs used to treat uncommon and rare diseases. Such drugs are considered orphans because the number of persons to be treated with them are too few to make their development, production, and marketing economically profitable. A rare disease has been defined as one that affects fewer than 200,000 people. In spite of the economics, by 1969 there were 26 pharmaceutical

---

[23] Ibid.

[24] *New York Times*, March 21, 1991, p. D10.

[25] FDA, Consumer Special Report, *New Drug Development in the United States*, pp. 55–57.

companies producing and marketing 92 orphan products (medical devices as well as drugs). For example, Hoffmann-LaRoche had developed some half-dozen drugs.

But the overall situation was sad, with known cures and alleviatives for some rare diseases unavailable. A particularly dramatic case unfolded in 1981, involving the plight of children suffering from Tourette's syndrome. The disease is characterized by bizarre, involuntary physical and vocal tics that vary in intensity throughout childhood and adult life. A drug that was not effective in all patients, haloperidol, was available in the United States. A second drug, peniozide, was more effective, was used abroad and in Canada, but had not been FDA approved for use in the United States. McNeil Pharmaceutical, the producer, believed the required clinical research would have been prohibitively expensive in view of the small patient population, and did not undertake the expense. The publicity associated with the situation generated public pressure, and the Congress responded with the 1983 Orphan Drug Act (a law that provided economic incentives to pharmaceutical companies to produce and market orphan drugs). Peniozide was approved by FDA following passage of the Act.

Generic Drugs[26]

These drugs are required by FDA to be in all scientific respects equivalent to the brand name drugs they purport to replicate. Most brand name prescription drugs are developed under a patent, generally a 17-year exclusive right to produce and market the medication. The patent is an incentive to the developer of the drug to engage in the extended and expensive research required, by guaranteeing him the sole marketing rights noted. Generic drugs, which are by law possessed of all the medical and therapeutic qualities of the original patented drug, may be made and sold by competing pharmaceutical firms only after the patent has expired. At that time, given the competition that develops and the fact that the generic product does not carry the original developer's research costs, its price is usually substantially less than the original brand name product.

Many consumers and some pharmacists, at least for a time, expressed fears that generics were not in all respects equal to their brand name sisters. The FDA made substantial efforts to combat these fears, emphasizing the requirements of law and their regulations. Unfortunately, in 1989

---

[26] Ibid., pp. 59–69.

it was revealed that a number of the protections required had been violated by some manufacturers. Part of the fault lay with an evidently overburdened FDA, which relied too heavily on manufacturer documentation that turned out to be deficient and in some instances fraudulent. Hopefully, that situation will be corrected, and generics will be as they are supposed to be.

Yet, as recently as February 28, 1991, the Bolar Pharmaceutical Company announced it would plead guilty to charges of illegally distributing adulterated generic drugs and obstructing government investigations.[27] Three Bolar employees, the research director and two government relations executives, pleaded guilty to the charges made against the company. The company was the nation's largest publicly owned generic drug manufacturer prior to its withdrawal of most of its product in 1990, the withdrawal following government allegations that Bolar had submitted bogus drug samples to FDA. The company announced it would pay $10 million in fines and $250,000 in litigation costs. Specifically, Bolar had submitted false samples of dyazide, a blood pressure drug originally made by Smith Kline Beecham. In the three years prior to its withdrawal from the market in 1990, Bolar's generic version of dyazide enjoyed sales in excess of $140 million. Concurrently, Smith Kline Beecham's brand version of dyazide suffered decreased sales of the drug amounting to $167 million. After Bolar's withdrawal of the generic version, sales of the brand name version recovered.

Some Ethical Issues

With the background provided by the pharmaceutical industry, it is not difficult to see several areas that can produce ethical issues. In each instance, undiluted concentration on maximizing short-term profits can lead to unethical, if not illegal, behavior.

First, the desire to achieve a scientific breakthrough and obtain the exclusivity granted by a patent may produce pressure to speed up required preclinical and clinical research. If this pressure results in more efficient research techniques with no loss of scientific accuracy, then there is no problem. But if it involves "shaving" the research effort by inadequate attention to harmful or dangerous side effects, then it is wrong. Even worse

---

[27] *New York Times*, February 28, 1991, p. D1 and 4.

would be distortion or falsification of the research results. Sadly, both types of activity have occurred.

Second, medications considered inadequately proven or unsafe in the United States have been distributed in foreign markets. We have already seen that the availability of drugs not yet approved by FDA is much greater abroad and is a source of substantial controversy. On the other hand, the record in the case of thalidomide, described earlier, is evidence of the degree to which the safety requirements of FDA do protect Americans. But the ethical issues are cloudier here than they are in connection with shaving research.

Third, the effort to preserve the market position of a brand name patented drug after expiration of the patent and the appearance of generic substitutes may inspire costly advertising campaigns, which add to the cost of the drug and thereby make it more expensive to those wanting it. Of course, this will increase the appeal of lower-priced generics, and thereby encourage the manufacturer of the brand name drug to twist his advertising so as to imply, with greater or lesser subtlety, that the generic substitutes are somehow inferior, either in composition, potency (degree of effectiveness), or speed of effectiveness. The FDA assures all that this cannot be the case, pointing out that its regulations prohibit any inferiority in generics. But violations do occur, and they provide room for creative copywriters.

Finally, but with no implication that the listing here is exhaustive, there is the matter of the development and production of orphan drugs. To some degree, pharmaceutical firms already produce these medications, and more so than before passage of the 1983 Orphan Drug Act. But there remain so-called cost-benefit issues, which can perhaps be brought together with this all-embracing question: Is there some point beyond which it becomes too costly for society to seek cures or alleviative treatments for all ailments? The question would make no sense on an ethical basis if society's resources were unlimited. But they are not unlimited. They are scarce relative to wants, and that is the profoundly fundamental problem that has bedeviled economists. Scarcity makes choice inevitable, in the case of medications and resources for fighting disease as well as in the case of opting for more of product A as against product B when one makes daily spending decisions. Put more dramatically in medical terms, when organs for transplanting are fewer than those waiting desperately to receive them, do we give a heart transplant to a 75-year-old heart patient as against one who is 25 years old? The answer seems so simple when the question is

posed that way. Of course, the younger patient should receive the preference, for he has the prospect of years of life in which to be creative and
productive, while the older person has already had that opportunity. But
make the choice more difficult. Suppose the 75-year-old is a famous, still-
productive scientist or artist, perhaps an Einstein, while the 25-year-old
has ordinary mental and physical endowments. The questions are easier
asked than answered.

ROLE OF THE CEO IN A REGULATED ENVIRONMENT

Our discussion of corporate culture in Chapter seven will conclude that
the values and attitudes of the chief executive are of critical importance.
While an established, traditional culture may withstand and undo a weak
CEO, it will not undo a strong one with a clear vision of organizational
mission and goals, and with a capacity to articulate them with some measure of charisma. He will rather reshape the traditional culture. These observations are relevant to any consideration of the role of the CEO in a
regulated environment.

The CEO in such a context can complain, object, and otherwise project a negative and combative attitude toward regulation. If, concurrently,
he exerts enormous pressure on his organization to maximize short-term
profits, and his decisions and actions reflect that as his overriding and paramount concern, then the organization is likely to fall into unethical and
possibly illegal activities. For example, a firm led by such a CEO is prone
to "shave" research efforts, and even to "doctor" the results. It is not likely
to spend time, effort, and money on orphan drugs. It is susceptible to using misleading, or even false, advertising to extend the market position
of a brand name drug against a generic one. If it manufactures generic
drugs, it is more likely than not to doctor the composition and potency
of the substitute, in an effort to keep costs down and short-term profit
high. It is more likely to use litigation to stymie regulatory efforts, hoping that an overburdened FDA, or other regulatory agency, may back off.
The list could be extended, but need not be, because the point is the importance of the CEO in setting the outlook and behavior of his organization.

By way of contrast, an ethical, strong CEO will quickly make clear
to everyone in his organization that no cheating or chicanery will be tolerated. Much more, it will be made clear that the organization must be and
is dedicated to serving the public good, and will do so by producing only

the highest quality product and selling it at a reasonable rate of return. Orphan drugs will be sought and produced, even though private efforts in this pursuit are subject to the need to earn a market rate of return for shareholders. If unintentional errors occur, or other crises unfold (like Johnson's and Johnson's Tylenol case), there will be no failure to confront the situation. There will be no double-talk. And the chief executive will be in the forefront, plainly in the lead of his organization and maximizing its efforts to achieve a solution.

The two extremes do not exhaust the range of CEO postures. There are degrees of difference as one moves from one extreme to the other. I am convinced that CEOs who appear uncertain in their attitudes and who waffle on issues other than maximizing short-term profit will fail eventually in a regulated environment. But they will be more the victims of their own uncertainty than creators of their downfall, because their organizations will fall into unethical practices by default of leadership, rather than by the design of an unethical CEO.

I do not mean to imply by the foregoing comments that CEOs in a regulated environment must accept every aspect of that regulation and the actions of the regulatory agencies involved. Government regulation is not perfect, either in its enabling legislation or in all the decisions and actions of enforcement. There are ample illustrations of the costs of ill-conceived, ill-drafted regulations, as there are of the costs and harmful consequences of rigid and inefficient bureaucracies. In such cases, the most ethical CEO has an obligation to speak out against bad policies and harmful implementation of those policies. But such opposition, when taken against a background and record of service and high product quality, is likely to command the high ground of public discourse. And that is a condition to be desired.

CHAPTER 6

THE MEDIA AND EXECUTIVE POWER

A STAB AT DEFINITION

The word *media* is a collective one, being the plural of *medium*. And, in this context, a medium is an "agency, means, or instrument."[1] Above all, the media are instruments of communication, and, in the broadest sense, they embrace all technologies and channels involved in gathering, sifting, and reporting information. Thus, they include the press (daily and periodical), publishing (books and magazines), television (which combines audio and visual), radio (audio), motion pictures, theater, and so on. Of course, so far-reaching a definition embraces a broader spectrum than we are really concerned about. Essentially, the media that is of concern here include press, TV, and radio, and only that part of them that cover organizations, both business and nonbusiness.

We are not interested in *The National Enquirer* or any other purveyors of imagined or actual scandals distributed at the supermarket's checkout counter. And we are not interested in the X-rated TV programming found, for example, on cable channel 35 in the Metropolitan New York area after midnight. We are interested in *The Wall Street Journal*, the *New York Times, Business Week, Fortune, Forbes, Barrons*, as well as other newspapers and periodicals. We are interested in those TV and radio programs which report news about business and business leaders.

---

[1] *The Random House Dictionary of the English Language*, unabridged edition, s.v. "medium." For an excellent discussion of CEO-media interactions, see: Steven Florio, *The Media and the CEO*, Joseph I. Lubin Memorial Lecture, February 20, 1991, Stern School of Business, New York University.

POWER OF THE MEDIA

Media power derives from its ability to influence and possibly direct public opinion, which, in a democracy, in turn affects legislators, legislation, and public policy. That this is so needs no elaborate proof. One need look only to the zeal with which dictators monopolize the media and treat as traitorous capital crimes any reporting of information not to their liking.

Our concern is with the power of the media to influence public attitudes on issues of major concern to business organizations in directions that are damaging to business, while not being productive of larger social or economic benefits. One may well ask, why would the media seek to exert influence in this way? The simplest and most attractive reason is out of conviction that the influence exerted is benevolent rather than malevolent. Such conviction may reflect ideological views antithetical to a market economy, or its handmaiden, the pursuit of private profit. And the fourth estate contains people having such sentiments. Less attractive reasons could include (1) an undue desire to win the notoriety (celebrity status) associated with "breaking" a story, the more scandalous the better; (2) the pleasure of exercising the power of the press, which can be as exciting as any exercise of personal power over other human beings; and/or (3) the personal financial gain that can be associated with the possession of media power. Without implying that any of these less attractive motivations apply, it is certainly true that leading TV anchormen, such as Dan Rather, Sam Donaldson, Tom Brokaw, Barbara Walters, and Mike Wallace are celebrities and usually command seven-digit annual salaries. Leading lights of the printed press are also celebrities, for example Russell Baker, Anthony Lewis, William Safire, Flora Lewis, Ann Quindlen, Paul Gigot, and Irving Kristol; but they do not generally command salaries equivalent to those received by major TV personalities. But all are powerful. They can damn or praise, strike down or raise up an individual or a company. And the object of their misrepresentation, when that is the message being disseminated, finds it hard to respond. After all, even a retraction, usually appearing inconspicuously in an inside page of a newspaper, is no match for the headline story that preceded it and which is being corrected. In short, the power to inflict harm is very great and unmatched by countervailing power. Invasions of privacy are not a defense for public figures. And litigation alleging libel is expensive, difficult under our laws, and unlikely to yield satisfaction to the accused.

MEDIA'S CORPORATE CULTURE

Viewed ideally, the media can be seen as the Sir Galahad at democracy's round table. That is certainly the self-perception characteristic of its members. They regard themselves as seekers of the truth, possessed of a profound responsibility to find it and publish it to the world. They are the ones who ferret out the information so vital to an informed citizenry as it makes its decisions regarding public policy. They see themselves as the guardians of democracy, and they take their mandate from the Bill of Rights and its guarantee of freedom of the press. In so portraying themselves, they can be insistent on their "rights" of access to information, as against the rights of others to privacy. And they can be arrogant in their intrusiveness, abrasive and unfeeling in their manner. One need only be reminded of the spectacle of the TV cameraman and accompanying newscaster as they push mike and camera into the face of the victim of some tragedy and inquire, How does it feel?

Perhaps there is no better example of the power alluded to and the celebrity status of a major TV personality than the CBS news special that celebrated Mike Wallace's career. Wallace is known especially for the show "60 Minutes," which interviews people deemed newsworthy and does investigative reports of various stories, such as the allegation that General William C. Westmoreland misled our nation about enemy strength in Vietnam, or the charge that the Audi automobile was defective in its design and caused tragic accidents as a consequence of sudden accelerations of power. Walter Goodman reviewed the special for the *New York Times*, under the title "Turning the Camera on a Feared Interviewer."

While noting that some of Wallace's interviews have produced libel suits, Goodman writes:[2]

> In the latest issue of the Videojournalist, a newsletter, Neil Postman, Chairman of Communication Arts at New York University, commented, "60 Minutes" is generally awful because the emphasis is more expose than understanding." He has a point, but the expose has long since proved its value, and Mr. Wallace, in league with his less famous producers and researchers, deserves credit for carrying on a useful tradition. What the expose lacks in

---

[2] *New York Times*, September 26, 1990, p. B3.

analysis and, occasionally, fairness, it often makes up for in revelations of facts and of personality. . . .

> Fairness does suffer. The camera assists Mr. Wallace by moving in so close on his prey that you can see the facial pores. A camera could give Mother Teresa a sinister look. Television will doubtless continue to exploit this technique until how one is made to look on the tube becomes grounds for libel. . . .

Mr. Goodman's readiness to accept unfairness in camera technique and analytical thoroughness seems cavalier, and without any evident appreciation of the damage inflicted on those who have been treated unfairly and/or inaccurately. The handling of the Audi story seems a good case in point. "60 Minutes," in its report, focused on a tragedy, in which a young mother inadvertently ran into her child. The mother had remained in the car (an Audi), while the child had gone to open the garage door. While the child was opening the door, the auto suddenly accelerated and crushed the youngster. The vividness of the tragedy and the publicity surrounding it and other reported incidents of similar failure of the vehicle resulted in a dramatic downturn in the sale of Audis in the United States. The car, which had been a well-regarded and successful seller, lost a major part of its market. Yet, exhaustive tests by governmental and other research agencies failed to show the car to be at fault. Instead, it appeared that drivers had inadvertently pressed their feet against the accelerator pedal instead of the brake, causing sudden surges of power and the resulting accidents. But it was impossible for Audi to win its case in the "court" of public opinion, although the facts are finally and gradually becoming more widely known.

There is an inherent oddity about the culture of the media. While it perceives itself as possessed of a profound public responsibility, its organizational structures are private and profit oriented. *The Wall Street Journal*, the *New York Times, Business Week, Fortune,* CBS, NBC, ABC, and so forth, are all private corporations concerned with bottom-line results. Indeed, most of them are public corporations, with their stock traded in public exchanges and with the same concerns as other corporations with price/earnings ratios and shareholder values. Indeed, I believe there is an internal split personality in this connection, with the news departments and the business managements feeling tension between their sometimes differing views of priorities in controlling costs and earning profits. Probably worse, from a societal point of view, would be the absence of such tension, with the profit criterion the sole and triumphant basis for decisions bearing on seeking and reporting the news.

COLLISION POINTS BETWEEN MEDIA AND OTHER BUSINESS CORPORATIONS

Whether pursuing the Holy Grail of truth and reporting it, seeking to entertain and titillate in the pursuit of profit, or simply pleasuring its practitioners as they exercise their power, the media can and will collide with those who are the subject of their investigations and reports. The underlying reason is that the media seek readers, listeners, and viewers, while nonmedia business organizations seek to be portrayed in a favorable light. The latter love "good news," but the former favor "bad news," news that has elements of the scandalous and the sensational. As one of my friends of the fourth estate once told me when I complained about his colleagues' concentration on the sour side of life, "When you cross the street safely, it's not news. When you get hit by a truck, it is."

Of course, there is a significant material side to the matter. The sensational and the scandalous sell papers, as they attract viewers to TV. In short, it is profitable. But, when such news involves business and businessmen, it can, and often does, harm profits and affect share values adversely. The case of Donald Trump is illustrative. A man of surpassing egoism, his appetite for personal publicity is insatiable. But he managed to mesh that appetite well with his business operations for a substantial period of years when real estate values were rising steadily. So, as he built a real estate empire with huge leveraging of debt, he co-authored *The Art of Deal*, which promoted his deal-making brilliance, bought Eastern Airlines Shuttle and converted it to the Trump Shuttle, bought Adnan Kashoggi's lavish yacht, "created" a board game bearing his name, and so on. Then, Martin B. Roffman, a little-known investment analyst published an opinion that Trump's Taj Mahal Casino was shaky, and that he was likely to experience cash-flow problems in meeting his interest and other commitments on debt. Trump reacted with howls of outrage, charging the man with gross incompetence and threatening litigation against the man's employer, Janney Montgomery Smith. The latter, evidently overwhelmed, discharged the analyst and subsequently was ordered by an arbitration panel to pay Roffman $750,000.[3] Concurrently, Trump and his wife separated, with enormous press and TV coverage. No longer able to manage publicity about his affairs, Donald Trump now became a victim. *The Wall Street Journal*

---

[3] *New York Times*, March 6, 1991 p. C1.

printed a page-one story indicating that he faced serious financial problems, and the story was shortly borne out by events. Trump was unable to meet required interest payments; extensive negotiations with banks and other creditors followed; his debts required major restructuring (which will need considerable time to complete, if they can be successfully completed); and his control over his business affairs was significantly circumscribed. In the meantime, divorce proceedings slipped into the background, and Mr. Trump seems now to prefer a lower profile, at least until such time as he may be able to surmount his problems.

Another case, referred to in a prior chapter, involved Leona Helmsley. Her story became a TV movie, titled "Leona Helmsley: Queen of Mean." She had for years advertised herself as the Queen of the Helmsley Palace Hotel and other Helmsley hotel properties. Since her trial and conviction for tax fraud (under appeal), she no longer so advertises herself, and, no doubt, she was not pleased with TV's portrayal of her.

Both the Trump and Helmsley cases involve personalities who are not likely to arouse sympathy. But the power of the media, evident in both, can be and is used in other cases where the right and wrong of the matter does not seem clear. In any event, the specific points of collision of interest between media and other businesses will usually involve these matters:

1. Alleged wrongdoing (e.g., dumping hazardous waste materials, other harming of the environment, unsafe practices, antitrust violations, fraud, etc.).
2. Labor disputes.
3. Industrial accidents (e.g., Three Mile Island, Bhopal in India, etc.).
4. Earnings outlooks.
5. Business personalities, with the Ivan Boeskys outnumbering the Lee Iacoccas.
6. Significant scientific and industrial breakthrough in research and development.

It is instructive that of the six possible points of collision, the media will likely focus on the sensational ones. And chief executives will be concerned with what is sometimes called damage control. Even in the case of scientific and research breakthrough's, where one would think media and business are in harmony, there is tension. The firm responsible for the breakthrough will worry about premature disclosure that can arouse unrealizable expectations in the public. It may also be concerned about disclosure of industrial secrets and possible loss of competitive advantage. The media is unlikely to have any such constraints.

Joseph A. Califano, Jr., then U.S. Secretary of Health, Education, and Welfare, and Howard Simons, then Managing Editor of the *Washington Post*, edited the proceedings of a conference that brought together dozens of leading journalists and business executives in the fall of 1977. Published with the title *The Media and Business*, the conference aim was an exchange of fundamental beliefs and differences, indeed an opportunity to "lock biases."[4]

Introducing the printed proceedings, Messrs. Califano and Simons summed up the conflicting attitudes of executives and media, saying, "To the businessman, too often the antagonism boils down to this—business builds up; the media tears down. To the media, too often the antagonism boils down to this—business always hides its wrongdoing; only the media penetrates this stone wall."[5] Additionally, businessmen complain that the media take advantage of the protection and cover given by the First Amendment and too often misuse the power of a free press to escape the same scrutiny, challenge, and accountability they demand of business. In this connection, many executives appear especially aggravated by a double standard that they accuse the media of using. The essence of that double standard is that the media claim absolute confidentiality as to their sources of information, but deny confidentiality to business and other societal institutions. Thus, while it is a crime for any party other than the media to induce someone to commit a crime, it is seen by the media as allowable to induce someone to steal a document and provide it with a copy. Or, while the average journalist says he or she will go to jail rather than reveal the source of a story if that source has asked for confidentiality, the same journalist will be quick to publish business and governmental secrets. What is perceived as hypocrisy by the business executive is seen as essential to the free flow of information to the media, and, through it, to the public. Without the protection afforded by confidentiality, the lives and livelihoods of news sources would be placed in jeopardy, and the media would have to rely on self-serving public relations handouts and press releases.

---

[4] Howard Simons, and Joseph A. Califano, Jr., *The Media and Business* (New York: Vintage Books, 1979), p. 27. The conference was sponsored by the Ford Foundation and these six major newspapers: the *Chicago Tribune*, the *New York Times*, the *Washington Post*, and *The Wall Street Journal*, the *Boston Globe*, and the *Los Angeles Times*.

[5] Ibid., p. 9.

Business executives, in addition, possess a characteristic that weakens their position, in regard to the media. They have typically risen through the hierarchy of business organizations, shielded to a large degree from public scrutiny and criticism. As Arthur Taylor, former president of CBS and present dean of Fordham University's business school, put it:

> Unlike politicians or public advocates, their professional skills usually tend to be directed inward, toward their companies, rather than outward toward the public. A middle-level corporation executive generally will not have to undergo the same rough-and-tumble give-and-take in the public arena from people who do not understand how business works that his or her counterpart in politics might have to. And when he or she gets to the top and becomes a captain of industry, the isolation will be even further enforced by a protective staff.[6]

FICKLENESS OF THE MEDIA

An important characteristic of sensational or scandalous news is that it commands a short public attention span. The appetite for new scandals and new sensations is immense, for yesterday's news quickly becomes boring and needs to be replaced by fresh news. The media feed this appetite, but this fact may be more a reflection of public fickleness and the media's own pursuit of profit than of an ethical failure to live up to overidealized self-perception.

Russell Baker, the brilliant columnist, captured the point in a column entitled "Presto! They Vanish." He wrote:[7]

> Troubles get boring. They wear out their welcome. The savings and loan crisis had reached that stage. So had homelessness.
>
> People were saying, 'I know homelessness is terrible, but I'm tired of it.' They were saying, 'Sure the savings and loan catastrophe may bankrupt the country, but it's been around longer than February now and I've had it up to here.'
>
> When things reach this stage, people need something to chase their troubles away. This is why the latest military expedition has been so refreshing. It has given us some new news.

---

[6] Ibid., p. 27.
[7] *New York Times*, September 4, 1990, p. A17.

Not good news. Good news doesn't perk people up. People say they want good news but they don't. For good news it's hard to beat the collapse of Communism and the end of the cold war, yet millions got bored with it overnight. Good news gets boring even faster than trouble.

What people really want is new news, and that's what Saddam Hussein's impetuosity and President Bush's military response have provided. The savings and loan problem has disappeared, as if by magic, the way headaches vanish instantly when exposed to the sponsor's tablets.

The significance of this fickleness is that it discourages painstaking, time-consuming, thought-provoking searching for truth. It encourages speedy publication, often with minimal verification. And it discourages careful follow-up stories to correct errors and/or false impressions left with the public. Yet, the corporation and individual who have been the subject of a story, most particularly a story that is felt to be inaccurate and distorted, want very much for their side to receive equivalent coverage. And equivalent coverage is almost never gotten, except perhaps for a few cases following litigation.

CEO'S RELATIVE WEAKNESS

The corporate chief executive who finds his company and/or his person the subject of adverse reporting is relatively weak against the media. The reasons are not difficult to grasp. First, the initiative rests usually with the media. Consequently, the role of the CEO and his company is essentially reactive, rather than proactive. Second, the channels of communication are controlled by the media (i.e., they are the channels). It is expensive for company and/or CEO to obtain equivalent, effective access to a communication channel, especially the one that first broke the story. Third, the CEO and his company typically lack the skill needed to respond (communicate) effectively. To note these sources of relative weakness, however, is not to say that America's CEOs and corporations are defenseless.

We are not concerned here with executive efforts relating to communication within the corporate organization, concentrating instead on communications with the media and the public served by the media. While the media generally control those channels of communication, by virtue of ownership, their control is not exclusive. Chief executives and their companies perform the following: (1) create public relations departments, employing professionals who are expert in gaining effective access to the media; (2) hire public relations firms as outside consultants, again to obtain professional expertise; (3) purchase advertising space in the media; (4) sponsor TV and radio programs, to build public goodwill; and (5) provide support for nonprofit educational, health, and welfare organizations, again to build public goodwill. These efforts are often benign, but they can be aggressive in pushing a particular corporate or executive viewpoint. In this connection, we shall speak of Mobil Oil and Herbert Schmertz, its long-time vice president for public affairs.[8] We will speak also of the extraordinary case of the American Express Company's covert attacks, through the media, on Edmond Safra, CEO of the Republic National Bank.[9]

Herbert Schmertz came to work for Mobil Oil in 1966 as a labor relations expert. But in 1969, he went to Raleigh Warner, Chairman and CEO, and William Tavoulareas, president and COO—the top executives of Mobil Oil—and suggested the company undertake an aggressive public relations posture. One side of his proposed campaign involved sponsoring top-quality TV programs ("Masterpiece Theatre"). The other side involved ads in leading newspapers upholding the virtues of free enterprise, and when Schmertz and his colleagues decided it to be appropriate, aggressive responses to media stories they regarded as biased or outright inaccurate. Mobil bought the strategy and it was applied vigorously throughout the decades of the 70s and 80s. However, following the retirement of Warner and Tavoulareas and the accession of Allen Murray as CEO, there seemed to be some toning down of pugnaciousness, although Mobil's ads (Thursday on the Op-Ed page of the *New York Times* and comparably high visibility spots) continue to run. It is worth noting that the Sunday, September 30, 1990, edition of the *New York Times,* had a special section celebrating the 20th anniversary of the paper's introduction of its Op-Ed page in 1970. Of the 20 pages making up the section, Mobil took 8 full pages, lauding the *Times* decision to feature diverse opinions opposite its editorial page. Mobil also reiterated its commitment to being represented on the Op-Ed page on Thursday, as well as announcing its forthcoming "Masterpiece" programs for the fall 1990 season. One thing seems certain: Mobil's activism has made it a more difficult target for aspiring media members. Critical stories are not cut off by Mobil's activities, but they

---

[8] Philip Weiss, "Up Schmertz, Down Schmertz," *Manhattan, Inc.*, November 1986, pp. 122–39.
[9] Bryan Burrough, "The Vendetta," *The Wall Street Journal,* September 24, 1990, pp. A1,8,9.

are likely to be more carefully researched and prepared before publication than might otherwise have been the case.

The American Express-Edmond Safra story is a far cry from the Mobil-Schmertz one. In its convoluted, complicated, and covert elements, it contains the elements of a first-class spy story, with allegedly secret meetings and underhanded operations across several continents. But one thing seems plain: there was an organized clandestine campaign, through stories planted in the media, by agents of American Express to discredit Edmond Safra, CEO of Republic National Bank. As reported in *The Wall Street Journal,* the essence of the story is this:[10]

> Slowly, with a hint here, a comment there, a question began to dawn on some American Express executives: Was a top aide to James D. Robinson III, the company's chairman and chief executive officer, up to something they would be wise to steer clear of?
>
> Harry L. Freeman was given to flashes of both brilliance and bad judgment, but Mr. Robinson's reliance on him was unquestioned. The two frequently began their day at 6:45 a.m. over a pot of coffee in the chairman's corner office. Special projects were Mr. Freeman's bailiwick, and associates say that didn't please the company's top lawyers, Gary A. Beller and Lawrence Ricciardi, who fretted that one of Mr. Freeman's operations might one day blow up in their faces. "We've got to stop this guy," Mr. Ricciardi said on more than one occasion. "He's going to destroy us."
>
> Few knew quite what Mr. Freeman was up to this time, but it was clear he had targeted one of the company's thorniest competitors, the international banker Edmond Safra, a man who some American Express officials were obsessed with defeating.
>
> When Matthew Stover, then an American Express public relations executive, asked about the project, he says, "I was always told, You don't want to know." Finally, in the summer of 1988, Mr. Ricciardi, the lawyer, confronted Mr. Freeman. "Harry, I don't know what you're up to," he said. "But if I were you, I'd stop what you're doing immediately."
>
> The warning was apt, but it was too late. In a stunning disclosure, American Express admitted last year that it had engaged in a covert campaign to ruin Mr. Safra's reputation by spreading rumors and articles in the international press. The company made a painful, public apology for what its chairman, Mr. Robinson, called an "unauthorized and shameful effort,"and paid $8 million to Mr. Safra and charities he selected. As part of the agreement, details of this shameful effort were to remain secret.

---

[10] Ibid., p. A1.

For American Express, a company that has enjoyed a virtually unrivaled reputation for integrity, the Safra affair reveals a willingness to engage in unseemly corporate revenge when confronting a rival, and, at the very least a jarring lack of oversight on the part of top company officials.

Despite regular contact with one of Mr. Freeman's operatives, there is no concrete evidence that Mr. Robinson knew of the smear campaign against Mr. Safra. Indeed, he and other top American Express officials, including Mr. Freeman, have vehemently denied any prior knowledge of the anti-Safra effort. Instead, they argue that a legitimate investigation of a competitor's activities was simply taken too far by overzealous employees.

The Safra affair is a story of corporate intrigue played out on three continents. Suspecting that American Express was behind the outbreak of specious stories that began surfacing in early 1988, Mr. Safra hired numerous detectives who engaged the American Express operatives in a cloak-and-dagger pas de deux that resulted in proof of the company's culpability roughly a year later.

There is another way for a chief executive to use a channel of communication, but it is outlandish and a return to an earlier era in American journalism; namely, to buy a paper or TV station and use it to convey the new owner's messages. There are some instances of important businessmen buying well-known newspapers, such as Leonard N. Stern's purchase of the *Village Voice* and H. Kalikow's purchase of *The New York Post*. But neither man has used his paper as his voice, and there is no indication of any such intention. Of course, their integrity of purpose need not be the hallmark of someone else who did want control to project a particular viewpoint.

INVESTMENT ANALYSTS, CEOS AND THE CORPORATE TIME FRAME

One segment of the media has special significance to the CEO, namely, investment analysts. Of course, the reverse is equally true, and analysts are deeply concerned with CEOs. The reasons are obvious: first, investment analysts, through market letters, the press, and the brokerage firms they advise, influence the purchase and sale of corporate securities and their market values. And those values are of major importance to CEOs, as they must be, because shareholders and directors so regard them. Second, the credibility of investment analysts, which is the touchstone of their reputation and livelihood, depends directly on the accuracy of their analyses and forecasts of earnings and corporate health. But that very accuracy depends, in turn, on their access to corporate financial data and its accuracy.

The CEO hungers for good news to be broadcast by the analysts; or, at the least, that bad news be put in the least damaging light. To that end, he/she has a powerful inducement to withhold or to color information made available to analysts. Further, given the isolation of many CEOs and their aversion to the give-and-take of possibly hostile questioning, they may avoid exposing themselves to the very analysts on whom they depend for a good press. And analysts will seek avidly to ferret out as much information as they can.

A third reason involves the time frame for the reporting of corporate earnings. Analysts are attuned to quarterly results, and their performance as experts is judged on the accuracy of their quarterly forecasts. But this time frame is very brief, and the undue emphasis it has received creates enormous pressure on CEOs to report ever more favorable quarterly results. With stock prices reacting rapidly to these reports, too many CEOs are seduced into unwise decisions and actions, aimed at avoiding the disclosure of negative news. Perhaps the most reprehensible decisions in this connection are:

1. Failure to write off bad inventories.
2. Failure to write off bad accounts payable.
3. Booking returnable dealer inventories as accounts payable.
4. Unwise, and, in the long run, damaging failures to replace and maintain plant and equipment.
5. Unwise curtailment of expenditures for research and development.

All these decisions will overstate earnings in the short run, but, if continued, doom one to disaster in the long run. And some of them, in particular the first three, can easily cross the line into fraudulent as well as misleading accounting.

The flow of information between analysts and corporate executives also involves these sensitive issues: (1) Should corporations arrange private meetings with investment analysts, thereby giving them a privileged position? (2) What and how much information should be divulged? (3) Does the disclosure of information in private meetings increase the danger of insider trading violations of SEC rules?

People favoring private meetings of CEOs with investment analysts argue that they enhance good will and thereby encourage more favorable reporting than might otherwise be received. Opponents of private meetings, to which news reporters are not invited, fear disclosures that will reveal inside information and become the basis for illegal trading activities. The proponents, however, feel that this danger can be avoided. Also, they think there is a significant disadvantage to meetings in which news reporters are mixed with analysts: namely, the business sophistication and interests of the two groups are so disparate that neither can be satisfied and the purpose of information transfer is harmed.[11]

The foregoing issues, as well as that of what and how much information should be disclosed, are highlighted by a controversy in mid-1990 between Caterpillar, Inc. and investment analysts.[12] Analysts had generally been issuing optimistic earnings forecasts for the company. By itself, that could reflect a general, if erroneous, opinion. But the analysts had attended a company briefing on June 25, 1990, at which it was announced that Caterpillar's Brazilian operations had slumped seriously. It was not announced at the meeting that the Brazilian operations had become much more important to Caterpillar's bottom-line results than they had been previously (i.e., 20 percent of earnings instead of 5 percent). Consequently, the stock dropped only slightly after the meeting. However, later in the day via a conference call, Caterpillar made a disclosure to analysts about the increased importance of the Brazilian operations. And the value of the stock dropped from $63 to $52 in two days, representing an aggregate shareholder loss of over $1 billion. Analysts were outraged that Caterpillar failed to make the disclosure in mid-March, when Brazilian prospects were allegedly clear to the company, so that an unwarranted run-up in Caterpillar's market value of roughly $700 million between mid-March and June 25 would have been avoided, as the subsequent losses of unwary investors could have been avoided. As Eric N. Berg of the *New York Times* asked:[13]

> Should a company alert analysts if it knows they are disseminating inaccurate information? Should multinational companies like Caterpillar be required to disclose their profits from individual countries if one or more of them is contributing disproportionately to the profits? Do Wall Street analysts—supposed to be the eyes and ears of investors—often make naive assumptions about a company's operations?

---

[11] *The Wall Street Journal*, section 2, December 17, 1986, p. 1.

[12] *New York Times*, July 17, 1990, pp. D1 and 8.

[13] Ibid., p. D-1.

I believe the answer to all three questions is yes. And I believe it is a wise CEO who opts for timely disclosure of significant corporate information. To fail to do so is to arouse suspicion and to harm credibility, which in the long-run is the strongest defense in the face of adversity. It is also true in our litigious society that any perceived failure to disclose will invite litigation and claims for damages by disappointed shareholders. As an example, a shareholder suit against Chase Manhattan Bank and its two top executives (William Butcher, chairman and CEO, and Thomas Labrecque, president and COO) was filed on September 25, 1990.[14] The lawsuit alleged: (1) Chase Manhattan's stock price was artificially inflated between January 27, 1990, when a dividend increase was announced, and September 21, 1990, when the dividend was cut in half, from 62 to 30 cents a share; (2) Chase Manhattan's management knew for several months that its loan loss reserves were inadequate and that it couldn't afford to maintain its common stock dividend; and (3) Chase Manhattan's failure to disclose its true condition in a timely manner intentionally misled investors by misrepresenting and not disclosing pertinent information about the company's loan portfolio. Chase Manhattan's stock, which traded at about $32 a share in mid-January fell to $11.125 per share by September 25, 1990. A spokesman for the bank said the suit was without merit. Without any knowledge of affairs at Chase Manhattan, I do know from personal experience as a bank director how drastically and suddenly loans can shift from performing to nonperforming, especially in a period when there is a free fall in real estate values (such as occurred in the Northeastern United States in 1990). That real estate was weak and likely to get much weaker was known to many well before September, 1990, which makes it something of a mystery that Chase Manhattan's management's outlook was optimistic enough to induce a decision to increase the dividend in January, 1990.

CRISIS MANAGEMENT, THE MEDIA, AND THE CEO

Business executives, *as citizens,* will interact with the media as they are called upon to undertake important tasks with government agencies. Examples are easy to find. Thus, in recent years, we have seen Lee Iacocca and William May, as chairman and president of the Statue of Liberty-Ellis

---

[14] *The Wall Street Journal,* September 26, 1990, p. C-15.

Island Foundation, working to restore both of those national monuments. In New York City, Felix Rohatyn has served with the city's Fiscal Review Board to oversee the restoration and maintenance of its fiscal health. In a matter of months, Donald Trump rebuilt the Wohlman Skating Rink in New York City's Central Park, an act which the city had failed to do over a period of years and with the expenditure of millions of dollars. And Peter Grace headed a national commission to study federal operations, with an eye to increasing efficiency and finding savings. In addition, there are the activities of executives at the state and local levels of government, with school boards and a multitude of other agencies.

Business executives will also interact with the media as they engage in charitable activities and in the support of education and the arts. Thus, endowments of museums, universities and colleges, medical centers, and religious institutions, by way of example, are reported in the press. We do not speak here of donor motivations, whether being purely unselfish and guided by the Golden Rule of ethical life, or in some measure reflecting a desire for a small piece of immortality. Instead, we speak of the activities of business executives, which will bring them to the attention of the media. And, from an ignoble aspect, we know that when scandal strikes in the personal life of a major business executive, that too will attract the attention of the media and result in publicity.

But, *in their activities as chief executives,* businessmen will typically interact with the media under two sets of circumstances: (1) a crisis involving their company or (2) economic developments affecting the earnings and stock values of their company's shares. Of course, a crisis (a sudden, drastic happening that was unforeseen) will have a significant impact on earnings and share values. However, how it is handled and the time available to make decisions are markedly different than in the case of business developments that emerge over a period of time. Of these two sets of circumstances, it is crisis management that is the most difficult and challenging for CEOs. One reason, and a major one, for this being true is the protective cloak of staff that usually insulates the CEO from the media. Another reason is the lack of training and skill that characterize most CEOs when confronted by TV cameramen and interviewers, or by investigative news reporters. The media people are in control of the cameras and questions—no small matter. They are prepared and "loaded for bear." The CEO usually lacks these strengths and is in a relatively weaker position. Further, and especially so in the case of TV, a crisis will probably involve complex and technical issues that are not compressible into 30-second "bites" for TV.

Into the context just limned, we now place the media representative who, in addition to seeking truth, may well be motivated by a desire to sensationalize and titillate, with an eye to attracting more viewers (TV) or more readers (newspapers, magazines), to winning a more prominently placed byline or story credit; or to advancing his/her personal career in the media. Also, media people must not be underestimated. They are intelligent and aggressive in pursuit of a story. And "a story" is usually one characterized by drama and conflict, rather than one that goes into careful, painstakingly researched details of highly complicated technical matters (like major oil spills). Villains command the headlines, and it is a temptation to convert a CEO caught by an unpredictable and tragic accident into a villain. Of course, there will be cases where a tragic occurrence is the result of executive and corporate misbehavior or negligence. In such instances, portraiture as a villain is within the realm of realistic, honest reporting.

Given a crisis, the well-advised CEO will move immediately to the front. He will not take refuge behind public relations staff and hired consultants. By so doing, he will project a picture of being in control and of caring. But he must also be forthright and ready to confront sensitive issues. Waffling on corporate readiness to do its utmost to meet and overcome the crisis will be damaging. Perhaps the most instructive cases are provided by James Burke, former CEO of Johnson and Johnson, and Lee Iacocca, CEO of Chrysler, on the one side, and Leonard Rawls, CEO of Exxon, on the other side. When Johnson and Johnson was shocked by the tragic discovery that some Tylenol capsules had been poisoned and had caused deaths, its then CEO, James Burke, stepped forward immediately and announced the withdrawal of all Tylenol capsules from the market. The immediate cost to the company was many millions of dollars. The longer-run cost was incalculable, for it could have meant the loss of future market share for the product. Burke also made it clear that the product would not be returned to the market until his company was reasonably certain it was available only in tamper-proof packaging. The effect of his actions was enormous. He achieved credibility and returned the public's confidence in Johnson and Johnson. And, when Tylenol was returned to the market, it quickly recaptured its market share.

When it was revealed that the Chrysler Corporation was resetting the odometers of cars used in testing, and selling them as new, Lee Iacocca stepped forward immediately. In terms of prior experience in Chrysler and other companies, the practice was not new. And the tested cars may actually have been mechanically superior to untested ones. But they were not brand new, as the public expected them to be! Lee Iacocca did not dissemble. Personally and in full-page advertisements in leading newspapers, he admitted what had been done, called it a mistake, said the practice was dumb, and promised there would be no repeat. That forthrightness helped preserve his credibility, which is a major asset of the Chrysler Corporation.

By way of contrast, we recall the experience of Lawrence Rawls, CEO of Exxon, when the company's tanker, the Exxon Valdez, went aground in Prince William Sound, Alaska, and spilled millions of gallons of oil into the bay's pristine water. Rawls relied on underlings and public relations staff. Only belatedly and reluctantly did he come forward personally. Further, the company's efforts at cleanup seemed confused and hesitant. And after a couple of years of cleanup activity and an estimated expenditure of $2 billion, neither Rawls nor his company could command good press. Instead, they had become the butt of comedians' jokes and cartoonists' jibes. The common judgment is that Exxon failed badly in its handling of the crisis. And the fault for that failure must be placed at Rawls' door. The sad aspect of the case is that there can be no doubt that Rawls acted throughout in what he thought was the correct manner. He was reported to have said he saw no reason for example, to fly immediately to Prince William Sound, examine the damage, and, at the spot, pledge Exxon's best efforts to overcome the damage. He believed he would be more effective remaining at headquarters, while the company's experts and staff handled affairs at the scene. Perhaps his own lack of experience before TV cameras and media representatives influenced his decisions. In any case, substantial long-lasting harm was done to his company's credibility and public standing.

A final word may be appropriate. CEOs would be well advised to obtain some training in appearing before TV cameras, in interviews, and in handling hostile questioning by media representatives. Mastering the art of the succinct statement could prove to be of immeasurable value.

CHAPTER 7

THE CHIEF EXECUTIVE AND THE CORPORATE CULTURE

MEANING

While *culture* has a variety of meanings, we are concerned here with its sociological sense, that is, "the customary beliefs, social forms, and material traits of a racial, religious, or social group."[1] Webster's dictionary further defines culture as "the integrated pattern of human behavior that includes thought, speech, action, and artifacts and depends upon man's capacity for learning and transmitting knowledge to succeeding generations." Sociologists also use the term *mores,* which Webster's dictionary defines as the "fixed morally binding customs of a particular group."

Several key ideas can be drawn out of the definitions and highlighted:

1. We are dealing with a group.
2. The group has certain customary beliefs, social forms, and material traits.
3. These beliefs, forms, and traits are fixed and morally binding on the individuals comprising the group.
4. Consequently, an integrated pattern of behavior characterizes the group.
5. That integrated pattern of behavior is reflected in the group's thoughts, speech, and actions.
6. The integrated pattern of behavior can be learned and transmitted to succeeding generations.

---

[1] *Webster's New Collegiate Dictionary,* s.v. "culture." Springfield, Mass., 1981 edition.

To this point, we are speaking in broad societal terms, that is, national characters or cultures, like the German, French, British, Russian, Japanese, or American. We know there is worldwide acceptance of the existence of national traits. But what about other groupings: for example, by religion (American Protestants, Catholics, Jews, and, increasingly, various Oriental and other religious strains)? As Americans, they share certain traits, which become stronger as the original immigrant generation is succeeded by second and third generation descendants. Yet they retain differentiating traits, beliefs, and customs defined by their various religious beliefs. Here we confront a basic notion in one of the definitions with which we began our discussion: namely, that the beliefs, forms, and traits comprising a culture are fixed as well as morally binding. When cultures clash, however, their beliefs are in conflict. Then, if the broader societal context is open and permissive (as in 1991 United States, as against 1991 Iran), one or both cultures can change.

Further, what about smaller groupings, such as a business corporation? And what about multinational (multicultural) business corporations, of which there are now so many in the world? In the first connection, it has become a widely accepted belief that business organizations can and do develop distinct corporate cultures. Further, it is accepted that those corporate cultures are important because they influence (some would say, set) the behavior of the human beings comprising the corporate entity.

All this brings us to some intriguing questions. What happens when a corporate culture faces a changed economic environment, one that requires new and different traits and behavior patterns? If the culture is fixed, does the corporate entity die? Alternatively, if the corporate entity is to survive, how is the corporate culture changed? Is an exercise of naked executive power required as the instrument of change? If so, how is the resistance of the traditional (the existent) culture to be overcome? In a multinational, multicultural organization, is culture clash inevitable, or can it be minimized, if not overcome?

Concerning the last question, the acquisition by the General Electric Company (GE) of the troubled French medical equipment manufacturer, Companie Generale de Radiologie, in 1988 provides a fascinating and illuminating case in point.[2] The acquisition seemed to be a brilliant move for GE, which wanted to achieve a major European position as a manufac-

---

[2] Mark M. Nelson and E. S. Browning, "GE's Culture Turns Sour at French Unit," *The Wall Street Journal*, July 31, 1990, p. A10.

turer of medical equipment. The French Company (CGR) had been government owned and as such had become accustomed to state subsidies and guaranteed purchases of its equipment (X-ray machines, CAT scanners, and other large diagnostic machines) by state-owned hospitals. Insulated from competitive market pressures, CGR suffered a massive culture shock when it was taken over by GE.

General Electric is a large, mature firm long known for the excellence of its management, both under its present chairman John F. (Jack) Welch and his predecessor, Reginald (Reg) Jones. But its culture changed when Welch succeeded Jones. The latter had a reputation as an industrial statesman, and under his sponsorship, GE had diversified and developed a large headquarters staff engaged in planning and other activities that presumably tie things together and avoid corporate anarchy. Also, Jones' personal style was "cool." Welch is a different personality, strong and aggressive. Under his leadership, GE divested substantial units and concentrated on several major manufacturing activities. Thus, in making the deal with CGR, it unloaded its RCA consumer electronics division to Thomson S.A. and ended up with CGR and $800 million in cash.

Having acquired the French entity, GE, apparently without having thought through the implications of its actions, took steps to convert CGR to the GE culture and way of doing business. To that end, GE arranged a training seminar for its European managers, including the French. To build a sense of company identity and team spirit, à la Americain, colorful T-shirts emblazoned with the GE slogan "Go for one" were left in the hotel rooms, with a note urging the managers to wear them to the seminar. The French found the arrangement distasteful, indeed humiliating, and strongly resented it. It was the opening round in what became a bitter, extended cultural clash. Other GE actions included changing CGR's financial control system by imposing a GE system said to be unsuited to the French reporting requirements; posting English language posters; flying GE flags; and generally, blanketing CGR with GE's presence in physical as well as organizational terms. Perhaps these actions would have been minded less if they had not been accomplished by a drive for efficiency and profitability. And that was undoubtedly the bedrock for the culture clash, the fact that turned distasteful behavior into something more. CGR was undergoing major restructuring, with plant closings and large layoffs (the number of employees has shrunk from 6,500 to 5,000). In this case, a culture clash was inevitable. But a different approach might have produced a different outcome.

The GE case will be badly misconstrued if it is taken as an example of bad behavior by ugly Americans. It is rather an illustration of the problems of cross-cultural corporate marriages, problems of major magnitude in an age of globalization. The validity of the point is demonstrated by the story of the acquisition of Diamandis Communications, Inc., a U.S. magazine giant, by Hachette, S.A., an even larger French magazine giant. Describing events subsequent to the acquisition, Patrick M. Reilly wrote in *The Wall Street Journal:* "The acquisition, in 1988, seemed a good idea at the time. . . . But Hachette's grand plan unraveled in a clash of French and American cultures and in a battle of egos. . . . Crossing international boundaries rarely turns out to be as easy as envisioned. . . . When business sours and difficult decisions must be made, once polite and cute cultural differences can turn to rudeness, stereotypes, and snippy backbiting."[3]

COMPONENTS OF CORPORATE CULTURE

What are the traits that are ideally sought in a corporate culture? Without implying an order of importance, the basic ones seem to be (1) a work ethic, (2) honesty/integrity, (3) a desire to serve others, or to be of service, and (4) a sense of individual worth, or of personal dignity. Other corporate characteristics, often identified as part of corporate culture, seem to be *derivative* of the foregoing four and include (1) quality of product and/or service, (2) customer satisfaction, (3) pricing policy, (4) job security as a high priority, and (5) participative management.

This schema envisages a two-tier cultural structure. The bedrock stratum, the core of cultural traits, is those values or norms central to the larger society itself. In the United States, they comprise the ethical and behavioral heartland of the Western world's Judeo-Christian ethic. They are the ideals that we believe should enlighten and guide us in our relationships with our fellow human beings, and that we teach to our children. So we praise those among us who display a work ethic, who take pride in their workmanship, and who seek faithfully to put forth their best efforts as they perform productive labor. We disdainfully regard those who seek to slide by with minimum effort, to obtain the fruits of the labor of others while

---

[3] *The Wall Street Journal,* February 15, 1991, p. A1.

withholding their own best efforts. And we honor those known for honesty and integrity. We elevate uprightness of disposition and conduct, the quality of straightforwardness. By way of contrast, we deplore lying, cheating, and stealing. By integrity, we mean more than simply innocence. We mean soundness of moral principle, the virtue of being uncorrupted and incorruptible. The call to be of service to others is deeply embedded in the Judeo-Christian religious ethos, in the concept of the brotherhood of man. Individualism, the notion that the individual has a supreme worth as a microcosmic entity apart from a macrocosmic group, flowered later in the history of man's development. The older and more common tradition emphasizes the social group, with the individual drawing significance as a member of the group, and having the obligation to subordinate his or her individual desire to the well-being of the larger entity. But, perhaps most notably in the United States, the rights of the individual have been elevated to a point where they often seem to overwhelm the well-being, even the safety, of the group (e.g., the manifold protections of the individual defendant in criminal trials).

Based on the foregoing cultural bedrock, U.S. corporate culture presumably emphasizes quality of output, customer satisfaction, and fair pricing. Job security is esteemed, but more so by workers than most managers. And participative management is intended to give voice to the importance of each individual's input and to improve the final outcome.

The list of cultural traits presents an impressive roster of societal and business organizational ideals, a seemingly pious parade. Yet to this point there is no reference to *profit,* the omission of which would be inexcusable. We are a capitalistic society, and our economic system is based on the operation of free markets in which businessmen seek profits. Indeed, profits are the market system's key to resource allocation and production priorities. They reflect the operation of Adam Smith's invisible hand, and permit millions of individual consumers to determine society's priorities in the production of goods and services. We cannot deny that the pursuit of profit is a central trait in our culture.

How does that pursuit conform with the other traits we so esteem? In theory, it conforms well. And, if recent history is any guide, it conforms much better than the dictates of central planners in a state-directed socialist system. In theory, the pursuit of profit does so because in a perfectly competitive market economy (in which consumers and workers, as well as owners and managers, are informed in their economic decision making) dishonesty, lack of quality, rigged pricing, and such could not win. The people manifesting such behavior would lose customers and workers and would not survive in business. But in the real world, markets are not perfect, and more often than we like, dishonesty, shoddiness, malingering, and exploitation of one person by another can exist, and even persist, and can produce profit. And that is a point of ethical collision and conflict that we will explore in a later chapter.

CORPORATE CULTURE AND EXECUTIVE POWER

It is generally believed that a corporate culture is an extension of the CEO, who puts his stamp upon it. It is implicit that the culture cannot be changed unless the CEO is personally and deeply involved in the change: that his/her behavior and actions manifest such involvement. Words are not the instrument of change. The CEO's behavior *is*. In fact, if the CEO's words are contradicted by his behavior, his words will probably be damaging to the organization's culture and effectiveness—for people will perceive the contradiction and will conclude that the actions, not the words, count. More importantly, they will believe a kind of duplicity exists, which in itself will damage morale and the ethical climate of the organization.

There is a caveat to the foregoing emphasis on the critical importance of the CEO's role and impact on corporate culture. In large organizations, with autonomous or nearly autonomous divisions, the head of a division can have a major impact on the larger organization itself. Alan L. Wilkins makes this point well in his *Developing Corporate Character; How to Successfully Change an Organization Without Destroying It*.[4] He describes the experience of Charles House, who was assigned to be research manager of a new ventures group in the Colorado Springs division of Hewlett-Packard Co. Finding a dispirited group of seeming misfits and has-beens, House defined a mission for the group, allocated funds to stimulate activities supportive of that mission, and involved himself deeply and directly with the individuals comprising the group. Thereby, he indicated his personal commitment. As a result, the group was energized and coalesced into a dynamic, enthusiastic, creative, and finally successful productive unit of Hewlett-Packard.

---

[4] Alan L. Wilkins, *Developing Corporate Character*, (San Francisco & London: Jossey-Bass, 1989), Chapter six, pp. 112–30.

My own experience as dean of the School of Commerce (now the Leonard N. Stern School of Business at New York University) was parallel. I was appointed acting dean in 1965, when the university central administration and trustees were seriously considering the school's demise. The school had by then ceased to be the enormous "cash cow" it had been historically. Also, it had come to be looked down upon as academically inferior. A core group of colleagues joined me in effecting a major turnaround. The school not only survived, it prospered mightily in the ensuing decades, and finally achieved a premier academic reputation and standing among the undergraduate divisions of the university, as well as externally. A part of that story was told by J. Victor Baldridge in *Power and Conflict in the University.* In his words,[5]

> Increasing admissions standards, emphasis on full-time students and faculty, and a general upgrading in quality changed the School of Commerce dramatically. Commerce was one of the schools most fully dedicated to the "school of opportunity" philosophy and had a large core of professors who fought strongly for this value when it was threatened. . . .
>
> Probably the majority of the Commerce faculty was opposed to major changes in their basic philosophy or to changes in admissions policies. Moreover, the administration's chief representative on the scene, Dean John Prime, was not totally convinced that the changes were desirable. Dean Prime resisted many of the changes, and his faculty was strongly behind him. A real power struggle developed, but in this battle the administration had most of the weapons. . . .
>
> For many months, the task of persuading the faculty to cooperate with the new changes went on against strong opposition. Finally two major changes in Commerce leadership were announced. First, in April 1962, Commerce was placed under an executive dean who headed both Commerce and the Graduate School of Business. Second, on September 1965, Dean Prime resigned and Dean Abraham Gitlow was appointed as local dean at Commerce. To no one's great surprise, both Executive Dean Joseph Taggart and Dean Gitlow favored the administration's plans for upgrading quality in the School of Commerce. *About that time the major breakthrough came in faculty cooperation.* [Italics added]

The culture clash that faced me when I entered the dean's office centered on two values that had been central in Commerce's culture from its

---

[5] J. Victor Baldridge, *Power and Conflict in the University* (New York: John Wiley, 1971), pp. 53–54. Reprinted by permission.

founding in 1900. First, the school focused generally on training accountants, bankers, managers, marketers, and businessmen. In that respect, it was practitioner-oriented, and, for its first six decades, its faculty was drawn heavily from people who had worked in the real business world as accountants, bankers, managers, and so on. While the faculty included professors who engaged in scholarly research and published, it was not characteristically composed of academicians. Second, the school was proud to be a "school of opportunity"; admission was easy (nonselective), but graduation was more daunting. Indeed, possession of a high school diploma, indicating completion of certain minimum requirements, coupled with the ability to pay the tuition, practically insured matriculation. But only about 30 percent of those admitted survived academically and graduated. Also part of the school of opportunity culture was to welcome part-time (evening) students, and thousands passed through Commerce's portals in the evening program.

These values were confronted head-on by NYU's decision in the 60s to upgrade itself and its divisions, some of which had already become prestigious, and to seek a place among America's first-rank research universities. President James Hester articulated the vision of a great urban university, in and of the city, yet characterized by high academic standards. NYU was to become a community of scholars in the teeming metropolitan center of New York. To help achieve that vision, a $25 million matching grant was obtained from the Ford Foundation. And the Washington Square area of Greenwich Village, famous as a center of intellectuals, writers, and bohemians, would become eventually the campus of the invigorated NYU.

A massive building program was initiated. After several decades and multiple crises, it succeeded, producing a residential university in place of the old commuter university on the subway, with a great library, student center, sports and recreation center, new academic buildings, multiple student residence halls, and substantial faculty housing.

But in the mid-60s, the critical turning point in the development of the university, the School of Commerce and its culture and values became the focus of the university's effort to implement its plans for transformation. Admission to the School of Commerce was to become selective, at least to the point of some reasonable comparability to the standards at the Arts and Sciences College. And the faculty was to become academically respectable, characterized by full-time academics possessing the Ph.D. degree and productive as research scholars. Of course, the curriculum would be changed radically, replacing the practitioner oriented courses that emphasized how-to-do, with more intellectually rigorous, theoretical ones.

The anticipated consequences of implementing these changes entailed a sharp reduction in school enrollments and an associated reduction in numbers of faculty. The latter connection also involved a change in the character of the faculty, from heavily practitioner-oriented to research-oriented academics.

Figuratively, blood was all over the place. The incumbent dean was forced into retirement. And I was appointed acting dean, with a clear mandate to change Commerce so that it conformed to the university's plan. Failing such conformance, it was made clear to me and to the school's faculty, the school would be discontinued. At least that was the threat, and it was made in such terms that it became believable.

A powerful group of faculty opposed the changes. They agreed that the school's traditions and values were correct and should not be abandoned. Undoubtedly, some truly believed that to be true. Others were opposed because the new values doomed them unless they could convert themselves into research-oriented academics. Such a conversion was difficult and painful, and most practitioner faculty fought against it. They believed they could muster support among prominent alumni of the school, some of whom were university trustees, and successfully blunt and ward off the central administration's drive.

The university president's key move, in terms of executive power, was to force the retirement of the incumbent dean and appoint me as the acting dean. I was known to be in sympathy with the university's plan, and I had the support of a core of highly respected, academically oriented faculty in the school.

I came into a position, as acting dean, where I was able to use another cultural trait of the School of Commerce. The dean's office had been able to exert great authority of position and had exercised that authority without much check by the faculty. Although my personal style and preference is for participative management, I used the dean's authority in my first week in office to force the resignation of a departmental chairman, who had assumed a leadership position among those opposing the changes demanded of Commerce. That move was a shock to the opposition and fractured their resistance to the curricular and other changes that followed in the next two to three years. Concurrently, an advisory faculty committee was elected to counsel me in curricular, compensation, admission standards, and faculty tenure decisions. Of course, the committee was comprised of those colleagues who shared my views, and who would be active supporters of them as they were presented to the faculty and then implemented. Regular meetings were instituted with departmental chairmen, to enhance and make effective communication between them and the dean's office. Plans were laid out and discussed. No effort was made to do things secretly. Promotion, tenure, and compensation policies were discussed openly. Faculty who appeared to be unable, or unwilling, to meet the new standards were seen personally, and given a candid explanation of what was needed to save the school, and how that affected their own positions.

As admission standards were raised dramatically, enrollments plummeted. Part-time faculty were laid off. Nontenured full-time faculty who did not seem likely to succeed as scholars were given notice of termination. And tenured full-time faculty were carefully reviewed. Those without the characteristics desired were divided into two groups: first, those who were near retirement age (68, under university rules, but 62 to 65 under social security eligibility rules) and had medical problems; and, second, those who were younger.

For older faculty, age 62 and over with medical problems, an early retirement buy-out plan was developed, based on several key elements:

1. While working, a faculty member faced deductions from base salary for social security and the university's TIAA-CREF[6] pension plan.

2. When retired, that faculty member's disposable income would no longer be subject to those deductions.

3. The university's contribution's for social security and TIAA-CREF would end when the faculty member retired, representing a saving.

4. Since enrollments were declining, replacement faculty would not have to be hired, so that a faculty member retired three to four years before age 68, as an example, would represent a saving to the university of that number of years of base salary, plus the additional contributions for social security, TIAA-CREF pension, unemployment compensation, and so on.

5. Given the prospective university savings associated with point four, the university could well afford to make a lump-sum contribution

---

[6] Teachers Insurance and Annuity Association-College Retirement Equities Fund.

of one to two years base salary to the faculty member's TIAA-CREF pension, bringing his or her after-tax disposable income in retirement up to or about even with what it would be if he or she worked to age 68 (the lump-sum contribution was allowable at the time under existing tax rules).

The arrangement was welcomed by several faculty suffering from medical problems. Word of mouth spread to others, including some older faculty whose health was fine. They came forward and requested similar deals, to which the university readily agreed. As a consequence, a number of tenured older faculty retired early. Younger tenured faculty who did not fit the academic profile of the future were interviewed and told candidly that, while they would be treated courteously in terms of teaching assignments, they should not expect to share in future salary increases. Also, leave arrangements were offered to make it easier for them to relocate, and a number accepted. Between 1964 to 1965 and 1969 to 1970, a full-time faculty of 97 was reduced to 51. In the same time span, part-time faculty was reduced from 58 to 11.

Along with changes in the type of courses offered, curricular reform involved a major reduction in number of courses (especially electives, which had proliferated when the school was a massive operation with thousands of students). The number of sections in multisection courses was also reduced. Consequently, average class size, while dropping, did not drop proportionately to the student enrollment. But it did drop significantly, making a more attractive teaching environment. Concurrently, the number of faculty, while sharply reduced, was not reduced in complete proportionality to the drop in numbers of courses and sections, enabling a cut in average faculty teaching loads. Smaller class sizes and teaching loads were critical ingredients necessary to effective implementation of the plan to upgrade the academic quality of the faculty.

But, while the foregoing developments were occurring, something immediate and very visible was needed as a morale booster. That something turned out to be a major physical overhaul and upgrading of faculty offices and the creation of an attractive faculty lounge. These physical investments were designed to communicate to the faculty that the drastic changes were supported by the university. But the university was unprepared to put up the $100,000 then needed to do the upgrade. So I took all the discretionary funds accumulated by prior deans, some $75,000, and told President Hester I would gamble it all if he would provide the other $25,000 needed. He agreed, and the job was done.

The School of Commerce was transformed. Enrollments dropped from over 2,500 in 1964 to a low 1,000 in 1972, and then rebounded to 2,500 by 1984. But the high school grade point averages of entering freshmen rose from 2.2 in 1960 to 1961 to 3.46 in 1990-1991, while combined verbal math SAT scores rose from 897 in the earlier year to 1,210 in the later one. In 1973, the undergraduate business school faculty was merged with that of the Graduate School of Business Administration, and today the faculty of the Stern School of Business is known internationally, highly esteemed, and, in a number of departments, preeminent in the field.

The massive transformation just described inspired a visiting accreditation team in the 1968-1969 academic year to make these comments:[7]

> The New York University programs in business at both undergraduate and graduate levels have standards of excellence manifestly exceeding minimum criteria of the Association. *The only doubt at all on this question might have arisen some four years ago when the School of Commerce had very large enrollments taught to a considerable extent by part-time faculty and some nonterminal full-time faculty.* . . . [Italics added]
>
> The most striking observation of the revisitation of New York University in 1969 is the spirit of change and innovation in an old and distinguished institution . . . ; we find a major qualitative thrust of gargantuan proportions in the critical characteristics of the School of Commerce over the last few years. This new direction plus new resources and new spirit would be hard to match nationally and is still going on.

But the transformation required the exercise of executive power. Initially, it was authority of position that carried the day. Over the longer run, the testimonials of my colleagues say it was authority of leadership.

A brief epilogue is needed for the sake of balance. The triumph of a research orientation as the acid test of academic and intellectual standing and acceptability was not without serious long-term cost to the overall educational mission of the school. Faculty interest in, and dedication to, the importance of classroom teaching and institutional needs, such as participation in curriculum development, declined as it did in other major U.S. universities emphasizing research. There was a sharp decline also in research oriented to the practical problems of the real, work-a-day world. The resulting imbalance in educational mission and responsibility is being

---

[7] School of Commerce, *1968-69 Dean's Annual Report* (New York: New York University, 1969), pp. 14-15.

confronted as the decade of the 90s unfolds. It is my hope, as it was my effort at the end of my deanship, to see a resurgence of faculty interest in classroom teaching, academic citizenship, and research oriented to the work-a-day world.

WINNING CONSENSUS WHILE TRANSFORMING CULTURE

Chapter One discussed consensus and the exercise of executive power. We saw then that winning consensus is a time-consuming process and, consequently, likely to collapse in a time of crisis induced by dramatic, sudden change. The consensus-winning process described there can now be enlarged by a brief description of Japanese practice, drawn from Howard S. Gitlow's log of a visit to Japan.

Gitlow refers to the Nemawashi and Ringi systems of management.[8]

Nemawashi literally means root (ne) spread out or binding (mawashi). It is the name of the procedure used to transplant old trees to new locations. One or two years before the transplant is to take place the roots are cut all around the tree, but the tree is left in place. In time, new young roots grow which make possible a successful transplant. So, nemawashi is a procedure of feeling out the situation in a company before a new policy is implemented; this is like cutting back the roots before the tree is transplanted. The feeling out process dramatically improves the probability of successful implementation of a new policy. Nemawashi probably originated in Feudal Japan. Its purpose was to allow the Shogun's counselors the opportunity to escape individual accountability, and hence, *harakiri* if they made a mistake that upset the Shogun.

Nemawashi has both an informal and a formal format. In informal nemawashi, a top manager sends a rough idea to a middle manager. . . . The middle manager then walks around to all of his peers and feels them out on how the rough idea could be best accomplished. It is a procedure of give and take, occupies a great deal of time, but leads to consensus and buy-in to the final plan. After consultation with all of his peers, the middle manager prepares a rough draft of the plan and shows it to all of his peers who then comment on the draft. After they all are comfortable with the draft, it is sent up to the originating top manager. The top manager then walks the plan around to all of his peers using exactly the same process as the middle

---

[8] From a privately distributed paper by Howard S. Gitlow, 1990.

manager. In this way, the time to make a decision is very long, but the time to implement a decision successfully is very short. In formal nemawashi, a middle manager prepares a draft plan and sends it up to the top management for their stamp of approval.

Ringi is a formal process of sending a draft policy up through the ranks of an organization. No nemawashi is needed for ringi. Ringi does not create the buy-in that is frequently necessary to effectively carry out a policy.

The foregoing account appears to confirm the general impression in America that a key element in Japan's success in producing products with a reputation for high quality is the emphasis on consensual decisions. Yet elsewhere in the Gitlow log of his journey we find

I met A . . . a professor of Sociology. . . . We discussed the reasons for Japan's success in industry. I said that I felt that Japanese culture created a penchant for teamwork, as opposed to the American penchant for individual work. A . . . disagreed that culture was the only factor; he even argued that culture might not be a critical factor. He said that if culture was the key ingredient to Japanese success in industry, why was Japan not an industrial power throughout history? Why has Japan been successful only in the last twenty years? *He argued that Japanese top management developed a method for deploying pressure throughout their organization which forced participation and teamwork* [Italics added]. Next, we discussed their performance appraisal system as being a key vehicle for the exertion of said pressure. For example, by placing on a supervisor's performance evaluation form, "What percentage of your subordinates are active in quality circles?" top management is able to focus pressure for the type of activity that they wish to deploy. *This view holds that a crisis must exist to motivate top management to create quality.* [Italics added]. This explanation is based on the belief that the Japanese industrial miracle was created, as opposed to being the result of a pre-existing natural condition. . . .

Gitlow's report is an eye opener. Japan has a homogeneous population, and its cultural characteristics do emphasize the group, teamwork, and consensual behavior. But change and the crisis it produces are the significant stimuli that brought about the contemporary "miracle" of Japanese manufacturing quality and economic growth. And, I suspect, the greatest change of the century was Japan's defeat in World War II. Out of the ashes of that debacle, out of that crisis, modern Japan rose Phoenix-like. It may not be a coincidence that Germany's postwar experience is similar. In both cases, there must have been leadership and the exercise of executive power. In Japan's case, a prewar reputation for producing shoddy, second-rate exports was transformed into the exact opposite.

ROLE OF THE CEO

It is a short step from the generalized observation that change and crisis push management to exercise leadership through the application of pressure through the organization, to the further observation that recognition of change and crisis, coupled with the creation and implementation of a program to overcome them, must originate with top management—with the chief executive.

The CEO is the major repository of a corporate culture. If a preexisting culture is in conflict with the requirements of new conditions, the CEO will have to change it, or eventually be driven out of office by it. Perhaps the sorry story of Frank Lorenzo and Eastern Airlines provides a case in point.

Lorenzo, perhaps more than anyone else, transformed the airline industry following its deregulation. Using Texas Air, his holding company, he took over Continental Airlines, placed it in bankruptcy, defeated its unionized workers and forced on them wholly new compensation structures and working conditions. Next, he absorbed Peoples' Express, which had grown rapidly until its culture of democratic worker participation and job transferability ran into conflict with the requirements of large size and organizational discipline. Finally, he acquired Eastern Airlines, where powerful unions (especially the machinists) had driven a previous CEO, the former astronaut Frank Borman, out of office. Lorenzo sought to replicate his Continental strategy at Eastern. But, at Eastern, he was fought tooth and nail, becoming involved in a lengthy and economically brutal strike. Lorenzo won the strike but lost the airline, because, after filing for bankruptcy, he was eventually supplanted by Martin Shugrue, appointed by the bankruptcy court to serve as Eastern's chief executive. Finally, having acquired a terribly negative public image as an airline executive, he sold all his airline interests to SAS (Scandinavian Airlines) and agreed to a negative covenant requiring him to stay out of the airline business for seven years. He was surely a CEO prepared to exercise executive power, and he did so with a will. But his authority of position did not yield long-run success when he failed to achieve authority of leadership. The solidarity of the pilots and the machinists at Eastern kept him from replicating his earlier success in transforming Continental Airlines.

Executive power is real and necessary, as is its exercise. But, minus leadership, it fails.

---

[9] Reported in the *New York Times* and *The Wall Street Journal*, August 9, 1990.

Another illustration of the point is provided by Robert C. Stempel's early actions as chief executive of General Motors. Unlike Roger B. Smith, his predecessor, Stempel confronted economic adversity and the need to retrench by cutting executive compensation first and substantially, followed by extensive cutbacks in the salaried and plant employee work forces. As Stempel put it, "The commander doesn't eat until the troops are fed."[10] The simple expression of sensitivity to feelings of fairness won him wide support in GM for decisions and actions of great unpleasantness.

CEO'S PERSONAL RESPONSIBILITY IN THE FACE OF FAILURE

In Japan, when corporate affairs go awry, the chief executive accepts responsibility and resigns. The organization failure is regarded as the CEO's failure, and, in President Harry S. Truman's famous dictum, "The buck stops here." That has not been accepted tradition and practice in U.S. corporate life. We have acted as though corporate and organizational failures can be attributed to shortcomings and systemic breakdowns for which the CEO is not, and should not be, culpable. We have recognized that subordinates may be the responsible guilty parties, and their detection and punishment should suffice.

Cases are easy to come by. We have witnessed the indictment of Eastern Airlines for deliberately falsifying maintenance records, an allegation implicating nine managers, for which the airline's top management denied any responsibility. And the General Electric Company agreed to pay a $16.1 million fine to settle charges that it had overcharged the Defense Department, but Jack Welch did not accept personal responsibility and resign. Similarly, the Northrop Corporation paid a $17 million fine after pleading guilty in February 1990 to charges of faking tests on weapons. The NYNEX Corporation admitted that 12 purchasing managers had attended lewd parties each year with suppliers, suggesting a conflict of interest.[11] To which can be added the Exxon Valdez oil spill case, where chief executive Rawls and his company suffered a major public relations debacle, to a significant degree related to his failure to step forward personally and deal directly with the situation.

---

[10] *The Wall Street Journal*, February 8, 1991, pages A1 and A4.
[11] *New York Times*, July 30, 1990, D1-2.

There are other, happier cases in the record of U.S. business, most notably Johnson and Johnson's handling of its Tylenol problem several years ago. In that instance, immediately after several people died following ingestion of Tylenol capsules that had been tampered with and poisoned, Johnson and Johnson, with its CEO in the lead, recalled all Tylenol capsules from the market and redesigned the product and its packaging to enhance their tamper-proof capability. The action cost millions of dollars, but it enlarged the company's credibility and reputation and was followed by Tylenol's recapture of its market. But James Burke, Johnson and Johnson's CEO, did not resign nor did anyone call for his resignation. Since the poisoning seemed to be caused by individuals external to Johnson and Johnson, no blame or culpability attached to its CEO, who, in fact was highly praised for his conduct. More recently, Perrier's sparkling spring water provided a case of a product removed from the market, while a deficiency (traces of benzene, which were not sufficient to be health-threatening) was corrected. Again, there was no CEO's resignation.

Perhaps a more striking example of the contrast between Japanese and U.S. attitudes is provided by the 1985 crash of a Japan Airlines Boeing 747, in which more than 500 people died. Yasumoto Takagi, the airline's president, traveled across the country and personally expressed his apologies to the victims' families, then retired. But T. A. Wilson, CEO of the Boeing Company, did not do so, nor did anyone think he should.

We are not dealing here with an issue of criminal culpability, where a CEO, or other member of top management knows of corporate wrongdoing, or, even worse, is a part of it. We are dealing with rather subtle and ethical issues, with questions like these: Should the CEO be expected to know what is happening in his organization? If the CEO does not know, why not? Even if the CEO does know, should he accept responsibility because the failure occurred during his tenure? Some think our culture has been deficient in not requiring a higher level of responsibility and accountability on the part of our CEOs, even if resignation is not required. It seems certain that the attitude of Robert Fomon, former head of the E. F. Hutton Group, is less acceptable than it once was. When E. F. Hutton was caught in an illegal check overdrafting scheme several years ago, Fomon, when asked about his responsibility, replied, "No chief executive can be held accountable for any single thing that happens in a corporation."

Representing an instance in which an American CEO was held responsible for corporate failure, Dr. Robert A. Fildes resigned as president,

CEO, and director of Cetus Corporation, a biotechnology industry pioneer.[12] His resignation followed the failure of an FDA (Food and Drug Administration) advisory committee to recommend Cetus's major drug, interleukin-2, for use. The drug is used to treat kidney cancer, and the Cetus Corporation was severely criticized for inadequate data and analysis in support of the drug's efficacy. Blame for the failure was placed on Dr. Fildes' shoulders. Significantly, the resignation was announced after a special meeting of the board of directors. It was also announced that Dr. Fildes would be replaced as CEO by Ronald E. Cape, Chairman of the Board and a founder of the company.

A particular aspect of CEO responsibility and accountability must be mentioned now, and we will return to it in the chapter on ethics. That aspect involves top management's responsibility for creating a corporate climate (culture) in which wrongdoing is condoned or encouraged. More specifically, I refer to the situation in which top management has exerted great pressure on employees to achieve certain corporate budgetary goals (e.g., sales, profits), and those goals are unrealistic; yet there is no recognition of that fact by top management. And top management evidences in no way to subordinates that the goals must not be achieved by unethical actions.

TIME, CHANGES IN THE ENVIRONMENT, AND CORPORATE CULTURE

Are the underlying cultural values and traits of an organization beyond change? If one looks only at the bedrock values of honesty and integrity, a work ethic, a desire to serve others, and a sense of individual worth, then one could argue that they *should not* change. But *should not change* is very different from *unchanging*. Thus, there are many in the United States today who lament the alleged loss of these values by the society and by its corporate organizations. We hear commonly of the "fast buck," of putting forth less than one's best effort, of looking out for "numero uno," and of disrespect for the rights of other individuals (even as the courts have extended those rights to protect criminal defendants and others). And

---

[12] Andrew Pollack, *New York Times*, August 17, 1990, pp. D1, 12.

this social and cultural deterioration is said to be reflected in corporate conduct, with Wall Street's orgy of fast-buck reorganizations and insider trading scandals during the decade of the 80s a prime example.

Perhaps the basic point is that change breeds uncertainty; uncertainty breeds fear; and fear brings challenges to the accepted traditions that presumably ruled conduct in less unstable times. In the broadest terms, one would be hard put to explain the decline and fall of earlier civilizations unless one accepted the idea that changes in the environment contribute to cultural changes. We suggested earlier that Japan's defeat in World War II may have been a major factor explaining its subsequent Phoenix-like rise and rebirth to economic prominence. Its prewar emphasis on the samurai tradition and militaristic expansion certainly was altered, and the energies formerly concentrated in those directions were shifted to the economic sphere, with stunning success. Now, older Japanese bemoan a lessening of adherence to traditional cultural values of hard work and abstinence (saving) in favor of increased leisure and consumption. Indeed, U.S. observers have argued that such changes are necessary to help redress the imbalance in the U.S.- Japan trade balance. By the same token, Japanese observers have argued that Americans need to work harder and save more (curb the appetite for consumption and satisfaction now). Could it be that U.S. victory in World War II contributed to our postwar behavior, but with reverse consequences to those experienced in Japan? Put differently, does affluence breed its own destruction, while poverty proves a spur? Categorical and extreme answers are likely to be wrong, but some grain of truth may still reside in what the questions suggest.

Again in broad societal terms, a technological breakthrough like the contraceptive pill proved to be a major factor changing sexual behavior patterns. Women undoubtedly felt freer than before, and men probably felt less responsibility for pregnancy. With some 44 years of experience as a university professor and dean, and based on changes in student behavior in the '60s and '70s, that certainly seemed to me to be the case. And the advent of the terrible AIDS epidemic in the '80s surely was a powerful factor encouraging the reemergence of monogamous relationships.

I suggest that what is true of society at large is also true of our business organizations. With the passage of time and changes in the environment due to technological developments, shifts in worker-management attitudes, the impact of government regulations relative to pollution and health, and so forth, corporate culture must and does change. It is no longer tolerable to pollute air and waterways. It is no longer tolerable to ignore hazards to employee health and safety. And it is no longer tolerable to minimize or disregard product or service quality. In short, changes such as these—and they are characteristic of trends in the United States as we enter the decade of the 90s—promise a higher level of corporate behavior and a more demanding type of corporate culture.

CHAPTER 8

ETHICS AND
EXECUTIVE POWER[1]

IS ETHICAL BEHAVIOR BY BUSINESS IMPORTANT?

Of course, it is! That answer may be so self-evident, so obvious as to make the question seem outrageous, or even stupid. But it is not obvious, because there are many people who focus exclusively on profit or shareholder value or market position, especially in the short-run time frame. Consequently, ethical behavior by chief executives and their corporations is of great significance.

Private enterprise, seeking profit in competitive markets, is what we are talking about when we speak of business. And private enterprise is a critically important institution in our society. If there is something inherently unethical or evil about the institution, then we are in very serious trouble. A society with a fundamental institution that is in basic and profound conflict with its moral culture is a house divided and cannot survive. And the Judeo-Christian mores central to our culture would be antithetical to business, if business was truly and inherently unethical. The fact is that there is a long-standing, chronic unease in Western culture between business and its profit-seeking motive and the self-sacrificing spirit that presumably motivates and energizes our society's religious and charitable activities. We preach that "Man does not live by bread alone," and we mean by it that there are values that transcend material wealth.

---

[1] These two books provide good background reading: Larue Tone Hosmer, *The Ethics of Management* (Homewood, Ill.: Richard D. Irwin, 1987), and William A. Evans, *Management Ethics, an Intercultural Perspective* (Boston: Martinus Nijhoff Publishing, 1981).

It is important to our society that its key institutions be perceived as being in harmony with its moral values, for that is the glue that holds us together. Business must behave so that its actions are seen by society at large as constructive and beneficial, and not as an institution designed to enrich an unethical few at the expense of the many. The role of chief executives is of key significance in this connection, for they must be the first to perceive and comprehend the vital importance of the matter. And their behavior as they influence their organizations in the pursuit of the goals of profit, market position, and so forth are critical. I emphasize behavior here, because it is what people do that counts, far more than what they say.

But the key criteria of ethicality are profits and the behavior of business and its CEOs in the pursuit of profits.

In January 1988, Touche Ross International, the prominent accounting firm, published the results of an opinion survey[2] of key business leaders, deans of business schools, and members of Congress on ethical standards and behavior. The response to the survey (1,107 respondents) indicated that the recipients of the survey instrument considered the issue important. Moreover, the respondents indicated overwhelmingly the belief that businessmen as a group felt it to be important. Ninety-four percent of the respondents said the business community was troubled by ethical problems. Less than one third (32 percent) believed the issue of business ethics to be overblown. This third placed principal blame for it being overblown on the media, and, to a lesser degree, on politicians.

The survey respondents, with some variation depending on industry or profession, agreed overwhelmingly that the CEO plays the most significant role in setting ethical standards. Seventy-three percent of all respondents expressed that opinion, while 25 percent thought it to be an employee's immediate supervisor. The remainder thought it to be the board of directors. But 79 percent of corporate officers and directors thought the CEO is the key figure. Deans of business schools agreed, but less strongly, while members of Congress (63 percent) think an employee's immediate supervisor is of key significance. The disagreement between businessmen, directors, and business school deans, on the one side, and members of Congress, on the other, runs through the survey, but there is no explanation offered. Interestingly, the age of the respondent influenced his opinion. Eighty-

---

[2] Touche Ross International, *Ethics in American Business*, New York, January 1988.

one percent who are age 65 years of age or older believe the CEO to be the key person, with only 18 percent naming the immediate supervisor, while only 57 percent of the respondents under 45 years of age named the CEO, and 39 percent named the immediate supervisor.

SHOULD ABSOLUTE MORAL STANDARDS DETERMINE ETHICALITY?

Orthodox religious views of morality see good and bad in absolute, rigid terms. An action is ethical or unethical. It is not partly right and partly wrong, with what is right possibly outweighing what is wrong through some exercise of proportionalism. Yet it is probably true that most Americans today accept the idea of proportionalism, which allows exceptions to absolute moral guides and permits ideas such as the greatest good for the greatest number.

Generally, unethical acts fall into two categories: (1) those that are *malum in se* (inherently evil and violative of mores and religious rules, like the Ten Commandments) and (2) those that are *malum in prohibitum* (wrong because they violate laws enacted by the state). I believe that attitudes respecting right and wrong in the second category tend to be less rigid than they do with respect to the first category, although there are undoubtedly significant degrees of reprehensibility attached to some violations of law as against others. Thus, violations of speeding laws will probably not be viewed as equal in moral seriousness to cheating on income taxes, or violating environmental, industrial, or safety laws. Yet, the former can cause death and destruction just as surely as the latter. Perhaps the scale of the harmful consequences is a factor, with the former viewed as inherently unlikely to be as severe in that regard as the latter. But, once again, this is a reflection of proportionalism.

Also, society's laws reflect its underlying moral values so that actions seen as inherently evil are also made illegal (e.g., murder, rape, and wanton destruction of property). Even in these cases, however, there is a basis for exceptions. For example, if abortion is murder, then is it justified to save the mother's life, or, more difficult, to avert the birth of a severely deformed or otherwise handicapped child? And what about an abortion where pregnancy occurred as a consequence of a rape? In business terms, is it wrong to discharge long-service, loyal, conscientious employees in order to improve operational safety (because the older employees are less able to handle new, complex, or hazardous equipment)?

Further, acts based on moral imperatives may be cited as justification for violating laws. This rationale is the basis for civil disobedience (i.e., actions against the law that are defended on the basis of a higher moral law). Thus, opponents of nuclear energy may attack atomic power plants and block entry and exit. Or advocates of affirmative action plans may be militant in their insistence that allegedly favored ethnic groups make way under some numerical plan for those who have not been so favored. In both instances, the activist will claim a moral basis as justification for any damage caused to property or persons.

Contemporary U.S. society is generally oriented in favor of proportionalism, although there are very active groups fighting to enact absolute moral rules into our laws, especially on the highly emotional issue of abortion. There are also those whose moral zeal in defending the quality of human life, as they see it, leads them to seek severe restrictions on such businesses as tobacco and liquor. Our nation's unhappy experience with prohibition was a traumatic illustration of where such attempts to legislate a rigid moral standard, no matter how well intended, can lead.

IS THERE A GAP BETWEEN IDEALIZED ETHICAL STANDARDS AND ACTUAL BEHAVIOR?

Perhaps this question is simply another way of viewing the matter of proportionalism. To the degree that idealized ethical standards are the equivalent of absolute moral standards, a gap between them and actual behavior is inevitable. The reason is that the world does not confront us with situations, conflicts, and choices that are necessarily and always absolutely good or bad, absolutely ethical or unethical.

I am reminded here of how strongly I was impressed years ago by the late Professor Thomas Nixon Carver's work *Essays in Social Justice.*[3] It had a chapter entitled "The Principle of Self-Centered Appreciation Commonly Called Self-Interest." I found his observations there prescient and richly supported by my own experience. Carver argued that kinship was a critical determinant in human behavior (i.e., we prefer ourselves to others, and those near to us in blood or group identity to those who are remote).

---

[3] Thomas Nixon Carver, *Essays in Social Justice,* (Cambridge, Mass.: Harvard University Press, 1915).

He argued further that the degree or intensity of our preference is related to the nearness of others. In a fascinating exercise, he related the preference born of kinship to our view of generosity and its opposite. Put bluntly, preferring one close in kinship may bring pain, even suffering, to those outside the kinship bond. And what is generous in the narrow frame becomes the opposite in the larger one. These consequences are clear in business organizations, as well as in other social, economic, and political entities. And it is easy indeed to translate Carver's observations into issues of what is ethical and what is not.

As a small example from the business world, we find successful fathers often insisting that incompetent offspring succeed them. Preference there can doom an enterprise and harm all whose lives have become entwined with it. In broader social and political contexts, we find everywhere the existence of nepotism. While preference based on kinship may be an aspect of nature, it seems to fail an ethical test when its result is harm to others. Thus, where kinship is coupled with incompetence, competence should rule and kinship fall as a criterion of organizational position.

Society's perception of a gap between actual behavior and idealized ethical norms can widen in at least two ways, assuming the idealized norms to be unchanged: (1) society's expectations of the degree to which actual behavior approximates the idealized norms may rise while actual behavior does not change, or changes in lesser degree than the change in expectations; and (2) the level of actual behavior deteriorates. I note these possibilities because so many people express the belief that the United States has suffered a widening gap between idealized ethical behavior and actual behavior due to the second reason—a real deterioration in actual behavior.

No doubt most older people hold that view. They think back to their youth and recall the devoted teacher who influenced them, and so on. They recall an age characterized by civility and, they think, characterized also by better behavior in an ethical sense. Being a senior citizen myself, I am strongly inclined to that view and find it most attractive. But simple acceptance of the view requires a significant exercise in forgetfulness.

In politics, I would have to forget Tammany Hall in New York, the Hague machine in Jersey City, and the Prendergast machine in Kansas City, as one would have to forget the infamous Tweed ring of the 19th century and others. In medicine and science generally, it would be necessary to forget the bitter resistance of the medical establishment to such pioneering advances as maintaining sterile conditions in hospitals, or the ridicule that initially met the work of Pasteur. In business, one would have to forget labor, environmental, and product safety conditions of past years as compared with those of the present.

In short, I cannot accept as proven fact that our society today is less ethical in its *demands* (expectations) of our businessmen, our political leaders, our doctors, our lawyers, or our teachers than its predecessors were. If anything, we demand a higher standard. Personal behavioral lapses viewed as slight offenses in earlier eras are now taken as evidence of serious character flaws and bring down prominent politicians (former Senator Gary Hart, whose 1988 presidential campaign was aborted by an extra-marital excursion, about which he subsequently was evasive). Businessmen who, in the past, would have been seen as savvy pursuers of profit are now scrutinized carefully as to the steps they take to that end. Seen in that light, I suspect that our disappointment with our present state reflects a demand for a higher standard of ethicality in *actual behavior* than was formerly accepted, coupled with the merciless magnification given to current events by the media and its enlarged power in this electronic age.

Robert L. Bartley, editor of *The Wall Street Journal,* in a commencement address at Babson College in May 1987, said: "We do not live in an age of moral collapse. We more nearly are in an age of moral zealotry. We are applying to ourselves, or at least to our public and private leaders, standards of ethics never before expected of ordinary mortals.[4]

In this connection, it is interesting to note that the Touche Ross survey earlier cited reported 96 percent of the respondents who are corporate officers or directors as believing that ethical standards (actual) vary among countries, and that the United States has the highest standards.[5] Ethical standards were also seen as high in Great Britain, Canada, Switzerland, and Germany, in that order. Members of Congress, while they agreed that the U.S. had the highest standards, did so in a lesser degree than did corporate officers and directors. And the ranking of the countries as to ethicality differed: United States, Canada, Germany, Switzerland, and Sweden, with Great Britain left out of the top five by members of Congress. Interestingly, respondents in telecommunications or the media, while agreeing that the United States is the most ethical country, did not rate it as highly as the other groups of respondents. Finally, it should be noted that 70

---

[4] *The Wall Street Journal,* May 18, 1987, editorial page.
[5] Touche Ross International, *Ethics in American Business,* p. 6.

percent of the corporate officers and directors surveyed were associated with multinational firms.

Given the globalization of national economies and the growth of multinational firms, variations in culture and in ethical standards from country to country become very important. Widely publicized scandals involving multinational U.S. firms led to enactment of the Foreign Corrupt Practices Act by the United States. Professors Laczniak and Naor, in an article entitled "Global Ethics: Wrestling with the Corporate Conscience," presented six propositions they thought would help multinational firms in handling ethical issues arising from cross-cultural variations:[6]

Proposition 1: When operating in international markets, there is no single standard of ethical behavior applicable to all business decisions. In contrast to domestic operations, a wide spectrum of standards and modes of ethical behavior confronts decision makers involved in situations that transcend national boundaries. This makes the development of a corporatewide ethical posture more difficult.

Proposition 2: The laws of economically developed countries, such as those of the United States, generally define the lowest common denominator of acceptable behavior for operations in those domestic markets. In an underdeveloped country or a developing country, it would be the actual *degree of enforcement* of the law that would, in practice, determine the lower limit of permissible behavior.

Proposition 3: The upper threshold of ethical behavior regarding either domestic or foreign operations is not clearly defined.

Proposition 4: Because of the visibility and their actual or potential impact on the economies of LDCs, multinational corporations have a heavier ethical responsibility than their domestic counterparts. Flagrant nonethical behavior may attract substantial attention in host countries and may generate regulatory action aimed at the offender or at multinationals in general. This may result in adverse publicity affecting operations in other markets as well.

Proposition 5: Because the top management of multinational organizations will tend to be less familiar with foreign markets than with domestic markets, and because of pervasive ethnocentric orientations, the likelihood of ethical misjudgments by top management regarding such markets will be greater.

Proposition 6: Concern for ethics seems to rise proportionately with the degree of a country's overall development. The higher a country's economic,

---

6 Gene R. Laczniak, and Jacob Naor, "Global Ethics: Wrestling with the Corporate Conscience," *Business*, College of Business Administration, Georgia State University, July–September 1985, pp. 3–9.

social, and technological development, the greater are the pressures in that country for higher standards of ethical business conduct. Conversely, the less advanced the level of economic development, the lower will be the concern within host countries with the ethics of business conduct.

Laczniak and Naor concluded:

It is becoming increasingly clear that, acting in their own self-interest, multinational corporations should consider themselves as change-agents of economic and social development. Willingly or unwillingly, their impact in foreign countries is often crucial and long lasting. Such influence on local cultures, institutions, religions, and ways of life therefore must be carefully ascertained. Companies should conduct periodic "ethical impact audits" to assess such effects. Ethical considerations must necessarily become a vital element in the multinational corporate planning process. Failing these, questions raised by multinational corporate behavior will result in regulations set by either the host government or larger regulatory bodies (such as the Organization for Economic Cooperation and Development or the United Nations) with regional or worldwide authority. Thus, it appears to be in the best interest of multinational organizations to set a single ethical posture for all worldwide operations, to set it at as high a level as possible and to implement it consistently and conscientiously.

DO CORPORATIONS AND THEIR CEOS INHERENTLY TEND TOWARD UNETHICAL BEHAVIOR?

I am skeptical of the degree to which one segment of society may be found to be significantly less ethical than another. I think mores are pervasive throughout a society, and conduct in medicine, law, politics, pedagogy, and business will be approximately comparable with respect to ethicality. Of course, some fields of activity claim to march to a higher and nobler drummer, such as religion, medicine, law, and pedagogy, and one hopes that they do. After all, these fields claim service to society as their goal, with no baser motivations such as material wealth or power diminishing the nobleness of their calling. But what is one to think in this respect when one reads about medical research, conducted in leading universities and research centers, which turns out to be "doctored"[7]; or when one cannot

---

[7] For a report of an extraordinary case involving Dr. David Baltimore, president of Rockefeller University, see the *New York Times*, March 26, 1991, pp. B5–B6.

escape the almost daily reports of malfeasance among public officials, of whom a great proportion are lawyers; or when one reads about ethical lapses in our educational system (improper payments to athletes, grade inflation, graduation of students who are inadequately educated and incapable of functioning at the level implied by their degree). And, perhaps most painful, cases like those of the TV preachers Jimmy Baker and James Swaggart.

It is congenial for those who are not in the business sector to take on superior ethical airs and behave as though there is something inherently nobler and more moral about their activities, but an objective observer is under no mandate to accept this view. One can question it, and one should. After all, the material advancement of mankind does not necessarily make us more brutish and immoral, any more than poverty can be demonstrated conclusively to be good for the soul and elevating to the spirit. The latter may shorten life and bring us more quickly to a spiritual afterlife, but it does not guarantee greater civility, consideration for one's fellow man, and ethicality in the here and now.

Despite what is said above, there is a deep-seated and, I fear, persistent notion that business is inherently less ethical than other pursuits. I believe that notion grows from these roots: that the pursuit of profits is morally questionable, and that materialistically oriented activities are somehow morally inferior to those that are service-oriented (religion, medicine, pedagogy, as examples). I do not accept these ideas. As an economist, I see profit as the guide to resource allocation and the indicator of society's preferences as reflected through the market system (assuming, of course, a competitive economy). Despite the shortcomings of that system, which exist and are significant, it has outperformed all alternatives in terms of human well-being. That being so, I feel no compulsion to complain about its shortcomings, or to act as though it is an inferior system. In short, profits are fine! Insofar as materialistically oriented activities are concerned, I perceive a false dichotomy between business and social service activities. The reason is simple. Despite protestations to the contrary, those who are engaged in service pursuits are also materialistically motivated. The daily press is filled with reports that confirm that fact, as does our personal experience.

The key issue involved in the ethicality of business behavior is the pursuit of profit. While it need not be so, it is too often the motive that leads many chief executives to close their eyes to unethical behavior or to condone it or to actively encourage it. In truth, the pursuit of profits can be seductive, can lead usually honest people into unethical practices, and provide convenient rationalizations for those practices. After all, in business, the bottom line is supposed to rule. While no one will confess publicly that any means to a profitable end is allowable, it is not difficult to succumb to the pressure to show good quarterly earnings results. Shareholders are watching. Investment analysts are watching. The business media are watching. The board of directors is watching. And there are devices at hand that can beef up short-run results, while a CEO comforts himself with the idea that their use will be temporary and will end as soon as some immediate difficulties are overcome. Thus, for example, bad inventories and accounts receivable can be carried as though they were good, so a firm doesn't have to write them off and negatively affect the bottom line. More reprehensible, even bordering on fraud, is carrying inventories that are in dealers' hands as accounts receivable. Shifts in the application of accounting principles can affect profits: for example, changing from LIFO (last-in, first-out) to FILO (first-in, last-out) in charging off bad inventories, and/or booking substantial maintenance expenditures as capital expenditures, so that they can be written off over a more extended time period. There is also the practice of shifting the "booking" of revenues and/or expenditures from the end of one month to the beginning of the next month, to alter the bottom line in the two time periods. Perhaps more serious is the misuse of planned budgets. In this case, CEOs can insist on an unrealistic profit goal, and pressure managers to produce a budget that anticipates achieving that goal. When reality intrudes, as it must, managers may do the things just noted, and others, to maintain the appearance of achieving the profit goal. But it is a false front doomed to collapse eventually. However, the CEO, if he is sufficiently blind, dishonest, and unethical, can blame his subordinates and deny responsibility for the outcome. Not a happy result and not one likely to sustain the CEO in his position over a long time span.

There are a variety of other unethical practices: (1) commercial bribery, to gain customers from one's competitors; (2) conspiratorial schemes to defame one's competitors (remember the case of American Express and Edmond Safra of Republic National Bank); (3) kickbacks (remember the NYNEX New York Telephone case); (4) misleading advertising and promotions; and (5) producing and selling shoddy products and services. Other unethical practices include unsafe plant operations, which may involve both inattention to hazardous conditions affecting employees and harming the environment (chemical discharge into waterways, air polluting emissions, illegal waste disposal). They would also include the discharge or forced early retirement of long-service employees without reasonable compensation arrangements. In this last connection, I will never forget a meeting between a small committee of deans, charged with studying a university financial crisis and recommending solutions, and a newly arrived president. During the meeting, the deans observed that the university had a moral obligation to a category of long-service but now redundant professors. The new president raised his hand and interjected, "Obligation? *I* have no obligation!" And the exchange ended.

A sad illustration is provided by Eastern Airlines, the late, great airline founded by famed Captain Eddie Rickenbacker—World War I ace and noted race car driver.[8] In a plea bargaining agreement announced on March 1, 1991, Eastern admitted it conspired to prevent the Federal Aviation Administration from determining if its employees and managers falsified maintenance records. Eastern, already bankrupt, shut down, and in liquidation, agreed to pay $3.5 million in fines. The allegation that Eastern had falsified maintenance records to keep deficient aircraft flying as it struggled to survive, was pressed by its striking unions. But management, prior to the appointment of Martin R. Shugrue, Jr., as trustee by Judge Burton R. Lifland of the bankruptcy court, insisted the allegations were false. And Mr. Shugrue also insisted they were false after he took over operations and unsuccessfully fought to save the airline. Andrew J. Maloney, the U.S. Attorney for the Eastern District of New York, observed that Eastern's upper management had intimidated its employees to keep aircraft flying, forcing employees to falsify maintenance records in a practice known as pencil whipping (making false entries in log books, work cards, and computer entries to indicate that work was done, when in fact it was not performed).

Another sad example is provided by the Beech Nut Nutrition Co., a company that once had a grand reputation for quality. Through worry over profits and poor judgment, Beech Nut fell into an ethical breakdown.[9] Beech Nut bought a juice concentrate, supposedly made from apples, and marketed it as 100 percent apple juice. But the concentrate was not apple juice, nor *any* kind of juice. Instead, it was a cheaper blend of synthetic

---

[8] *New York Times,* March 2, 1991, pp. Y19 and 31.

[9] Chris Welles, "What Led Beech Nut down the Road to Disgrace," *Business Week,* February 22, 1988, pp. 124–28.

components that tasted and looked like apple juice—in short, a "chemical cocktail." The Beech Nut employees involved were not hardened criminals engaged in a brazen swindle, at least as they saw it. They were honest, well-respected people. But Beech Nut was under great financial pressure, and the phony, cheap concentrate saved millions of dollars. Of course, the perpetrators had to convince themselves that their activity was only a small case of cheating that hurt no one, because the concentrate was not harmful to health. It just wasn't apple juice, which is what the company said it was.

The background of the case covered some dozen years, beginning in 1973 when Frank Nicholas, a Pennsylvania lawyer, and his investment group bought the Beech Nut baby foods division from its then owner, Squibb Corp. The baby food division had never been a robust profit producer and had been sustained by more profitable divisions, such as chewing gum. Further, Nicholas acquired the baby foods division almost entirely with borrowed money, laying large interest costs on the already strained operation. Consequently, the firm's 80-year-old plant in Canojoharie, New York, was neglected, and the marketing outlays of the dominant firm in the market (Gerber Products Co., with 70 percent market share) could not be matched. Losses mounted. By 1978, Beech Nut owed millions of dollars to suppliers. Since products containing apple concentrate accounted for 30 percent of Beech Nut's sales, savings from a cheaper concentrate would have a major impact on corporate finances and might keep the company alive. Nicholas denies any knowledge of using an artificial apple juice concentrate, but he sold the company to Nestle in 1979 for $35 million. Nestle invested an additional $60 million, to increase marketing budgets and boost sales. But red ink and cost pressures continued.

In any case, in 1977, before the sale to Nestle, Beech Nut agreed to buy apple concentrate from Interjuice Trading Corp., a wholesaler whose prices were about 20 percent below market. The low price raised suspicions among chemists in Beech Nut's R & D Department, but there was no certain test that could prove adulteration. However, some procedures could indicate evidence of the use of inferior, artificial ingredients such as corn sugar. Based on these procedures, Beech Nut's chemists concluded the Interjuice product was adulterated and possibly wholly artificial. By 1981, the chemists were so strong in their opinion that Jerome J. Li Cari, director of research and development, sent a memo (August 1, 1981) to his superiors, stating he believed Interjuice's product to be adulterated. No action was taken and Li Cari resigned a few months later.

The "can of worms" burst open in mid-1982. The Processed Apples Institute, Inc., whose members made products from fresh apples, were deeply concerned over the sale and use of cheaper substitutes parading as the real product. They hired a private investigator to visit the plants of firms engaged in selling apple products and to notify them that, with the results of a new testing procedure and documents retrieved from a Dumpster near the plant making Beech Nut's concentrate, proof now existed that the supplier's product was adulterated. The investigator asked Beech Nut to join other juice makers in a lawsuit against the supplier.

If Beech Nut had behaved as a victim at that point, on the basis that earlier evidence was inconclusive, they probably would have escaped with a modest fine. But Beech Nut, while it did cancel its contracts to buy the concentrate, refused to join in the lawsuit and refused also to cooperate with it. Worse, the company continued to sell the products made from the fake concentrate, which it had in its inventory (some $3.5 million worth). In fact, Beech Nut continued to sell mixed juices from the fake concentrate until March 1983—months after its eventual recall of straight apple juice. The ultimate upshot was a 1986 indictment (470 counts) of Beech Nut and its two top executives (Neils F. Hoyvald, president, and John F. Lavery, operations chief). In November 1987, Beech Nut pleaded guilty to 215 felony counts and admitted to willful violations of the food and drug laws by selling adulterated apple products from 1981 to 1983. And so a proud corporate name was dragged through the mud.

The pursuit of profits by use of devices described earlier and in the Beech Nut case presents examples of unethical activities. Let us make the matter more complex. Take a company that is profitable, has an excellent reputation for quality products, and is known for the humaneness of its treatment of employees, but its profitability is significantly less than is found in its competitors. I refer specifically to the Campbell Soup Company, to which reference was made in Chapter 1. There, we noted the early retirement of R. Gordon McGovern as CEO of Campbell Soup. What is relevant at this point is the ethical aspect of the case, the relationship of his retirement to profitability. Campbell Soup is a company with an outstanding reputation for ethical behavior, for producing high-quality products, for generous treatment of its employees (including continued operations of plants that had become marginal in efficiency and profitability), and for exceptional concern for and involvement in community matters. It was also a company with majority ownership held by the members of the Dorrance family (the heirs of its founder). In 1989, John T. Dorrance,

Jr., patriarch of the family and Campbell's long-time CEO, died. Campbell's ethical behavior and corporate culture were an extension of the character of John T. Dorrance, Jr. He was willing to accept less-than-maximum profitability in order to have his company do the things he believed to be ethical. And the force of his personality and his position in his family enabled him to exercise leadership power to that end. Thus, Claudia H. Deutsch wrote in the *New York Times*,[10] "R. Gordon McGovern catered far more to Mr. Dorrance's interest than to those of shareholders . . . Mr. Dorrance's gentle prodding . . . made Campbell one of the first companies to provide on-site day care centers, to give extensive notice of plant closings to workers, even to keep plants open longer than was financially sensible to preserve jobs. . . ."

With Mr. Dorrance's death, a desire for greater profitability emerged among some family members, some of whom indicated restiveness through a reported interest in selling their Campbell stock. The board of directors, perhaps reflecting a greater sensitivity to shareholder desires, also became restive. Actions that John T. Dorrance, Jr., did not take (e.g., plant closings, employee layoffs) and that R. Gordon McGovern did not want to take were pressed by board members with some insistence. So Mr. McGovern resigned, was succeeded by two other corporate executives, and the market value of Campbell's stock immediately rose on that news.

Question: Given the profitability of Campbell, even though less than it could have been with greater efficiency, was it ethical for the board to pressure Mr. McGovern? Given the investment of their savings by stockholders, was it ethical for Mr. Dorrance to weigh the interests of stakeholders (employees, community, etc.) relative to shareholders as highly as he did? Is it ethical for employees to press for greater benefits and to be satisfied with a lower level of efficiency than is possible at the expense of shareholders, and possibly consumers who may consequently pay higher prices? Remember proportionalism, for these questions do not permit simple responses as to good or bad.

An especially complicated ethical issue involves so-called fetal protection policies adopted by a number of firms. These policies deny jobs to fertile women where, in the event of pregnancy, the materials and processes inherent in the job could endanger the health and development

---

[10] *New York Times*, April 11, 1989, p. D2.

of a fetus. Some women and civil rights groups are challenging these policies in the courts, charging discrimination. The companies' defense is the unethical character of allowing women to endanger unborn fetuses. There is also an issue of liability. What is right?[11]

Profit and its pursuit *do* exert pressure on personal and corporate actions that will have substantial ethical implications. Consequently, it would be easy to damn them as the spawn of Satan, and as inherently bad. But that would be a grave mistake. We have the most dramatic evidence today of the evils inherent in nonmarket, nonprofit-seeking economies, and they outweigh by far the ethical problems that may be associated with profit-seeking in a competitive market economy. It seems to me that only a fool, or a fanatic blinded by his adherence to a false ideology, could continue to prefer state-controlled systems to ones that rely on private enterprise and the much-maligned profit motive.

METHODS FOR ENCOURAGING ETHICAL BEHAVIOR

The Touche Ross International survey of business leaders, business school deans, and members of Congress, cited earlier, indicated that 39 percent of the respondents considered the adoption of codes of ethics in business to be the most effective method of encouraging ethical behavior.[12] Thirty percent thought a more humanistic curriculum in business education would be helpful and 20 percent considered legislation helpful. Looking at the other side of the coin (i.e., views as to which of these methods were least effective), 55 percent of the respondents believed legislation to be least effective, while 26 percent of them thought a more humanistic B-school (business school) curriculum least effective, and 18 percent considered codes of ethics least effective.

But there is an anomaly, because a majority of respondents from the eastern part of the United States, as well as a majority of those in the securities; aerospace and defense; drugs, pharmaceutical, and cosmetics; and manufacturing industries believed that legislation was effective in improving business ethics. Of course, these industries are regulated to a significant degree. Of interest also is the fact that B-school deans were less optimis-

---

[11] *The Wall Street Journal,* October 8, 1990, p. A1 and 5.

[12] Touche Ross International, *Ethics in American Business,* p. 14.

tic than bankers and lawyers as to the effectiveness of a B-school's curriculum in encouraging ethical behavior in business.

In an article entitled "Developing the Ethical Corporation," Professor W. Michael Hoffman reported[13] the results of a survey of the 1984 *Fortune* 500 industrial and 500 service companies. The 28 percent survey response rate (279 responding companies) revealed that 80 percent of the respondent firms were taking steps to encourage ethical behavior. Professor Hoffman observed:[14]

> Most of these corporate attempts need to go much farther before they will be successful. . . . Although 93 percent of the responding companies taking ethical steps have written codes of ethics in place—representing almost a 40 percent rise over a study for the Conference Board 20 years ago—only 18 percent have ethics committees; only 8 percent have ethics ombudsmen; and only three companies said they had judiciary boards. It is difficult to understand how codes can be overseen and enforced adequately without a committee or ombudsmen assigned to that task or how alleged violations of codes can be adjudicated effectively and fairly without a board or committee for that purpose. Furthermore, the communication of the codes seemed suspect . . . almost all the companies communicate them to their employees through printed materials but only 40 percent do so through advice from a superior, 34 percent through an entrance interview, and 21 percent through workshops or seminars. Only 11 percent post them in the workplace. Writing a code of ethics is an important first step toward building an ethical corporation, but is just that—a first step. To be effective, it must be backed up by other kinds of support structures throughout the organization to insure its adequate communication, oversight, enforcement, adjudication, and review.

The Wall Street Journal reported the results of a study of 202 corporate codes of conduct[15] and found these subjects included at least 75 percent of the time: (1) relations with the U.S. government (86.6 percent); (2) customer/supplier relations (86.1 percent); (3) political contributions (84.7 percent); (4) conflicts of interest (75.3 percent); and (5) honest books or records (75.3 percent). But these subjects were *not included* in at least 75 percent of the codes: (1) personal character matters (93.6 percent);

---

[13] W. Michael Hoffman, "Developing the Ethical Corporation," *Business Insights*, School of Business Administration, California State University, Long Beach; vol.2, Fall 1986, pp. 10–15.

[14] Ibid., pp. 11–12.

[15] *The Wall Street Journal*, October 9, 1987, section 2, p. 1.

(2) product safety (91.0 percent); (3) environmental affairs (87.1 percent); (4) product quality (78.7 percent); and (5) civic and community affairs (75.2 percent).

Examining this data, as well as the results of other studies, Professor William Frederick of the University of Pittsburgh noted that corporations with codes of ethics are actually cited by federal agencies more often than those that lack such standards. He added the opinion that the reason was that the codes themselves typically emphasize improving the companies' balance sheet. He commented further: "A company is like the military. The law comes down, and then people see how much they can get away with." Not a happy comment, but certainly one emphasizing the key role of the CEO.

Before leaving this matter, it should be noted that there has been some Congressional interest in legislation that would expand the responsibility of the accounting profession in its auditing activities. Specifically the *Deloitte and Touche Review* reported that several members of the House Committee on Energy and Commerce proposed an amendment to the Securities Exchange Act of 1934. The amendment would expand the responsibility of independent auditors in connection with evaluating a public company's internal control structure and the reporting of illegal acts.[16] Although this legislation is far from being enacted, it does indicate the extensiveness of concern over business ethics.

DO BUSINESS SCHOOLS HAVE A RESPONSIBILITY?

Despite the pessimism expressed by B-school deans in this connection, they and their schools have a substantial responsibility. The B-school's mission is to educate management, and B-schools pride themselves on the number of their alumni who become chief executives and members of top management. To emphasize techniques aimed at achieving maximum profitability while ignoring ethical considerations would be a travesty of the mission, and a gross disservice to students and society. Yet there is a substantial disagreement among B-school professors and deans about the matter. Some think student character is already formed by the time students get to the school and cannot be changed by ethics courses or

---

[16] *Deloitte and Touche Review*, September 24, 1990, p. 1.

discussions of ethics. They believe family, church, and earlier educational experiences have been the critical forces. Then, there are those deans and professors who, while agreeing that family, church and earlier education are of major importance, think the B-school can be a significant factor— and should try.

In a particularly perceptive article, William G. Scott and Terence R. Mitchell identified certain basic weaknesses in management education, as it related to ethical issues, and proposed several remedial avenues of action.[17] The basic fault Scott and Mitchell found in management education is that it promotes *a monodimensional, single-set value system*. This value system emphasizes the market as its fundamental reference point in decision making. Indeed, they say the *only* reference point. The market is seen as so important because it is objective, capable of rigorous analysis, viewed as possessing predictive power, and a guide for the allocation of resources. It is an important corollary that quantitative methods and scientific analysis are most efficient in obtaining market knowledge, as well as knowledge of human behavior in markets. As a consequence, the B-school curriculum emphasizes subject areas that are market directed and quantitatively oriented such as accounting, finance, operations research and statistical analysis, and economics—with marketing, management, policy, and strategic planning also highly regarded. A second fault of the value system is that it *promotes certain myths:* it sees the primary role of the CEO as being that of the "shaper and manager of shared values in an organization, as the creator(s) of symbols, ideologies, language, beliefs, rituals, and myths." Consequently, as Peters and Waterman pointed out in *In Search of Excellence,* management works to form people and their values so that they will conform to such values as productivity, teamwork, and excellence.[18] Of course, this role of the CEO and top management is a central point of this book, and I do not back away from it. Instead, as will be pointed out, the B-school must affect the future CEOs it educates to see and act in a multidimensional, ethical way as they exercise their power. They must be made to understand that faith in the market system, faith in scientific and quantitative methods, and faith in myths do not alone prepare them for the moral choices they will face as executives.

---

[17] William G. Scott and Terence R. Mitchell, "Markets and Morals," *Selections,* The Magazine of the Graduate Management Admissions Council, Autumn 1986, pp. 3–8.

[18] T. J. Peters and R. H. Waterman, *In Search of Excellence* (New York: Harper and Row, 1982).

Scott and Mitchell proposed five avenues of action to change the usual, monodimensional B-school approach:

1. Strongly encourage the inclusion of ethical and moral issues in all functional area courses (use of lectures, cases, or other means would be decided by the professor).
2. Establish ethics courses and incorporate them in the required curriculum.
3. Encourage and nurture the creation of informal enclaves, in which morals, values, and management ethics are discussed (these enclaves or groups would be independent of formal academic programs, would be public, and would hopefully be in some respects like the great salons of earlier years in stimulating social as well as intellectual interaction).
4. Work to get the support of the professional management associations (e.g., Academy of Management, American Society for Public Administration) for student development in ethics, as well as the inclusion of ethical issues in papers published by the major academic journals.
5. Establish an independent national institute for the study of the moral philosophy of management. The central element for such an institute may already exist in the Ethics Center, in Washington, D.C.

The first three proposals are most immediate to the B-schools, with the last two involving existing and proposed external agencies. However, I would include the accrediting agencies as a major actor, especially with respect to the curricular and other standards they apply in deciding on accreditation (for example, American Assembly of Collegiate Schools of Business).

In short, B-schools have a responsibility. And the Scott-Mitchell proposals are well conceived. In particular, the first three fall within the direct power of the B-schools to implement.

CHAPTER 9

EGOISM, EMPIRE BUILDING, EXECUTIVE POWER, AND ESTIMATING RISK

LEVERAGING FRENZY OF THE 80s

The decade of the 80s was an extraordinary period in the history of U.S. business. It was characterized by multibillion dollar leveraged buyouts (LBOs), mergers, and takeovers of major corporations, financed by newly created types of securities. Among them were high-yield, high-risk bonds, and certain preferred stocks, with the former quickly labeled as junk bonds. Deal-making became frantic, as investment firms fought for the incredibly large fees to be gained when deals were consummated. The key was debt, and the source of corporate capital shifted from equity (stock) to debt, and from debt provided by commercial banks and subject to their traditional concern for capacity to repay, to debt in the form of junk bonds. The frenzy finally collapsed following the huge RJR Nabisco $25 billion LBO by Kohlberg, Kravis, Roberts (KKR), the exposure of insider trading and other scandals involving Wall Street, the bankruptcy of Drexel Burnham Lambert (the leading junk bond firm), the failure of several substantial LBOs, and the collapse of the junk bond market.

Debt is identified as the key to the frenzied financial activity of the era. But large-scale leveraging, to a degree previously unacceptable, was the Achilles heel that finally brought the house down. Leveraging involved the multiplication of the power of a limited amount of equity capital to magnify itself enormously, so that corporate cats were able to conquer and take over corporate elephants. It was not unusual in this type of financing to find one part equity to nine parts debt. Inherent in these proportions is very great risk exposure, for the debt and its interest (which was high) had to be repaid, eventually if not in the short term.

What inspired corporate chief executives to assume such risk? The rationalizations, readily available, will be examined later. But the reason goes beyond the rationalizations, at least in a considerable number of cases set in motion by management, or in which management was reacting to an external bid that put a company "in play." And the reason, I believe, has to do with CEO egoism, urge to empire-build, and determination to retain executive power.

SOME DATA ON THE DECADE

The 10-year period from 1979 to 1988 witnessed an enormous increase in going-private leveraged buyouts (i.e., LBOs of public companies that became private). Table 9–1 shows the number of transactions in the decade, their total dollar value, and their median and average (mean) values. The data exclude management LBOs.[1]

Table 9–1 is striking. The number of going-private LBO transactions rose almost eight-fold from 1979 to 1988, while the total dollar value of the transactions increased an almost incredible 95.8 times. Such a relatively greater increase in value of transactions, compared with number of transactions, reflects the increase in megadeals. This is confirmed by

TABLE 9–1
Going-Private LBO Activity, 1979–1988 (In Millions of Dollars)

Year	Number of Transactions	Dollar Value	Average Value	Median Value
1979	16	$ 636.0	$ 39.8	$ 7.9
1980	13	967.4	74.4	25.3
1981	17	2,338.5	137.6	41.1
1982	31	2,836.7	91.5	29.6
1983	36	7,145.4	198.5	77.8
1984	57	10,805.9	189.6	66.9
1985	76	24,139.8	317.6	72.6
1986	76	20,232.4	266.2	84.5
1987	47	22,057.1	469.3	123.3
1988	125	60,920.6	487.4	79.8

---

[1]Michelle R. Garfinkel, "The Causes and Consequences of Leveraged Buyouts," *Federal Reserve Bank of St. Louis Review*, 71, no. 5 (September/October 1989), p. 25.

a look at the change in the median value of the transactions. If we use the extreme values in that column to measure growth (i.e., 1979 ($7.9) and 1987 ($123.3)), the increase is 15.6 times. If we allow for inflation during the period, the growth in the average value of transactions is more striking, from $50.6 million to $400.5 million in 1982 dollars, a real annual growth rate of 25.8 percent.[2] The existence of megadeals explains why the average value so greatly exceeds the median value.

If we turn to value created for shareholders, such as the premium in the price paid by the LBO over the value of stock shares prior to the initial announcement of the LBO, then we find that the average and median premiums averaged some 36.3 and 30.6 percent, respectively, from 1979 to 1988. These figures exclude 1979, which showed extremely high values compared to the other nine years in the decade, when they were relatively stable. Including 1979, the average and median value premium percentages rise to 43.3 and 34.1, respectively.[3] We should note that the calculation of the premium compared the closing market value of the stock five days before the initial announcement of the LBO with the price per share paid by the LBO.

EGOISM, LEVERAGING, AND RISK

The financial risk inherent in magnification of debt as the primary source of corporate capital was enlarged enormously by the number of financial instruments, many of them newly created during the decade of the 80s, which effectively *postponed* payment of interest and repayment of principal for several years into the future. Pushing payment back in time makes it possible to enlarge the amount of debt that can theoretically be financed, and so increases the leverage.

A particularly creative debt instrument in this connection is the so-called payment-in-kind (PIK) bond. Instead of the bondholders receiving their interest payments in cash, they receive them in additional bonds that mature at a later date. What an extraordinarily imaginative creation of the human mind! A claim to a money payment is satisfied by an additional claim to a money payment, all in the future. The device was so

---

[2]Ibid., p. 25.
[3]Ibid.

attractive to the financial deal-makers that it was extended to preferred stocks, and some deals included PIK preferred stock.

The underlying idea of postponing is enlarged further by the rise of "balloons," scheduling payments so that they are relatively small in the short term and become substantially larger as time passes (i.e., they balloon). This concept is enhanced by creating tiers of debt (a mezzanine). An interesting borrowing of terminology from theater design, a mezzanine involves financing structures in which there is a base of secured securities (backed by pledged assets) and then a variety of convertible and/or nonconvertible unsecured bonds. The high-yield, poorer-quality paper (junk) matures in the more distant future: hence, mezzanine.

What arguments are advanced by the proponents of leveraging and the corporate divestitures and restructurings that typically follow a leveraged buy-out? Probably the major ones are (1) operating efficiency is increased and costs reduced, especially when management is included in the LBO and has the personal incentive to achieve those objectives; (2) debt is a financially superior source of capital than equity because interest is tax-deductible while dividends are not; (3) the cross-subsidization of marginal and unprofitable divisions in corporate conglomerates is greatly reduced, if not ended, by the pressure to repay debt; (4) value is created, especially for shareholders, as corporations undervalued by the market are subjected to buy-outs; and (5) generally, it is beneficial for the nation if U.S. top corporate management is shaken out of its comfortable post-World War II torpor, and leveraged buy-outs are seen as one means to that end.

Undoubtedly, many corporations operate at inefficient levels, with earnings below what is possible with achievably greater productivity. Of course, management must bear the responsibility. But it had enjoyed a quarter century without serious foreign competition (1945–1970), and slackened in pursuing innovation in major basic industries. A tacit partnership had grown up between big business and big labor, discussed in an earlier chapter, under which inflationary wage-benefit increases were accepted by management, along with increasingly inflexible and expensive work rules. And top management adapted itself readily to corporate perks that provided a lavish life-style. The hallmarks of corporate status and chief executive stature became corporate jets, corporate limousines, corporate-subsidized apartments and country club memberships, corporate art collections (sometimes displayed in the CEO's home), corporate yachts, and so on.

That interest is tax-deductible while corporate profits are subject to double taxation (first as corporate profit and second as dividends) is undoubtedly a major artificial stimulus to the use of debt as a source of capital. Of course, debt involves risk, and the greater the debt the greater the risk. But in the go-go '80s, most eyeglasses were fitted with rose-colored lenses, so leveraging debt looked like a marvelous means to multiply financial power and build empires. Given chief executive appetites fed by egoism, and fee-seeking investment and banking deal-makers who fed that egoism, the temptation to overeat was all too often irresistible.

While egoism and fees were sparks, the LBO conflagration was enormously enlarged by the conglomeration drive of the '60s. That was a period when cyclically sensitive corporations sought complementary companies in a diversification drive designed to smooth earnings over the business cycle. It was popular to believe that management skill was portable across all industries and technologies, so that a management efficient in one industry would be equally efficient in others. It was believed also that economies of scale would be achieved by merging and slimming headquarters staffs. Events disproved the beliefs. Managements competent in one industry failed in others. Not always, but with sufficient frequency to undo the advantage expected. And headquarters staffs mushroomed, as new layers of management were created to deal with diversified corporate divisions. Inherent in this situation was the fact that some corporate divisions were marginally profitable, or unprofitable. And it was equally inherent that the profitable divisions would cross-subsidize the others and enable top management to continue acquisition errors at great cost.

To the degree an LBO drove stock values up, shareholder value was created. Although a significant part of this value was often gained by arbitragers who speculated on anticipated increases in a stock's value when a company was put in play, it is undeniable that a substantial part also went to long-term shareholders. From a macro standpoint, it can be argued that this gain in value was more a transfer than a real growth, for divestitures and liquidations involved large losses to discharged employees, discontinued suppliers, and depressed communities But the market's focus was on the change in shareholder value.

While describing the advantages of LBOs, we touched on some inherent disadvantages, namely, those aspects of the transactions that increased risk. Of course, the major disadvantage is the ability provided by leveraging to overvalue a corporation (i.e., its *real* ability to repay under economic conditions less optimistic than those used in LBO forecasts and cash flow projections). Consequently, more debt is assumed than can actually be managed. It is important to recognize that LBO cash flow forecasts play down corporate earnings (profits). The reason is simple. The corporation being bought is going private, and being taken out of trading on the public stock exchange. Quarterly earnings and market stock values are no longer relevant. What counts now is the capacity (cash flow) to repay debt plus interest. In these forecasts, depreciation for capital replacement is included in cash flow, because such replacement can be postponed while the set-aside for the purpose is reallocated to debt repayment and interest. Further, a significant portion of corporate profits formerly going for taxes is now diverted to tax-deductible interest payments. This segment of cash flow projections involves a kind of government (societal) financing of leveraging. And so we find in LBO cash flow forecasts such odd-sounding acronyms as EBDIT (earnings before depreciation, interest, and taxes).

When seeking ways to increase cash flow, to expand the magnitude of possible leveraging, the creative deal-maker and egoistic CEO do not stop with depreciation and corporate taxation of profits. They closely examine research and development (R & D) expenditures, as well as spending for normal capital maintenance. Once again, the temptation to cut back these expenditures is limited only by the conservatism of the principals (CEO and deal-makers). But their egoism and desire for huge financial gain and fees too often propel valuations into the ether. Cutbacks in R and D, normal capital maintenance, normal marketing, and so forth, are destructive to corporate health and viability in the long run. A small but interesting illustration is provided by the case of a newspaper, *The New Haven Register.* In 1989, Ralph Ingersoll, Jr., and E. M. Warburg, Pincus and Co. paid Mark Goodson, the game show entrepreneur, some $245 million for the paper. About $200 million was financed by debt. The *New York Times* reported that the paper's top executive Thomas P. Geyer was discharged because he objected to a second round of employee layoffs within one month.[4] Reportedly, Geyer believed the new layoffs would harm the paper's new coverage and delivery service standards.

A further danger that contributes to overvaluing and overleveraging arises once a company has been put in play. When an LBO is announced, anyone able to put together a financing package can bid. In short, an

[4]The *New York Times,* October 17, 1990, p. D19.

auction takes place, and, in an auction, competitive bidding pressures can build to a frenzy based on considerations unrelated to financial facts (i.e., egoism, desire to retain status and power, desire to gain status and power, the primal urge to win a fight). In short, sense is succeeded by emotion. And estimations of risks are overcome by the intensity of those emotions.

Once a company has been overvalued and overleveraged, the new owners are confronted by heavy interest and debt repayment obligations. The earlier overly optimistic assumptions collapse before harsh financial realities. At that point, the stimulus to engage in unethical and even fraudulent practices becomes very great. An immediate likelihood is the preparation of unrealistic budgets, based on optimistic assumptions involving projected sales revenues and cost reductions. Top management may press middle management to show the expected budget results. Frightened middle managers may oblige by misstating actual revenues, carrying bad accounts receivable, shifting the accounting recording of sales and expenditures over time periods, emasculating capital maintenance, and so on. And, for a brief period, the financial facade may appear all right when the corporate body is actually rotting from within. Recall the Beech Nut case.

Finally, harm is done to stakeholders, namely employees, suppliers, and their communities. I do not speak here of a transfer effect, the losses to these groups as against the gains to shareholders. Nor do I speak of losses to workers whose wages and benefits were bloated by years of tacit union-management partnership in passing excessive costs on to consumers unprotected by competitive product markets. In such instances, suppliers and the corporation's communities benefited from a transfer at the expense of consumers. I speak instead of healthy companies thrust into financial ruin by frenzied overleveraging, fed by egoism and empire-building run wild. One need think only of Robert Campeau and the effect of his activities on Federated Department Stores and Allied Stores. In such cases, jobs were lost, suppliers hurt, and communities subjected to suffering where there was no prior mismanagement.

The psychological climate of the late '80s was well reflected by Michael J. Murray and Frank C. Reid, of the Continental Bank of Illinois, in an article entitled, aptly enough, "Financial Style and Corporate Control."[5] In an introductory paragraph to the article, they said

---

[5]Michael J. Murray, and Frank C. Reid, "Financial Style and Corporate Control," *Journal of Applied Corporate Finance*, spring 1988, 1, no. 1, pp. 76–84.

Who will control the process of realizing values inherent in a particular business? If the answer is to be "management," then *a more assertive financial style and an accelerated financial restructuring timetable may be required* to accompany any necessary business restructuring activities. In the new financial environment, *failure to take the initiative* to implement prudent, well-reasoned financial restructuring *may allow outside interests to re-define the game*. Management would thus lose control of the value creation process. [Italics added][6]

The ceremonial obeisance to prudence, reason, and "necessary" restructuring should not blind the reader to the basic issue of control and the naked assertion that, if management didn't take on corporate debt and leverage to finance shareholder special dividends and/or buy-backs, then outsiders would "raid" and management would be out. Indeed, the opening paragraph of the article went on to say,

Any management team charged with responsibility of creating value for public shareholders must come to terms with two facts: (1) the supply of capital for corporate control transactions is quite large and (2) much of this capital is managed by individuals or entities which actively seek undervalued situations. We have all heard about the "corporate raiders" and their ability to draw funds from the high-yield ("junk") debt markets. . . . [7]

Note the overriding emphasis on management's responsibility to enhance and *realize* shareholder value. One of the leading proponents of this managerial responsibility, and critic of the failure of many managements to carry it out, is Michael C. Jensen, Edsel Bryant Ford Professor of Business Administration at the Harvard Business School. Jensen perceived and exposed a collision of interests between shareholders and management in a number of the corporate diversification programs associated with the growth of conglomerates in the '60s. He focused on mature companies that generated what was called "free cash flow" (i.e., cash in excess of the amount that management could profitably reinvest in its existing businesses).[8] Confronted with that situation, management could exercise either of two options (or some combination of them): (1) pay out the excess cash to shareholders in the form of large special dividends or stock repurchase

---

[6]Ibid., p. 76.

[7]Ibid.

[8]See Mark L. Mitchell, and Kenneth Lehn, "Do Bad Bidders Become Good Targets?" *Journal of Applied Corporate Finance* 3, no. 2., Summer 1990, p. 61.

arrangements or (2) reinvest the excess cash in acquisitions (i.e., diversification), even if they yielded returns below the corporate cost of capital. The latter course of action involved corporate growth, with management gaining control over more operations, more employees, and so forth. Of course, this expansion of control was also an expansion of executive power and status. Jensen charged that, given this conflict of interest between shareholders and management, the former lost. It followed, as day does night, that corporate takeovers and LBOs financed by debt and involving large leveraging were good for shareholders and society. They introduced a needed discipline that compelled management to return value to shareholders rather than to reduce and dissipate it in value-reducing, but ego-enhancing, acquisitions. Corporations taken over could be broken open by divestitures that would unlock value and return it where it belonged—to shareholders.

The foregoing limns the psychological climate and the major rationale underlying the leveraging frenzy of the 80s.

FRUEHAUF, RELIANCE ELECTRIC, AND RJR NABISCO CASES

The *Fruehauf* case involved a management-led LBO.[9] Subject to an unfriendly takeover bid by Asher Edelman in 1986 and pursued relentlessly by Merrill Lynch to do a management LBO, management agreed to fight Edelman's bid. What transpired was described by Robert Siefert, former president and chief operating officer of Fruehauf and board chairman and CEO of Kelsey-Hayes, a major division of the corporation. Edelman originally approached management with a plan to increase shareholder value. The goal would be accomplished by selling off a major part of the firm. But top management was adamant against divesting the Fruehauf trailer operations and Kelsey-Hayes, which they regarded as the core divisions. They explained their position as being based on a commitment to employees, customers, suppliers, and local communities (stakeholders).

Edelman proposed his own slate of directors, and a vicious proxy battle occurred with "personal accusations and vitriolic language . . . the order of the day." Emotions on both sides rose to a fevered level. Backed by

[9]The Continental Bank, *Journal of Applied Corporate Finance* 3, no. 2 (Summer 1990), pp. 13–15.

Merrill-Lynch-arranged financing, management waged a bidding war against Edelman. There were hectic attempts at negotiation and lawsuits. Finally, Edelman retired from the bidding, and the last management bid succeeded. But the price was very high, and, as subsequent events showed, too high. Cut to its essence, the capital structure involved $25 million of equity and $1.185 billion of debt (actually $250 million consisted of PIK (payment-in-kind) preferred stock, with $510 million in junk bonds and $425 million in a bridge loan provided by a group of banks).

The next two years were difficult, although noncore businesses were divested. While Kelsey-Hayes almost met its profit targets, the trailer and maritime divisions were buffeted by adverse changes in the economic environment, to which management and the investor group did not respond timely or in a way needed to overcome the problems. In the third year, major corrective steps were taken. Excess plant capacity was closed, and branches were shut down. Management and staff cutbacks were made, and other cost reduction programs were taken. Still, the debt-service burden was too heavy, and management proposed a recapitalization. Unfortunately for management, when it was making its presentation to the bondholders, a Canadian company entered the picture and offered to better any proposal put forward by management. At that point, management recognized defeat, and the company was put up for auction. Eventually, Fruehauf avoided bankruptcy, but the trailer operations and Kelsey-Hayes were sold off (the heart of the business, which management had been so adamant to keep).

Summarizing the experience, Robert Siefert said, "All in all, . . . the Fruehauf operation failed not because the company was not a good operation, but rather because the level of debt was too high." In amplifying this judgment, he made these observations: (1) everyone, including Edelman, overestimated the value of the real estate and of the divisions to be sold; (2) everyone failed to recognize changes in the trailer industry, which affected profits adversely, and failed also to estimate adequately the potential cost of unfunded liabilities and environmental problems; (3) emotions dominated negotiations and bidding, resulting in a final stock price much higher than the real underlying value of the business; (4) too much time was taken before meaningful actions were taken to conserve cash and pay down debt. Siefert believed that the Fruehauf LBO erred also in issuing public common stock, which denied management the benefits of going private, and in placing management restricting powers in the hands of bondholders and stockholders. In his words, "Management needs to retain as much flexibility as possible in entering into these transactions!"

The *Reliance Electric* case provides a counterpoint to Fruehauf, for it was a successful management LBO. But it was successful precisely because it avoided the errors of judgment and the excessive debt that characterized Fruehauf. A major reason was the absence of an emotional bidding war.[10]

Reliance Electric was a subsidiary of Exxon, the huge oil company. In 1986, Exxon decided to sell the subsidiary to the Reliance management and a group of investors (Citicorp Capital Investors and Prudential Bache Securities). Although other purchasers were interested and bid, all prospective buyers sought to retain the Reliance management. As a result, all bids were conditioned by Reliance management's estimates of the value of the business and the amount of debt it could handle. When the buy-out was completed in December 1986, total debt amounted to $1.263 billion, of which $1.2 billion consisted of bridge (temporary) financing. Long-term financing was completed in the first quarter of 1987, comprising $650 million of senior bank debt, $450 million of subordinated high-yield (junk) notes and debentures, $120 million of preferred stock ($90 million of which was later exchanged into a junior subordinated debenture), and $10 million of common stock. Although the equity base was 10 percent of total capitalization, if $120 million of preferred stock is included, the true equity base (the common stock) was under 1 percent of the total. Even the inclusion of the $30 million of preferred stock remaining after the exchange into junior subordinated debentures brought the equity portion to less than 5 percent of the capital involved. This capital structure surely represents leveraging on a proportionately grand scale.

Yet the Reliance Electric LBO was a success, and all participants agreed it was essentially due to the business not having been overvalued and subjected to an unsustainable level of debt. In fact, debt was reduced by a net of $606 million, or about 48 percent, in the three years following 1986, while investments in technology and new product introductions were increased. Market share expanded, and employment increased in those business units that were retained. Explaining these excellent results, John Morley, president and CEO of Reliance Electric, noted: (1) the LBO financial forecasts were conservative; (2) financial flexibility was a fundamental

---

[10]Ibid., pp. 15–17.

element in the capital structure, so that divestitures and asset sales could be pursued in the most advantageous ways; (3) clear and straightforward corporate goals were set, with a clear recognition of the importance of early reduction of debt without compromising investment in technology and new product introductions; (4) effective communication of corporate goals to all employees was maintained; (5) powerful financial incentives were established for management and employees, to insure everyone's maximum effort toward achievement of corporate goals; and (6) the crossover from an almost single-minded focus on debt reduction to a more balanced strategy of business growth and continued debt reduction was anticipated.

To repeat, the major element accounting for the success of the Reliance Electric LBO was price, the avoidance of overvaluation and overleveraging. And the basic reason these risks were avoided was the key role of management in determining value and debt levels. But management was able to play this role only because there was no external bidder ready to bid and buy without the participation of management. In the Fruehauf case, Asher Edelman was prepared to oust management, and the spark needed to ignite an emotional bidding war was present and struck.

The ultimate LBO of the frenzied 80s, both in scale and in suspense, involved *RJR Nabisco*, America's 19th largest industrial company. It also involved several of America's largest chief executive egos: Ross Johnson, president and CEO of RJR Nabisco; Henry Kravis, partner of Kohlberg, Kravis, Roberts (KKR); and Peter Cohen, Chairman and CEO of Shearson, Lehman, Hutton. There were also a number of other powerful personalities associated with other investment firms. And attorneys were omnipresent.

Ross Johnson apparently became fearful he would lose control of his empire after the market crash of October 1987 reduced RJR Nabisco stock value to some $40 per share from over $60. At first, he toyed with the idea of a management LBO. Then, he accepted the idea and took the steps that put the company in play. Peter Cohen, desperate to make Shearson, Lehman, Hutton a major player in the LBO activity that was making fortunes for other firms and individuals, agreed to unprecedented concessions to Ross Johnson, to win Johnson's acceptance of Shearson as his LBO partner. And Henry Kravis, who had been pursuing Johnson to do an LBO for over a year and who considered KKR to have a "lock" on megadeals, was outraged at what he perceived to be Johnson's perfidy in selecting Shearson over KKR. He also considered Cohen impertinent to presume to compete with KKR.[11] Once Johnson's management LBO bid was announced on October 20, 1988, the play was set in motion and the contestants, captured by their pride and driven by their powerful egos, fought a historic financial battle characterized by frantic competitive bids. Of course, the legal, banking, and investment firm fees involved were astronomical on a deal that ultimately went for some $25 billion.

Since Ross Johnson, as chief executive of RJR Nabisco, made the key decision to do the management LBO and thereby raised the curtain on the ensuing action, some background bearing on his personality and outlook is appropriate. Born Canadian in a family of modest means, Johnson was truly a self-made man. While his early years in business did not indicate the success that would later follow, he was driven by ambition. Ultimately, his drive to succeed was rewarded, and he achieved the position of chief executive of Standard Brands, a large food-manufacturing firm. To become CEO of Standard Brands, he ousted Henry Weigl, his predecessor. That story and the story of subsequent events in Johnson's career are told by Bryan Burrough and John Helyar in *Barbarians at the Gate*.[12] Burrough and Helyar, telling of the ousting of Weigl and his succession by Johnson, point out that very quickly after Johnson ousted Weigl, he revealed a penchant for lavish living, supported by corporate resources. Prior to succeeding Weigl, his salary was $130,000 and Weigl's, as CEO, was $200,000. Soon Johnson, as CEO, was making $480,000. Johnson did not restrict this largess to himself. Many of Standard Brands' executives enjoyed a doubling of their salaries, and the company's compensation of its management went from the bottom of the industry to the top. But salaries were only a part of the story. Company apartments for top executives, a private box at Madison Square Garden, and country club memberships, as well as stretch limousines and corporate jets (his penchant for private jets flowered later) became a hallmark of his executive style. As Burrough and Helyar put it: "He (Johnson) had an overriding

---

[11]Henry Kravis flatly denies these allegations. See *Fortune*, January 2, 1989, p. 70. This issue of *Fortune* contains both Henry Kravis' and Ross Johnson's own accounts of what happened, and is significantly different in a number of details from the Burrough and Helyar account. But the latter account seems to me to be more objective.

[12]Bryan Burrough and John Helyar, *Barbarians at the Gate* (New York: HarperCollins Publishers, 1990). Copyright © 1990 by Bryan Burrough and John Helyar.

rule he felt free to invoke at any time. The chief executive can do whatever he wants."[13]

By 1981, Johnson was in his late 40s, but restless and unready to age gracefully. He was an avid sportsman and golfer who loved to hobnob with famous athletes. He used them extensively in his corporate advertising and treated them lavishly in compensation and perks. He also divorced, and married a 26-year-old woman, an action not uncommon among powerful corporate chief executives.

In March 1981, Robert Schaeberle, Chairman and CEO of Nabisco, called Johnson. As a result, the two men met. They liked each other (Johnson was a gregarious man, a natural salesman with a fund of stories and easy to like), and they agreed to merge their companies. The merger, creating Nabisco Brands, involved a $1.9 billion stock swap. Since Nabisco was the richer and more powerful firm, Schaeberle became chief executive and chairman, and Johnson, president and chief operating officer. But, while that was the arrangement on paper, Johnson soon became the real chief. He managed it by ingratiating himself with Schaeberle so that the latter supported Johnson's every initiative, including enormous increases in both their salaries and bonuses, as well as those of other executives. Also, the company endowed a professorship in accounting at Pace University in Schaeberle's name.

Johnson was not a sycophant. He was a man of some business talent, and he proved that in the "soft cookie" battles of 1982 to 1983. Cookies were a mainstay of the Nabisco product lines, and cookies generally were a multibillion dollar business. Frito-Lay Inc., a competitor, introduced a new product, soft cookies, into the Kansas City market in mid-1982. The new product quickly captured 20 percent of that market. Soon, Procter and Gamble entered the fray with a Duncan Hines brand of soft cookies. By mid-1983, Nabisco put their own line of soft cookies, Almost Home, on the market. While Nabisco did not win in the Kansas City market, it did overcome its competitors in the rest of the country. The results were clear by 1984. Schaeberle, now an unqualified admirer of Johnson, retired as chairman and CEO and made Johnson chief executive.

Less than a year later, early in 1985, Johnson received a call from J. Tylee Wilson, chairman and CEO of RJ Reynolds Industries, the tobacco

---

[13]Ibid., p. 23.

giant. The men met. RJ Reynolds bought Nabisco for $85 a share ($4.9 billion), and Johnson became president and chief operating officer. He was able to retain company apartments for all the top officers of Nabisco. And five Nabisco directors were added to the Reynolds board, making a 20-person RJR Nabisco board. Of course, this gave Johnson one quarter of the combined board, since his relationships with the Nabisco directors were excellent. Being especially sensitive to CEO-board relationships, Johnson quickly sensed considerable tension between Wilson and the directors of the former RJ Reynolds board—fertile ground for Johnson, who moved first to establish close working relationships with Wilson and to win his confidence. He succeeded, as he had with Schaeberle at Nabisco. But it must be observed that his success reflected the excellent job he did in merging Nabisco and Del Monte (a subsidiary of RJ Reynolds), as well as in divesting certain divisions of the merged RJR Nabisco. Johnson's second step, as before, was to cultivate the directors, a course encouraged by Wilson.

Johnson's chance to oust Wilson came when the RJR Nabisco board discovered that Wilson, without consulting it, had authorized the expenditure of some $68 million in a research project to develop a smokeless cigarette (eventually named Premier). The directors were outraged: first, because the aggregate spending on the project, which exceeded the limit allowable without board approval, had been effected over a five-year period in small increments; and, second, because Wilson, the CEO, had demonstrated a complete lack of trust in the directors to keep the project secret. Yet, hundreds of employees were working to produce the smokeless cigarette. The board's outrage burst at a meeting in July 1986.

Johnson precipitated matters by calling several directors and telling them he planned to leave RJR Nabisco, possibly to become CEO of a British food firm. He expressed his intention strongly, saying he felt he had done what he could at RJR Nabisco, and further advancement there was not possible since Wilson was CEO and clearly the board's choice. But Charlie Hugel, a key board member, persuaded Johnson to meet and discuss the possibility of his taking over Wilson's job. Johnson agreed with Hugel's idea, and the latter brought along an overwhelming majority of the board members. When Wilson realized what was happening, he arranged a handsome departure deal and resigned. And so, having merged Nabisco into RJ Reynolds in 1985, Johnson became chief executive of the combined giant a year later.

As head of America's 19th largest company, Johnson's penchant for lavish living truly expressed itself. A new headquarters was magnificently decorated with expensive antiques. Even middle-level managers were given a country club membership and a company car (worth up to $28,000). But the most extreme example of lavishness was seen at Atlanta's Charlie Brown Airport, where Johnson ordered a new hangar built to house RJR Nabisco's corporate fleet of 10 planes, which was known as the RJR Air Force. Adjacent to the hangar, a three-story headquarters was built to manage the movement and maintenance of the aircraft, as well as the fleet's 36 pilots. The three-story building featured Italian marble floors, tinted glass exterior walls, a striking three-story entry atrium, inlaid mahogany walls and doors, and so on.

Johnson saw to it that the directors were well taken care of. Burrough and Helyar describe this aspect of things as follows:[14]

> The directors found that all their needs were now attended to in detail. Bill Anderson of NCR slid into Sticht's chairmanship of the International Advisory Board and was slipped an $80,000 contract for his services. Johnson disbanded RJR Nabisco's shareholder services department and contracted its work out to John Medlin's Wachovia Bank. Juanita Kreps was given $2 million to endow two chairs at Duke, one of them named after herself. For another $2 million, Duke's business school named a wing of a new building "Horrigan Hall" . . . Ron Grierson was also being fussed over lovingly. . . .
>
> Holdovers from Johnson's Nabisco board did especially well. Bob Schaeberle was given a six-year, $180,000-a-year consulting contract for ill-defined duties. Andy Sage received $250,000 a year for his efforts with financial R and D. In an unusual move, Charlie Hugel took Sticht's post as the ceremonial "non-executive" chairman of RJR Nabisco, for which he received a $150,000 contract. By naming him chairman, Johnson hoped Hugel would cement his increasingly close ties with the board.
>
> At the same time, the number of board meetings was slashed, and directors' fees were boosted to $50,000. Wilson had allowed board members to use company jets only for official business. Johnson encouraged them to use the RJR Air force anytime, anywhere, at no charge. "I sometimes feel like the director of transportation," he once sighed after arranging yet another director's flight. *"But I know if I'm there for them they'll be there for me."* [Italics added]

---

[14]Ibid., p. 97.

All the pieces were now in place, with Johnson believing his board was in his pocket. Then, on October 19, 1987, the stock market collapsed. RJR Nabisco dropped from the mid-60s per share to the low 40s. And there the stock stayed. Everything positive that happened, like a 25 percent profit increase reported in December, failed to move the stock up. Of course, at a price in the low 40s, the company made an attractive takeover prospect, a point that attracted the attention of syndicated columnist Dan Dorfman and others. Among them was Clemmie Dixon Spangler, Jr., president of the University of North Carolina and a man whose family was one of RJR Nabisco's largest shareholders. Spangler was most unhappy at the decline in the value of the stock. He arranged to meet Johnson and proposed a LBO. Johnson managed to deflect Spangler, but he increased his efforts to boost the stock's value. With the approval of the board, he undertook a major buy-back of RJR Nabisco stock at prices between $52 and $58 a share. After spending $1.1 billion, the price of the stock sank right back down.

By late spring 1988, anyone with an interest knew Ross Johnson was concerned about RJR Nabisco's stock price. He was bombarded by dealmakers anxious to arrange an LBO. Although he denied any interest in the idea, pointing out that his life-style was great, it is not believable that he did not envisage the possibility of its loss through a takeover, even though a hostile takeover had two major hurdles: (1) the loss of existing top management and (2) the mammoth size of the financing that would be needed. Finally, Johnson decided to do a serious exploration of a management LBO. Being a director of American Express, he turned to Shearson, Lehman, Hutton, its investment banking subsidiary. Why didn't he give more serious thought to KKR, Henry Kravis's firm, which appeared best prepared to do a megadeal and which had pioneered the LBO? A significant clue is offered in Burrough and Helyar's account, as they describe a meeting between Jeff Beck, of Drexel Burnham Lambert, and Henry Kravis. Beck had been pursuing Johnson and suddenly found the latter not taking his calls. Becoming suspicious, he called Kravis and suggested they meet Johnson. Kravis agreed, but Beck suggested there would be a problem. *When Kravis asked what the problem was, Beck replied it was Johnson's insistence that he have control over the new company's board. And that was a concession that Henry Kravis had not and would not make.*

In early and mid-October 1988, Johnson and Peter Cohen of Shearson hammered out the details of an LBO bid at $75 per share. Johnson would have the control he demanded, and the lavish corporate lifestyle he loved would not be interfered with. Kravis would never have acceded to such demands, but Cohen was determined to make Shearson a major LBO player, and he surrendered. Johnson would have control over the board, and a very rich financial package. Johnson's top management group would get 8.5 percent of the equity, with a tax compensation loan from Shearson to finance it. Johnson's personal share (one percent) was estimated to have a potential value of $100 million within five years.

On October 13, Johnson called Hugel, a key director, and asked him to head the board's independent committee. Subsequently, the committee's membership included Martin Davis of Gulf and Western; William Anderson, former NCR chairman; John Macomber, former Celanese chairman; and Albert Butler, a Winston-Salem businessman. On October 20, the LBO was announced, stunning Henry Kravis who must have felt he was treated cavalierly and unfairly, as well as Jeff Beck of Drexel Burnham Lambert and other important financial people. And so the war began!

The details of the war consume another 300 pages of the Burrough-Helyar book. What counts here is that estimations of financial risk changed substantially in the heat of battle. As the bids ratcheted up from $75 to $106 and $108, and the total amount of money involved from some $17.6 billion to $25 billion, powerful, clashing egos drove the principal actors beyond what they would have done in a less frenzied atmosphere. Interestingly, as the bidding intensified, Johnson was forced to concede the very things he insisted on most strongly in the beginning. The richness of his own and management's cut had to be scaled back substantially to make possible Shearson's ultimate but losing bid. And it was plain that the eventual price of the LBO made impossible a continuation of the lavish corporate living so much esteemed by Johnson.

No less important was the fact that once RJR Nabisco was put in play, the board's independent committee became boss. They were not in Johnson's pocket, and it was an illusion for him to have ever believed otherwise. The danger of their exposure to personal liability for failing to get the best value for shareholders became the critical criterion of their deliberations and final decision to sell to KKR. Henry Kravis won the war with a final bid of $109, even though the independent committee's investment adviser could not say that bid was definitively better than Shearson's $112 (which included paper whose actual value was uncertain). But the lawyers and RJR Nabisco board members finally found in KKR's favor on a variety of grounds which they believed made his $109 bid the superior one.

Looked at in the spring of 1991, over two years later, RJR Nabisco has completed a number of divestitures. But its long-term fate is not yet certain. However, unlike other excessively leveraged buyouts, this one has got the continuing great financial resources of KKR behind it. Thus, after the junk bond market collapsed in 1989 to 1990, KKR announced a substantial refinancing of RJR Nabisco. By putting in over $1 billion of additional money, they were able to effect a significant restructuring of the company's capital profile. With that combination of elements, the greatest LBO of the time may succeed, and, in the language of the financial theorists, "create value." It would be a fascinating finale. Whatever the outcome, it will be studied in the years ahead.

It is appropriate to recall at this point that one of the advantages claimed for LBOs is that they shake professional managers out of complacent risk-averse sloth, and compel them to become more entrepreneurial and efficient. But the odds favor that outcome only when a business has not been overvalued and overleveraged.

ENTREPRENEURS AND PROFESSIONAL MANAGERS: DO THEY VIEW RISK DIFFERENTLY?

Perhaps the most astute observations on this question were written by Moses Shapiro, late Chairman and CEO of General Instruments Corporation:[15]

The entrepreneur . . . is an extremely independent, self-moving enterpriser. *He has placed himself in a situation that is fraught with risks and uncertainties because he needs that way of life.* Decision making and other forms of authority he vests in himself and himself alone, and he keeps his hands on all phases of the business. He is essentially a generalist, understanding production, moving deftly in financing, creative in marketing, quickly grasping the significance of data, and highly intuitive. He enjoys risks, not because he needs danger in his life, but because in risks he can prove his value. Moreover, risks provide fast feedback and the feedback is in the form of a quick, concrete and reliable statistic-profit. But, it is important to remember that his primary motivation is not profit, but what profit represents: individual achievement. . . . In my experience and in the experience of others, large corporations are not really centered in a vision of the future but rather on

---

[15]Moses Shapiro, "The Entrepreneurial Individual in the Large Organization," in Jules Backman, ed., *Entrepreneurship and the Outlook for America,* (New York: The Free Press, 1983), pp. 63–64.

the success of the past and the present, their public statements to the contrary notwithstanding. Indeed, the function of a large corporation is typically to preserve (and, if possible, to enlarge) a position already attained and to administer an empire already conquered. *These tasks are best accomplished by professional managers working in teams.* In such an environment, it is natural that change works best when it comes slowly.

Observing that the dichotomy between the entrepreneur and the professional manager is not so absolute as it may seem, Shapiro adds that in many ways the entrepreneur is similar to the innovative corporate manager. He goes on to note that two conditions are prerequisite to the successful inclusion of entrepreneurial types in large corporate organizations: (1) top management must have strong egos, a high tolerance for people who cannot be ordered about, who argue back assertively, and whose strong drives and opinions are likely to upset many to whom they nominally report; and (2) careful, continuous attention to internal communications, so that the creative entrepreneurial types are not smothered by mountains of red tape and inflexible relationships that inhibit the free interchange of ideas.

If these conditions are satisfied, then Shapiro suggests that there are organizational structures that enhance the possible coexistence and cooperation of risk-averse professional managers and risk-seeking entrepreneurs in the configuration of the large corporation. Among these possible structural arrangements, he notes franchises, corporate spin-offs, new ventures, assignment of authority and responsibility for new product development to an internal entrepreneur, and the establishment of big business small investment companies, that is, big business backing, in the form of capital invested, for newly established autonomous corporate entities (the big business is simply an investor and exercises no authority over the management of the small business).[16]

---

[16]Ibid., pp. 67–75.

CHAPTER 10

EXECUTIVE POWER AND THE EXPANDING ROLE OF WOMEN IN ORGANIZATIONS

SOME RELEVANT TRENDS

Division of labor on the basis of sex is probably as ancient as humankind, stretching back into prehistory and the primordial beginnings of our species. As an example, writing about the stone age primitives of Mount Hagen, New Guinea in my doctoral dissertation, I observed: "There is a division of labor on the basis of sex, . . . it may be said that women do the chores, while the hard physical labor is reserved to the men. Women perform labor such as cooking, cleaning grounds, weeding grounds, tending pigs, making bilum net baskets and garments etc."[1] Later and more explicitly, I added, "The heaviest, physically most arduous labor is performed by men and the tasks which are more tedious but require less strength are performed by women."[2]

Skipping millennia in the evolution of human society and coming to the 19th century, we arrive at that time when the ancient division of roles by sex began to break down. Women began to enter the labor force (i.e., the proportion of the population employed for remuneration, and to escape from "obligatory domesticity)."[3]

---

[1] Abraham L. Gitlow, *Economics of the Mount Hagen Tribes, New Guinea* (New York: J. J. Augustin, 1947), p. 39.

[2] Ibid., pp. 63–64.

[3] Excerpts from *The Economic Emergence of Women*, by Barbara R. Bergmann. Copyright ©1987 by Basic Books, Inc. Reprinted by permission of Basic Books, Inc., a division of HarperCollins Publishers, p. 3.

Barbara Bergmann, in *The Economic Emergence of Women,* points out that:[4]

In 1870, only 14 percent of women of working age in the United States were employed. . . . the percentage of women in the job market . . . doubled . . . between 1870 and 1940, and then doubled again between 1940 and 1986. By 1986, 56 percent of women were in the job market, and the percentage was still growing. Of women under age sixty-five, about two-thirds are now in the labor force. . . . The decade of the 1970s . . . marked the beginning of an era in which an employed woman could see herself as part of a majority, and within the mainstream. By the same token, the 1970s marked the start of minority status for the woman devoted exclusively to domestic service at home for husband and children.

Bergmann believes these profound changes reflect technological change and advances in labor productivity, which vastly increased the money (market) value of women's labor and made the economic (opportunity) cost of continued domesticity too high to be sustainable. She believes they also reflect the long-term decline in the birth rate, for today, women average half as many babies as in 1900 and one fourth as many as in 1800. The lower birth rate leaves more time for paid employment outside the home. And, in a circular and self-reinforcing way, the expanding opportunity for paid employment reduces the number of children that women—and many men—want to have. To this must be added a further significant technological advance, the development of more reliable, more convenient, and easily available birth control techniques.

Despite these profound changes that have been transforming the traditional roles of men and women, equality of economic result is still unachieved. Women's earnings are typically less than those of men, and the movement of women into formerly male-dominated occupations, especially management, still is lagging. There is considerable debate about whether the continued, though lessening, disparity between women's and men's earnings reflect market forces or discrimination, but there is far less argument over the impact on men of the massive emergence of women in the labor force. The latter, although slowly and haltingly, are being confronted by the need to reexamine their own responsibilities and role in the home and in the care of children, as well as in their conduct and attitudes in the workplace.

---

[4]Ibid., p. 5.

Narrowing the scope of our attention from sweeping societal changes to the narrower focus of women's progress in management, we find substantial overall progress coupled with a failure as yet to achieve equality with men, especially in the ranks of top executive positions.[5] While the proportion of women in executive, administrative, and managerial positions rose from under 6 percent in 1960 to 30.5 percent in 1980, a substantial growth, they remain a minority. And a 1984 estimate indicated that only 1,000 women, as against 49,000 men, held top policy-making positions in major corporations in 1984.

But attitudes appear to be changing. Robert L. Dipboye, based on an exhaustive survey of relevant research, reported that "the percentage of managers favorable toward women in management rose from 9 percent in 1965 to 33 percent in 1985 among male managers, and from 48 to 68 percent among female managers. The percentage agreeing that they personally would feel comfortable working for a woman rose from 27 to 47 percent among male managers and from 75 to 82 percent among female managers. Perhaps the most dramatic change was in beliefs regarding women's desire for management responsibilities. In 1965, 54 percent of the male managers and 50 percent of female managers agreed that women rarely expect or want authority. In the 1985 survey, these percentages had dropped dramatically to 9 percent for the men and 4 percent for the women."[6] But other evidence indicates a significant sentiment against women in management continues among college students, both women and men.[7]

Examining the research relating to sex-characteristic stereotypes, Dipboye distinguished between *nonmanagerial* women and *managerial* women, making the general point that the former display significant differences as compared with the latter in such stereotypical masculine traits as aggressiveness, tendency to dominate, and competitiveness.[8] *Managerial*

---

[5]Robert L. Dipboye, "Problems and Progress of Women in Management," in Karen Shallcross Koziara; Michael H. Moskow; Lucretia Dewey Tanner, eds., *Working Women, Past, Present, Future,* Bureau of National Affairs, Washington, D.C. chapter 5, pp. 118–153, copyright Industrial Relations Research Association, University of Wisconsin, Madison, Wisconsin.

[6]Ibid., p. 120.

[7]Ibid.

[8]Ibid., pp. 122–123.

women do not seem markedly different in these traits from managerial men.[9]
Dipboye added:

> The research on characteristics of managerial and nonmanagerial women suggests that aspiring managerial women are as likely as aspiring managerial men to possess the requisite traits of the successful manager and to achieve success in management. Nevertheless, the research on nonmanagerial women suggests one reason why women continue to be underrepresented in management. Regardless of the validity or invalidity of the stereotypes of women, many women appear to have been socialized to conform to traditional female stereotypes and, consequently, have much more limited occupational aspirations than do men. Thus, the total pool of qualified women is smaller than it should be because of the biases of many women against a managerial career.[10]

While managerial women appear to match managerial men in the traits important to career advancement and success, they lag in reaching the top ranks of executives, and they lag in compensation. Dipboye suggests the reasons "include exclusion from informal relationships with male peers, biases in the perception and evaluation of their performance in supervisory roles, . . . greater conflicts between work and family roles, sexual harassment, lack of sponsors, and biases in job assignments."[11]

CHANGES IN LAW

The huge expansion in the market-related activity of women was for many years associated with the enactment of legislation designed to protect them (and children) from exploitation by unscrupulous employers. Protective labor laws reflected a societal view of women as weak, defenseless, and requiring the protection of laws enacted by moral men in a male-dominated culture. There was concern also that women who worked for excessive hours and/or in heavy, arduous physical labor might be harmed and suf-

---

[9]Ibid., pp. 123–124. For a vigorous debate on this proposition, see Judy Rosener, "Ways Women Lead," *Harvard Business Review*, November–December 1990; and "Ways Men and Women Lead," *Harvard Business Review*, January–February 1991, pp. 150–60.

[10]Ibid., pp. 126–127.

[11]Ibid., p. 130.

fer impairment for their role as mothers. Consequently, state laws set maximum daily or weekly hours of work for women, prohibited or regulated night work, and limited the occupations in which women could be employed. These laws have been almost completely erased since the passage of Title VII of the 1964 Federal Civil Rights Act.[12]

Title VII and the emergence of a militant feminist movement marked a watershed in society's attitudes and behavior relative to women's role in the workplace. The collapse of the laws regulating hours of work did not command significant media attention. But the steady penetration of women into occupations previously regarded as male preserves did. The daily news frequently reported lawsuits by women demanding access to employment as police, fire fighters, teamsters, construction workers, and so on. And the military opened its doors to women recruits, including the portals of the academies that trained career officers: West Point, Annapolis, the Air Force Academy.

Problems of sexual harassment and discrimination did not disappear. But they were increasingly met by expensive lawsuits against employers who could then find themselves subject to affirmative action programs dictated by the courts. Affirmative action is a hotly debated subject, especially when it appears to involve numerical hiring and staffing goals that seem akin to quotas.[13] Barbara R. Bergmann, in *The Economic Emergence of Women*, is a strong supporter of affirmative action programs, even if they occasionally and in some degree harm groups outside the favored groups. She believes the benefits to those favored outweigh the damages to those not favored. In any case, it is certain that chief executives and top managers, whether male or female, must wrestle with these problems.

Perhaps affirmative action would generate less heat if it was ineffective. But the general perception among men and women in management appears to be that civil rights legislation and legal action have had a significant effect on women's opportunities in the workplace. Robert L. Dipboye reported that "in a 1965 *Harvard Business Review* survey, 71 percent of men and 55 percent of women rejected the idea that new laws would expedite progress of women in management. In a 1985 replication of this survey, only 16 percent of the men and 26 percent of the women believed

---

[12]U.S. Department of Labor, Women's Bureau, *1975 Handbook on Women Workers*, Bulletin 297, U.S. Superintendent of Documents, Washington, D.C., 1975, pp. 329–333.

[13]Barbara R. Bergmann, *The Economic Emergence of Women*, chapter 7.

that civil rights laws have had no impact on equal opportunity."[14] But neither men nor women seemed receptive to affirmative action when it was implemented through preferential treatment. Dipboye added:[15]

> In a recent Gallup survey of 1,562 adults, 85 percent of the men and 84 percent of the women said that ability should be the main consideration and only 9 percent of the men and 11 percent of the women said there should be preferential treatment to correct past discrimination. . . . Fernandez (1981) found that 47 percent of white male managers believed that affirmative action has hurt their chances for promotion and 84 percent believed that it had lowered general hiring and promotion standards. Moreover, women leaders who are believed to have been selected as leaders on the basis of their sex have been shown to have received lower evaluations from their subordinates than women who are believed to have been selected on the basis of ability. . . .

PROBLEMS IN THE PATH TO THE EXECUTIVE SUITE

Title VII of the Civil Rights Act of 1964 aims at overcoming the effects of discrimination, and it provides a basis for legal action and affirmative action programs. It has also had an impact on sexual harassment, which involves more than making sexual submission a condition of employment, promotion, or improvements in salaries and/or other aspects of compensation. It can include offensive teasing, gestures, and unwanted physical contact. It can also include behavior that unreasonably interferes with a person's work performance or creates an intimidating, hostile, or offensive work environment.[16]

Of course, sexual harassment and discrimination are serious problems, and present significant barriers to the advancement of women into the top echelons of corporate management. But these problems are obvious, and society's attitudes and the law have moderated them, even though they remain significant. Other barriers to the advancement of women in management are perhaps more subtle, but nonetheless important. They include (1) the biological time clock and the desire for motherhood; (2) the pres-

---

[14]Robert L. Dipboye, "Problems and Progress of Women in Management," p. 137.

[15]Ibid., p. 137.

[16]*New York Times*, November 9, 1990, p. B5. See also "Ending Sexual Harassment: Business Is Getting the Message," *Business Week*, March 18, 1991, pp. 98–100.

sure of primacy in the two-career family; (3) nepotism in the workplace; and (4) social awkwardness at work and "on the road."

Nature itself has imposed a differentially disadvantageous burden on women, for it is their sex that suffers the exclusive capability of bearing children. Conception is a shared sexual responsibility, but childbirth belongs solely to women. No less significant in our consideration of barriers confronting women seeking top management positions is the fact of the biological time clock. Men may continue to father children well into their senior years, but women face the fact of menopause in their mid-40s to mid-50s. And the risks of significant medical problems for mother and fetus increase importantly as women advance in age beyond the early 30s. While these risks are abated somewhat by the development of tests such as amniosynthesis, they continue to be greater than in the case of pregnancies in younger women.

In this physiological context, we must place the career woman of today. Let us picture her as having received a baccalaureate degree at age 20 to 21, spent a couple or three years in a full-time job, returned to graduate school for a M.B.A. degree, which she has completed after two years of full-time study, and now being about four years into full-time corporate work on a management track. She is now 28 to 29 years of age and, like her male counterpart, on the verge of significant advancement into middle- and upper-management levels during her 30s and early 40s. At the most critical point in terms of future career progress, when career demands place greatest pressure on the primacy of career over other goals, consciousness of the biological time clock becomes increasingly intrusive and compelling. Obviously, not for all women. But for many it does.[17]

And once a woman opts to have one or more children, the primacy of career advancement appears to be inexorably undermined. While many may argue that it should not be so, the harsh fact is that the responsibility and burden for nurturing children still falls mainly on women, including career women in two-career families. Dipboye observes:[18]

> Women in general experience more role conflicts than do their male counterparts, and this role conflict serves as another barrier to women managers

---

[17] An excellent discussion of these issues is Felice N. Schwartz, "Management Women and the New Facts of Life," *Harvard Business Review*, January–February, 1989, pp. 65–76.

[18] Dipboye, "Problems and Progress of Women in Management," pp. 135–36.

seeking to advance in their careers. A major source of role conflict appears to be conflict between household responsibilities and organizational duties. *Even women managers as high as the vice presidential level report that they carry a disproportionate share of the responsibility for home chores* . . . Strober (1982) found in her 1978 survey of the 1974 Stanford MBA graduates that the women managers mentioned discrimination and *conflict with family roles* . . . as the most serious problems they expected to face in achieving their career goals. . . . "

An important illustration of the point being made is provided by the case of Diane McCourtney.[19] Mrs. McCourtney lost her job when she was absent from work for many days because her infant son was ill and she was unable to arrange suitable child care. Mrs. McCourtney has no quarrel with her employer, Seagate Technology, recognizing its problem of getting its work done. What angers her is the fact that she has been denied unemployment benefits, on the ground that loss of her job was due to her own decision to stay home and care for her child, and, consequently, was her own fault. Currently (Spring 1991), Connecticut, the District of Columbia, Maine, New Jersey, Rhode Island, and Wisconsin have laws requiring employers to provide unpaid leave to workers with sick children, and the state of Washington provides leave when a child is terminally ill. Several other states allow state workers to take such leave but have no provision covering private employers. But these laws are different from unemployment compensation and involve only *unpaid leave.* Consequently, the problem is real and common. In any case, Mrs. McCourtney is appealing her case to the Minnesota Court of Appeals. Its outcome is being closely watched.

A particularly high-profile illustration of the different impact of parenthood on women as contrasted with men is provided by the cases of Meredith Vieira and Connie Chung. Both are celebrity TV network newswomen. Meredith Vieira was dismissed from CBS's "60 Minutes" because she insisted on a part-time work schedule, so she could spend more time with her young son. Don Hewitt, producer of "60 Minutes," insisted the show needed a full-time commitment. Connie Chung, age 44, announced publicly in July, 1990, that her weekly CBS series, "Face to Face with Connie Chung," would be cut back to less frequent specials because she had

---

[19]*New York Times,* March 2, 1991, p. 48.

"to take a very aggressive approach to having a baby." During the Gulf War, when she was coanchor of a report on the war, her performance was criticized by Tom Sholes, the *Washington Post* TV critic, as confused. He discovered, between the first and second editions of the paper carrying that criticism, that her performance might have been related to certain medication. He softened his criticism for the second edition. In an article in the *New York Times*, Caryn James asked, "Would he have done the same if he had learned, for instance, that Dan Rather had been taking painkillers for extracted wisdom teeth?"[20]

Caryn James added,

A front-runner for Ms. Vieira's "60 Minutes" job is Lesley Stahl, the Margaret Thatcher of television news. A White House correspondent and the moderator of "Face the Nation," Ms. Stahl happens to be a mother but does not trail that image on the air and has not asked to work part-time. Known as a tough reporter, she has an iron-lady image that virtually makes her an honorary man.

That option is the traditional and unfortunately still the safest one for women who want to be taken as seriously as men, but it doesn't begin to address a problem that will only become more common. Quick, think of a TV reporter who is an expectant father. As long as none come to mind, television newswomen who are already juggling motherhood and careers will have another tricky balancing act: how to be mothers and still be considered first-rate reporters. In that, Connie Chung and Meredith Vieira *are valuable examples of what not to do.*" [Italics added]

Reference has been made to the differentially greater burden on women in two-career families. The reference related to the usually greater pressure on women to carry a heavier portion of the housekeeping and nurturing responsibilities than males do. To some degree, this is a cultural holdover, and a consequential one, of society's traditional view of male-female divisions of responsibilities. But it still reflects a real struggle over primacy in the two-career family.

The struggle reflects psychological as well as economic elements. On a purely economic basis, the primacy issue ought to be resolvable on the basis of an analysis of which career looks most promising in terms of future success and achievement of material well-being. But on a psychological basis, a decision that the woman's career is more promising is also

---

[20]*New York Times*, Section 2, March 17, 1991, p. H33.

a decision that appears to brand the man's outlook and career a relative, and hence a real, failure. This is a harsh conflict of interest between husband and wife, and many two-career families founder on the rock of whose career has primacy. It is no answer to the problem to say that men should be objective, for too many will not see the issue in that light. What they are more likely to see is a test of the wife's love, loyalty, faith, and confidence. And, sorry to say, it is probably true that many more men expect the support of their wives on this issue than wives expect the support of their husbands. And so, even today, the man's career is likely to have primacy. In this connection, Dipboye notes women managers mentioned the difficulty of integrating their own careers with those of husbands as one of the most serious problems they faced.[21]

The problem of primacy in the two-career family is not limited to the relative burden of housekeeping chores and nurturing. It arises also in connection with relocation. Where one career requires a change in location while the other does not, even a successful resolution of housekeeping and nurturing chores can come apart.

Nepotism, the perception as well as the reality of favoritism unrelated to ability and performance, but rather on the basis of a spousal relationship, is a problem where women (and men) in two-career families work in the same corporate context. The problem is intensified where one of the marriage partners is in a reporting relationship to the other. Performance critiques, job evaluations, decisions on promotion and compensation, job assignments—all of these and more aspects of working relationships become more complicated and subject to divisive and maritally damaging tensions in two-career families where the dual careers are juxtaposed.

Even when there is no favoritism, there is a strong tendency by other people in the workplace to attribute advancement of one spouse by the other to nepotism rather than to ability and performance. And the perception of favoritism can unfortunately be almost as damaging to the corporate atmosphere as the reality would be.

Perhaps I reveal now some biases of a septuagenarian person. But it seems to me that there are subtle problems that can arise in connection with work "on the road," such as travel assignments to clients or customers, or to conventions and other out-of-town meetings, where coworkers of

---

[21]Dipboye, "Problems and Progress of Women in Management," p. 136.

opposite sex are thrown together away from home for days at a time. All their time is not devoted to work. There are some social elements built into the shared time, such as dinner in the hotel dining room or elsewhere. I neither believe nor suggest that, given opportunity, inclination follows automatically. But opportunity does give ground for temptation, and temptation can condition inclination. And an integral part of the problem noted now is the attitude of the spouse of one or both of the coworkers who are on the road. To what degree and with what frequency are spousal relationships poisoned by suspicions? I don't think any evidence is available as an answer. On the other hand, I do think the point has some substance and warrants thought by executives who seek the most constructive ways of employing the talents of executives of both sexes. By way of example, the *New York Times,* in an article entitled "Curbing Sexual Harassment in the Legal World," observed that, while few suggest that sexual harassment is particularly prevalent among lawyers, "several characteristics of the legal world have aggravated the problem there. They include *long hours, frequent travel,* the autonomy of law partners, the entry of large numbers of women at junior levels. . . . "[22] (Italics added)

Data exist to support the point that the problems discussed above are significant, especially those relating to motherhood, child-rearing, and primacy in two-career families. *Fortune* analyzed the career paths of men and women who received M.B.A.s in 1976 from 17 of our nation's most selective B-schools.[23] Ten years after graduation

> Significantly more women than men . . . dropped off the management track. . . . [T]hey left positions where they either managed other people or were clearly on their way to doing so. Fully 30% of the 1,039 women from the class of 1976 reported they are either self-employed or unemployed, or they listed no occupation. Men bailed out too, but the percentage is much smaller. Some 21% of the 4,255 men listed either self-employment or no occupation.. Even those numbers probably understate the difference. Telephone interviews with a random sample of over 50 of the women in the 30% group indicate that many work only part time out of their homes, or do not work at paying jobs at all. Phone interviews with 50 men chosen at random from the 21% found that 29 are in fact working for companies, 19 are self-employed, and only two are unemployed.[24]

---

[22]*New York Times,* November 9, 1990, p. B5.

[23]Alex Taylor III, "Why Women Managers Are Bailing Out," *Fortune,* August 18, 1986, pp. 16–23.

[24]Ibid., pp. 17–18.

Other research supports *Fortune's* data. A 1985 study of 401 women M.B.A. graduates of the University of Pittsburgh between 1973 and 1982 reported that 34 percent of them had dropped out of the labor force at one time or another. But among men graduates, the percentage was 19.[25] *Fortune* asks,[26] "Why are women dropping out?" and suggests it is because: (1) they think it is harder for them to get ahead than it is for men, so they conclude the climb to the top isn't worth the effort and sacrifice; (2) they suspect they are discriminated against in compensation; (3) they find themselves stifled by organizational rigidities, which make adjustments for motherhood more difficult than parenthood is for men; and (4) they are shunted away from exciting and more important operating assignments into staff positions in purchasing, personnel, and public relations. In the last connection, the *New York Times* reported a lawsuit alleging sexual discrimination by Ms. Nancy O'Mara Ezold against Wolf, Block, Schorr and Solis-Cohen, a prominent Philadelphia law firm. Among other allegations, Ms. Ezold claimed "that she had been told that she could become a partner if she was willing to take over the firm's domestic relations department, an area to which women were traditionally assigned, but that she would never be more than an associate in the litigation department."[27] She alleged further that the firm assigned her to less complex cases and to fewer partners than it did the men, so that she was denied exposure vital to a favorable decision on partnership. Significantly, federal district judge James McGirr Kelly ruled in her favor and held the law firm guilty of sex discrimination in denying her a partnership. While the judge's decision will probably be appealed, the case and its initial outcome seem significant.

Of the several problems facing women on the management career track, *Fortune* expresses the opinion that the major ones involve (1) raising a family and (2) tensions in a two-career family. Mary Anne Devanna in a study of Columbia M.B.A.s from the classes of 1969 through 1972, reported that only 58 percent of the women were married, compared to 73 percent of the men. And Josephine Olsen, a researcher at the University of Pittsburgh, observed that women with a managerial career are less likely to be married and have children than are men.[28] In two-career fam-

---

[25]Ibid., p. 18.
[26]Ibid., pp. 18–19.
[27]*New York Times*, November 30, 1990. p. B12.
[28]Alex Taylor III, "Why Women Managers Are Bailing Out," p. 19.

ilies, *Fortune* notes, the failure of the babysitter to arrive or the unexpected closing of the nursery can create a crisis. Who will stay home and tend to the children? Put differently, whose career is to be primary? Conflicting travel schedules can mean little and harried time together, while job changes and/or relocations are also sources of severe tension.[29]

ARE THERE PSYCHOLOGICAL BARRIERS WOMEN FACE IN SEEKING AND EXERCISING EXECUTIVE POWER?

Nina L. Colwill reviewed the research on the exercise of interpersonal power, noting that sex differences have been represented by two different literatures—one dealing with *power bases or resources,* the other dealing with the *communication of power.*[30]

The major work relating to power bases or resources was done by F.R.P. French and B. Raven, who identified five bases of power: the power to reward; the power to punish; the power of position—which they termed legitimate power; the power arising from special knowledge or expertise; and referent power (i.e., power gained through perceived similarity or attraction). Later, Raven added the power derived from the possession of information sought by others, (i.e., information power). Although French and Raven considered these power bases distinct, I perceive overlaps. For example, legitimate power (i.e., the power of position) has in it the power to punish or reward, which would seem to make the latter two derivative powers. Similarly, information power gives its possessor the power to share or to withhold information, which is surely power to reward or punish. Nonetheless, the identification of power bases is instructive and useful. Subsequently, L.A. Dunn studied perceptions about the appropriateness of reward and punishment as power strategies for women and men, and reported that concrete rewards and coercion are perceived to be masculine modes of influence.[31] Johnson observed that women tend to have different types of power bases than men, and she distinguished three power *dimensions* along which men and women differ:[32]

---

[29]Ibid., p. 21.

[30]Nina L. Colwill, "Men and Women in Organizations: Roles and Status, Stereotypes and Power," in Koziara, Moskow, and Tanner, *Working Women, Past, Present, Future,* pp. 105–106.

[31]Ibid., pp. 105–106.

[32]Ibid., pp. 106–107.

1. Men are more likely to exert *direct* power by openly and overtly issuing orders or requests; women are more likely than men to employ *indirect* power techniques, the goal of which is to conceal the source of influence from the person being influenced.

2. Men are more likely to bargain with *concrete resources* like money, strength, and knowledge in their influence attempts; women tend to employ *personal resources* such as affection or approval that depend upon personal relationships for their maintenance.

3. Men tend to stress their own *competence* when trying to influence others, by drawing attention to their expertise, information, or physical strength; women are more likely to employ *helplessness* to stress their weakness or their incompetence.

If Johnson's schema has any validity, women face serious psychological as well as societal barriers in their pursuit of careers in management, and most particularly when their goal is top management. Of course, we can assume that the behavioral traits noted are not genetic in origin, but the result of many generations of socializing influence to conform to particular patterns. And this assumption draws some support from the existence of powerful personalities of the female sex. In recent history, such dominant, aggressive people as Margaret Thatcher, England's recent prime minister; Golda Meier, Israel's late prime minister; and Indira Gandhi, late assassinated prime minister of India, come to mind. Thatcher was referred to as the Iron Lady, and the others were equally famous for strength of will. In any case, to the degree women have been conditioned to behave in ways that inhibit their successful exercise of power, they need to be aware of that and prepared to adjust to a more masculine mode. But that is not a proposition that all will readily agree upon.

Thus, Sally Helgesen suggested that women create unique, workable organizational structures suited to their behavioral patterns.[33] She says:

> Women, when describing their roles in their organizations, usually referred to themselves as being in the middle of things. Not at the top, but in the center; not reaching down, but reaching out . . . Inseparable from their sense of themselves as being in the middle was the women's notion of being connected to those around them, bound as if by invisible strands or threads. This image of an interrelated structure, built around a strong central point and constructed of radials and orbs, quite naturally made me think of a spider's

[33]Sally Helgesen, *The Female Advantage, Women's Ways of Leadership*, (New York: Doubleday, Currency, 1990), pp. 45–47, 50.

web. . . . Jokingly called the Girl Scouts' "Wheel of Fortune" by Peter Drucker, the wheel actually spins; most management staff jobs are rotated every two or three years . . . there is no up or down. . . . The contrasting models also reveal different notions of what constitutes effective communications. Hierarchy, emphasizing appropriate channels and the chain of command, discourages diffuse or random communications; information is filtered, gathered and sorted as it makes its way to the top. By contrast the web facilitates direct communication, free-flowing and loosely structured by providing points of contact and direct tangents along which to connect.

Helgesen overdoes the rigidity of the hierarchical structure as an inhibitor of communication, and she seems to overlook the emergence of more horizontal and diffuse structures. Further, in her eagerness to decry top-down authority she ignores the possibility of stress in the web structure as individuals perceive themselves as being at or near the periphery. Significantly, she says about her women executives, "Nor are their organizations run as participatory democracies, with everyone contributing in a haphazard way. The women are authorities as much as if they sat at the very top of a hierarchical ladder, but that authority has more subtle ways of manifesting itself."[34]

Helgesen's construct of a circular organizational structure, a web or wheel with a hub and a network radiating outwards, is not uniquely female. James R. Houghton, CEO of Corning, Inc., has explained his organization's structure in these words:

Since 1983, we have been experimenting with ways to make our management structure conform better to our business structure. As a result, Corning is now what we call a "global network." We use the concept of network in the broad way: A network is an interrelated group of businesses with a wide range of ownership structures. Although diverse, these businesses are closely linked.

Over the years our network strategy evolved from our basic businesses, which we visualize as four segments of a wheel: consumer housewares, specialty materials, telecommunications, and laboratory sciences.

Mr. Houghton continued:

We have found that the successful operation of a global management network requires a new mind-set. *A network is egalitarian.* There is no parent

---

[34]Ibid., p. 53.

company. A corporate staff is no more, or less, important than a line organization group. And, being a part of a joint venture is just as important as working at the hub of the network.[35]

Returning to the literature relevant to the communication of power, Colwill noted such subconscious means of communication as verbal (i.e., the language we use); paraverbal (i.e., the way we say the words we use); and nonverbal (i.e., body language, such as posture when standing or sitting, etc.). As an example of paraverbal means, she observes that "men interrupt more than women, and women allow themselves to be interrupted more than men do. Women are also more likely than men to yield, to agree, and to praise; men talk at greater length and make more suggestions."[36]

Once again, we are confronted by psychological as well as social traits that represent barriers on women's path to the executive suite. At this juncture, it appears appropriate to recall the earlier reference to managerial and nonmanagerial women, a reference that suggested that the former possessed the traits characteristic of managerial men. It is implicit that these traits contribute to success in a management career, and hence are desirable. There are subtle degrees involved. As an example, assertiveness is desirable, and aggressiveness can be useful, but bullying would not win votes of approval as a means of successful management. Also, there is an implication that women generally are nonmanagerial in disposition, while men are managerial. Again, there is a matter of degree. After all, there are significant numbers of nonmanagerial men, just as there are numbers of managerial women. The distribution of these traits between the sexes is the important issue; that is, a substantially larger proportion of women are possessors of nonmanagerial traits than in the case of men.

Despite the barriers discussed, there is significant progress compared to earlier times. Heidrick and Struggles, the executive search firm, surveyed women corporate officers in 1980 and 1986. In its 1986 survey, published in 1987, Heidrick and Struggles report that the percentage of women officers who are at the vice presidential level or above increased from one third in 1980 to 80 percent in 1986. And, where a majority held the title of assistant or corporate secretary in 1980, only 10 percent were in those positions in 1986.[37] Progress is also evidenced by the fact that

---

[35]James R. Houghton, *New York Times*, September 24, 1989, Business Section, p. 3.

[36]Nina L. Colwill, "Men and Women in Organizations: Roles and Status, Stereotypes and Power," p. 109.

[37]Heidrick and Struggles, *The Corporate Woman Officer* (Chicago, Ill., 1987), p. 3.

44 percent of the women officers report backgrounds in finance and general management, while 29.1 percent report background in public relations, communications, personnel, sales, and marketing.[38] Overwhelmingly, women advance in their organizations through promotion from within (68.5 percent), with such advancement more marked in nonindustrial organizations (73.2 percent) than in industrial ones (58.6 percent). Advancement through recourse to an executive search firm was more important for women in industrial organizations (12.8 percent) than in nonindustrial ones (7.1 percent). Personal references accounted for advancement to the present position in the cases of 13.9 percent of the women corporate officers.[39] A significantly higher percentage of the women executives reported possession of graduate degrees in 1986 than in 1980 (43.3 percent as against 25 percent).[40]

But having reported the foregoing data, the Heidrick and Struggles survey reveals some heavy personal costs for the women executives. Of the 1986 respondents, 81.5 percent reported making personal sacrifices because of career demands, with 90.5 percent of the highest paid among them ($160,000 plus per annum) reporting personal sacrifices.[41] Listing type of sacrifice made by reported order of importance, we find (1) decision to have children (30.3 percent); (2) success of marriage (17.1 percent); (3) decision to marry (14.5 percent); and (4) effectiveness as a parent (13.1 percent). Of those women executives who had married, 21.3 percent were separated or divorced and not remarried, while 16.7 percent were divorced and remarried—making 38 percent of the total in these two categories. Another 2.8 percent were widowed, with half of them remarried. And 19.4 percent of the women executives were single and never married.[42]

Of the married women executives, 68.3 percent were wed to business executives, or professional men, so that a large group were involved in two-career families.[43] Interestingly, another 11.4 percent were married to retired men. When relocation conflicts arose in the dual-career fam-

---

[38]Ibid., p. 5.
[39]Ibid., p. 6.
[40]Ibid., p. 7.
[41]Ibid., p. 11.
[42]Ibid., p. 9.
[43]Ibid.

ilies, 20.7 percent of the women reported the decision as to primacy was made on the basis of the more highly compensated person's career. Another 15.7 percent decided on the basis of which career seemed to offer the greater long-term potential. In 11.4 percent, the spouses took turns in making the career decisions, while in 8.6 percent a commuting marriage was the arrangement. And in 6.4 percent of the cases, separation or divorce resulted. Significantly, among the most highly compensated women executives ($160,000 plus per annum), only 9.4 percent of them reported a dual-career decision on the basis of the more highly compensated person, while 25 percent reported a commuting marriage.

When asked which criteria were most important to their success, the women executives responded hard work, intelligence, and leadership ability.[44] These responses are almost identical to those of other senior level executives. With respect to satisfaction with their careers, 87.5 percent reported their satisfaction as very high or high; 32.9 percent indicated very high and 54.6 percent indicated high. More than four of five corporate women officers enjoyed counsel and support from mentors (knowledgeable counselors) and sponsors (influential supporters). But 52.6 percent reported that they did not believe networking in professional women's organizations helped advance their careers.[45] Finally, 79.8 percent indicated they believed that such female qualities as intuitiveness, sensitivity, and a preference for cooperation over confrontation are becoming more important as our economy shifts from an industrial to a service emphasis.[46]

WOMEN IN THE BOARDROOM

There is a wide disparity of views as to whether or not progress has been made by women in achieving corporate directorships. In 1987, Dipboye wrote,

> The gains women have made in occupying positions on corporate boards appear even smaller than at the top management levels. Only 367 women, compared with 15,500 men, hold board positions in the top 1,300 public companies in the United States, and among the 6,543 directorships in the Fortune 500,

---

[44]Ibid., p. 13.
[45]Ibid., p. 14.
[46]Ibid., p. 15.

a mere 2.8 percent are occupied by women. . . . The lack of women on boards is not surprising considering that board positions are usually filled from the ranks of senior management in other firms and there are still very few women at the highest levels. Elgart . . . claims that there are qualified women, however, and they have been systematically excluded from directorships. Consequently, corporate boards retain "the historic white male profile that has existed since the days when boards were invented!"[47]

But the 1987 Heidrick and Struggles survey of women executives reported that "substantial gains have been made by responding women officers in the area of outside directorships. Today, more than one fourth of these executives hold board seats in *organizations other than their own,* in contrast to seven of eight who held no such positions six years ago."[48] And the Heidrick and Struggles data for 1987 is strongly supported by its results in 1988 and 1989 (Table 10–1). The 1988 to 1989 results show an increase in one year (1988 to 1989) of women on the corporate boards covered by the survey from 5.7 percent (1988) to 12.7 percent (1989). Note should be taken not only of the greater than doubling of the overall percentage, but also of the appearance of black and Hispanic females, as well as the 40.8 percent increase in the percentage of white women.

The disparity of views is really not a mystery. First, it is undoubtedly still true that a small percentage of corporate directors are women. But, second, that percentage is growing, and will continue to grow as more women move into top management. And I believe that outcome is as inevitable as it is desirable.

Although the trend favoring increasing numbers of women directors appears clear and conclusive, the statistical data emerging from surveys shows substantial variation. Thus, if we compare the results of the Korn/Ferry International Board of Directors Study in 1989 with the data from Heidrick and Struggles, we find the former reporting a far larger percentage of boards with women members. The Korn/Ferry study showed 59.1 percent of the boards as having women members in 1989, up from 45.0 percent in 1985. Parenthetically, it showed 31.6 percent of the boards as having ethnic minority members in 1989, up from 25.4 percent in 1985. Both women and ethnic minority board members were drawn overwhelmingly from academicians, CEOs and COOs of other companies, and the

---

[47]Dipboye, "Problems and Progress of Women in Management," p. 119.

[48]Heidrick and Struggles, *The Corporate Woman Officer,* Chicago, Illinois, December 1986, p. 6.

TABLE 10-1
Director Population by Race and Sex, 1988 and 1989

	Percentage	
Race and Sex	*1988*	*1989*
White males	92.2	82.2
White females	4.9	6.9
Black Males	1.6	2.6
Black females	0.7	3.1
Hispanic males	0.2	0.5
Hispanic females	0.0	2.6
Asian/other males	0.3	2.0
Asian/other females	0.1	0.1

Source: Heidrick and Struggles, *The Corporate Woman Officer,* p. 9. It should be noted that the survey covered board chairmen of the nation's largest industrial and service parent companies listed by *Fortune.* Of 859 chairmen invited to participate, 264 completed questionnaires were received (i.e., a response rate of 30.7 percent). The results may not be an altogether accurate picture of the larger universe because of the response rate.

senior executives of other companies.[49] Perhaps the disparity between the Korn/Ferry and Heidrick and Struggles surveys is attributable to differences in the universes surveyed, as well as in the response rates. Heidrick and Struggles surveyed 859 chairmen (response rate of 30.7 percent [i.e., 264]) of our nation's largest industrial and service companies listed by *Fortune.* Korn/Ferry surveyed 1,000 companies (response rate of 42.6 percent, [i.e., 426]), including the *Fortune* 500, the *Fortune* 100 major service companies, the *Fortune* 50 major banking institutions, 50 major insurance companies, 50 major diversified financial companies, 50 major retailers, 50 major transportation firms, and 150 selected smaller firms.

COMPENSATION ISSUES

Reference has been made to a disparity between the earnings of women and men executives, with the former lagging behind the latter. Reasons put forward to explain the discrepancy include (1) discrimination; (2) the frequency with which women drop out of the work force and interrupt

---

[49]Korn/Ferry International, *Seventeenth Annual Study of Board of Directors,* 1990, pp. 15 and 24.

their careers to have children and to nurture them, as compared with men, so that their relative job effectiveness and productivity are reduced; (3) the allegation that women have lower expectations and aspirations than men, especially with respect to compensation; and (4) where averages are given for broad categories of women and men managers, the data for women are lowered because relatively more of them are newcomers to the ranks of executives and to management positions in previously male-dominated industries and occupations.

The fourth reason is not substantive; that is, it does not go to the heart of the matter. It deals essentially with statistical and computation issues of comparability of data, not with the underlying reasons for differentials in earnings of seemingly comparable male and female managers. The third reason suggests that lower expectations on the part of women facilitate discrimination and their exploitation by employers who deny them the true value of their labor. But the first reason argues that sex differentials in earnings reflect discrimination. And the second reason suggests that there are valid economic and market forces that explain those differentials. Convinced feminists are inclined to dismiss the second reason as rationalization minus merit, while most economists and business executives are inclined to give it weight.

I believe both sides are partly right. Undoubtedly, there is a significant degree of discrimination, although the force of law, court decisions, and changes in social attitudes are diminishing its power. There is also a real economic and market issue of relative value of labor power as between managerial careers differentiated by degree of absence from the job and significant interruption in continuity of employment. Feminists may and do argue that women ought not to suffer a relatively greater burden of such interruptions and absences. And abstract concepts of justice make that argument appealing. But nature dictates that childbirth is uniquely specialized to women by the facts of physiology, and, despite the reality of diminishing discrimination, that fact continues to cause substantial differences between the usual career patterns of men and women managers.

Some comment is called for on the issue of equal pay. There should be no argument if the term means equal compensation for equal output. Where men and women are comparable in job performance, there is no justification, either in economics or morality, for any difference in compensation. Where performance differs, however, a basis exists for a differential in earnings. And this brings us to the concept of equal worth, which is often propounded as a basis for equal pay. The concept of worth gets away from market criteria and introduces value and compensation criteria, which are reminiscent of the medieval notion of the just price. Thus, instead of examining job performance, the proponents of equal worth seek to compare educational backgrounds and other nonperformance related criteria as the basis for compensation decisions.

The concept of equal worth, as just presented, takes us to a never-never land, for it goes beyond the question of whether women M.B.A.s working as C.P.A.s in accounting firms, for example, should earn as much as men so employed. It goes to the question of their earnings relative to men M.B.A.s working in other fields, assuming they are alike in all respects except occupational field. In fact, the concept of equal worth goes far beyond the matter of sex. Should Ph.D.s, male or female, earn the same because they are Ph.D.s, regardless of their field of work (classicists as against nuclear scientists; sociologists as against computer scientists, etc.)? And, sad to say, doctorates in philosophy are not homogeneous with respect to the intellectual rigor required to earn them, nor are the institutions that award them equally rigorous. These are sensitive issues, but well known to academicians who are painfully aware of academia's hen-pecking order. Or why should entertainers and sports figures earn astronomical sums while educators and other presumed producers of social well-being earn much less? In short, equal worth moves away from market forces to abstract notions of social value, and *compensation so decided will reflect the concepts of justice of those individuals with the power of decision.* Nonmarket pricing leads to severe distortions of supply and demand, with consequences we now see revealed in extreme form in the collapsed communist economies of eastern Europe.

These general and conceptual considerations should not obscure the results of a recent survey of salary differences between male and female M.B.A. graduates of 20 leading business schools.[50] *Business Week* magazine surveyed 3,664 of the 1990 M.B.A. graduates. The survey revealed that a female M.B.A. from a top-20 school will receive an average of $54,749 in her first year after graduation, but the average male M.B.A. will receive $61,400 (12 percent more).

Business Week comments that the disparity is not explained away by claiming that women enter lower-paying fields. The magazine adds, "Even when grads are grouped by industry entered, women still show lower start-

---

[50]*Business Week*, October 29, 1990, p. 57.

ing salaries . . . companies and schools generally deny that discrimination accounts for the differences in starting pay. Some recruiters say women M.B.A.s have less work experience and technical training than men. Others argue that women are taking lower-level positions that carry smaller paychecks. The size of the overall discrepancy, however, suggests that there may be a bit of a head-in-the-sand attitude at work here."[51]

Table 10-2 summarizes *Business Week's* findings for the five schools with the largest sex differentials in salaries and bonuses and the five schools with the smallest sex differentials (out of the 20 leading schools surveyed), as well as by industry.[52]

Even a cursory examination of Table 10-2 indicates a complex bundle of forces at work, forces operative in addition to any sex discrimina-

TABLE 10-2
Male and Female M.B.A. Compensation* per Annum after Graduation 1990

By School	Men (dollars)	Women (dollars)	Discrepancy (percentage)
MIT	77,539	58,500	32.5
Virginia	67,397	54,306	24.1
UCLA	62,785	51,147	22.8
Columbia	65,009	54,817	18.6
Rochester	46,521	40,367	15.2
Average	61,400	54,749	12.1
Stanford	80,412	74,925	7.3
Dartmouth	57,393	54,643	5.0
Michigan	54,058	51,702	4.6
Berkeley	54,322	52,934	2.6
Cornell	53,762	54,433	−1.2
By Industry			
Info Systems	50,441	38,950	29.5
Management	58,434	51,445	13.6
Consulting	72,704	66,731	9.0
Marketing	53,134	49,902	6.5
Finance	56,664	54,840	3.3

*Salary plus bonuses.

Source: *Business Week*, October 29, 1990, p. 57.

[51]Ibid., p. 57.
[52]Ibid., p. 57.

tion. For one thing, we have the great disparity in salaries and bonuses by institution, with the range of variation much greater for men than for women. Thus, for men, Stanford M.B.A.s received $80,412 while Rochester M.B.A.s received only $46,521, a differential of 72.9 percent in favor of Stanford. For women, the range of variation was from $74,925 at Stanford to $40,367 at Rochester, a differential of 85.6 percent. Why should the *internal* variation for women be relatively so much greater than for men? Further, and recognizing the magnified impact on an average of extreme variants at the ends of a distribution, let us see what happens when the two extreme outlier institutions (Stanford and Rochester) are removed. When that is done, the range of variation for men goes from $77,539 at MIT to $53,762 at Cornell, a differential of 44.2 percent. And the range of variation for women goes from $58,500 at MIT to $51,147 at UCLA, a differential of 14.4 percent. Note that the internal range of variation for women is now not only smaller than for men, but much smaller (14.4 percent against 44.2 percent). *Observe also that Stanford M.B.A.s who are women received salaries and bonuses of $74,925, a sum surpassed only by male M.B.A. graduates of Stanford and MIT.* Why were women M.B.A. graduates of Stanford deemed to be worth so much more than male M.B.A. graduates of 18 leading B-schools (the exceptions being only Stanford and MIT)? Finally *Business Week*'s averages are affected greatly by the huge disparity between male and female M.B.A. salaries and bonuses at one institution (i.e., MIT). None of what is said is believed or intended to disprove the existence of some degree of discrimination. What is intended is a sense of skepticism as to the degree of the disease, or the simplistic ease with which the data is taken as indicating more than it probably does.

I checked *Business Week*'s survey results against those for men and women baccalaureate graduates of the undergraduate college of the Leonard N. Stern School of Business at New York University, a leading institution for which data were readily available to me. According to the school's placement office, of the some 400 graduates per year in 1989 and 1990, there were no differences, overall or by field, in the salaries received by men and women. There were differences, for both men and women, by field, ranging from 1990 average salaries of $32,000 in accounting to $28,500 in management and marketing. In 1989, the top salaries were also in accounting ($31,000) and the lowest in marketing ($27,500). In 1989, management salaries amounted to $27,800.

If sex differentials based on discrimination are prevalent and persistent, then why does it not show up in the baccalaureate data? Does something happen in the five or more years between receipt of the baccalaureate and receipt of the M.B.A. that affects the outcome? Do prospective employers perceive a significantly greater likelihood that the M.B.A. women recipients will drop out of the job market in the coming 5 to 10 years and thereby be more costly to train relative to continued job performance than men M.B.A. graduates?

The questions are complex. The available data are still inconclusive. And consequently, the answers are very difficult to come by.

ENTREPRENEURSHIP

Note has been taken of the tendency for a significant proportion of managerial women to drop out of jobs in large corporations.[53] While some of these women withdraw entirely from the labor force to devote themselves to their children, increasing numbers decide to become self-employed, frequently as part-timers, working from their homes. According to *Fortune* magazine, the areas of work most favored by these women are consulting, retail sales, and educational services, followed closely by public relations, real estate, and advertising.[54] Today, the existence of computer networks offering access to home-based PCs and modems provides the technical data processing and communications ability to enlarge the capacity of the self-employed woman to offer service. It is worth noting that the number of firms owned by women has risen significantly since 1982. A recent report from the U.S. Census Bureau[55] revealed that firms owned by women increased 57 percent from 1982 to 1987 (from 2.6 million to 4.1 million). And the receipts of these firms grew from $98.3 billion to $278.1 billion. While part of the increase can be attributed to a change in Internal Revenue Service regulations that gave tax advantages to business firms filing as subchapter S corporations,[56] there can be no doubt that a substantial part of the growth reflects real expansion in the number of women owned firms.

---

[53]Alex Taylor III, "Why Women Managers Are Bailing Out," p. 19.

[54]Ibid., p. 19.

[55]*Deloitte and Touche Review*, December 17, 1990, (90/26), p. 2.

[56]Subchapter S corporations avoid the double taxation involved in the corporate income tax. They are closely held firms and are allowed to pass corporate net income through directly to the owners. In that respect, they are treated for tax purposes in a way similar to the treatment accorded to partnerships.

But these women are not typical entrepreneurs: the founders of businesses that employ other people and expand as they experience success. Of course, some do found such enterprises, and some are established from the start as full-time entities. But, at least in the present, a very large proportion are part-time and home based. It is worth observing that in the full-time business enterprise, the woman executive-owner has maximum flexibility to decide her own priorities between job-related and home-related work.

The essential point is that self-employment is one important way that managerial women take their fate into their own hands. If corporate United States wants to keep these women with them, then greater efforts will have to be made to accommodate the profound desire for motherhood and child care. And that means that chief executives, and their colleagues in corporate top management, will have to think creatively and spend the money required to arrange leaves of absence, child care, flexible work hours, flexible work locations, and so on.

It is heartening that some CEOs and their top managers are already acting, especially in the area of child care. Thus, IBM announced that it "would spend $3 million in 1991 to build five child-care centers near its offices and plants around the country to serve 530 preschool children. It said it would spend an additional $500,000 in communities that have large populations of I.B.M. workers to improve existing daycare centers and to recruit and train people who care for children in their homes.[57]

Another illustration is provided by Tenneco Inc. In 1988, James L. Ketelsen, Tenneco's CEO, established eight advisory councils composed entirely of women, a central one at the Houston headquarters and the others as satellites at each corporate division. The mission of the councils was to help him promote women in the organization.[58] Since coming into existence, the councils have suggested, and Tenneco has implemented, bonus plans that penalize male managers who fail to promote women; benefits plans designed to meet women's needs; and networking gatherings attended by Mr. Ketelsen, Tenneco's division chiefs, and as many as 200 Tenneco women. Before the introduction of the councils, only 10 women were found in Tenneco's upper management. Today, there are 30. Other corporations with active programs to promote women into upper management levels include Dow Chemical, Ryder Systems, Honeywell, Equitable Life As-

---

[57]*New York Times*, December 12, 1990, p. A20.
[58]*New York Times*, December 6, 1990, p. F25.

surance, and Polaroid. In all these firms, substantial budgets are provided for meetings and research. All are run by high-level women executives, who are treated as business advisors, not as political adversaries.

So significant efforts are underway. And the odds are good that the talent gained and retained by such efforts will prove well worth the cost in energy and money.

CHAPTER 11

WINNING AND KEEPING
EXECUTIVE POWER

SIGNIFICANT TRAITS

Chapters one and two discussed two traits: *leadership* and *psychological maturity*. Leadership is the ability to envision organizational goals and bring people in an organization together in support of those goals, so that the corporate entity becomes more than the sum of its individual parts and is magnified in purpose and strength. Of course, leadership so defined is inherently neither democratic and participative nor authoritarian and dictatorial with respect to decision making. So detestable a figure as Adolf Hitler aroused the admiration and ardent support of multitudes, just as his great wartime opponents in the democracies did; Franklin Delano Roosevelt, Winston Churchill, and Charles de Gaulle. So other traits are also significant.

Psychological maturity is vital to a sense of confidence, which makes an executive comfortable with strong colleagues who feel free to express contrary opinions and to argue in support of those opinions. A psychologically mature executive will be less likely to be corrupted by the possession of power—less likely to become authoritarian and dictatorial. And the organization led by such an executive will be less likely to make judgmental mistakes, or if mistakes are made, less likely to persist in them to the point of producing organizational catastrophe.

Without any intent of indicating order of significance, other traits needing note are (1) heart (i.e., courage, perhaps stubbornness); (2) competence; (3) integrity; (4) intelligence; (5) health (i.e., physical fitness, which enables hard work); (6) foresight; (7) willingness and ability to listen (i.e., to hear and to understand what other people are saying, even when it is contrary to one's own opinion); (8) sensitivity to the feelings and reactions of others; (9) desire and ability to communicate, rather than simply to issue orders; (10) ability to relax and not to be *unduly* worried and stressed by the problems that are part of any leader's position; to maintain a sense of calm under pressure, which transmits a sense of confidence to colleagues and prevents panic; (11) pragmatism (i.e., an ability to concentrate on the things one can affect and avoid dissipating energy and time on the things beyond one's power); and (12) ego, which is a sense of self-respect that identifies oneself with one's organization and seeks self-satisfaction through the achievements of the organization, rather than through the exercise of power over other human beings.

The foregoing is an imposing list of traits. If found combined in a single individual, we would be looking at a superman or superwoman. The odds imposed by reality suggest we are not likely to find any executive possessing all the traits noted. But some are essential to success, at least as I see success. These most important traits are leadership; psychological maturity; character; courage; competence (of which intelligence is no doubt an ingredient); foresight; health; and ego. Perhaps a few additional words about courage are appropriate. Under this rubric I embrace ambition, the desire to succeed and the stamina to persist in the face of setbacks.

Some additional words about character are also called for, especially since it is so often true that scoundrels achieve executive power and outstanding success. So it was that Ivan Boesky several years ago delivered a commencement talk at a major western university and extolled the virtue of greed. Indeed, many people view the decade of the '80s as the quintessential era of greed and self-seeking materiality. Whether true or not, it is the period that produced a national frenzy of LBOs, mergers, and acquisitions. It is also the period that witnessed the application of RICO (the Racketeer Influenced and Corrupt Organizations Law) to white-collar crime, an application that brought down Ivan Boesky; Michael Milken; Drexel, Burnham, Lambert; and made a shambles of the junk bond market and many of Wall Street's high flyers. No doubt I reveal a personal bias here, but it is one I hold strongly and without apology. I am convinced that integrity is vital to true leadership and the correct exercise of executive power. It is not a matter of Leo Durocher's infamous dictum that "nice guys finish last." It is a matter of having and leaving a good name, of having a reputation for honesty and honor. And that is something society still holds high, and properly so.

The other traits are desirable, but do not seem to possess the same degree of importance. Thus, there are successful executives who are notorious for being arrogant, insensitive, dictatorial, impatient, disinterested in others' opinions, and generally nasty of temperament. Anyone interested in examples can find them in the periodic publication by *Fortune* of the "toughest bosses in America."[1] They may be disliked and even feared by subordinates, but they have achieved and do hold executive power, and they have been successful.

WHAT PREPARATION, IF ANY, IS IMPORTANT?

We noted that competence and intelligence are two important traits contributing to getting and keeping executive power. But intelligence is transmuted into competence through learning, both from formal education and life experience. Allen E. Murray, chief executive of the Mobil Corporation, certainly had this in mind when he spoke at the Leonard N. Stern School of Business Graduate Division of New York University, saying:

> I received my business administration degree at night from NYU while working for Mobil during the day. I've always been good with numbers, and I think most of the successful CEOs I know are numbers-oriented people. I was also able to take about a year of law school at night which helped me in later years when I was negotiating for the company. Although my formal education was not all that extensive, what I learned in my many different jobs with Mobil gave me a wide background in planning, accounting, manufacturing and marketing. One of the real strengths of Mobil is its career development process, and I have been the beneficiary of a system that puts talented people in jobs of increasing responsibility and diversity. These jobs have made me a good problem solver, a good manager and a good communicator.[2]

Mr. Murray's comments are certainly consistent with the results of a *Fortune* 1985 survey of the chief executives of the 500 largest industrial

---

[1]Steven Flax, "The Toughest Bosses in America," *Fortune*, August 6, 1984, pp. 18–23; and Hugh D. Menzies, "The Ten Toughest Bosses," *Fortune*, April 21, 1980, pp. 62–72.

[2]Notes for remarks at Graduate Division, Leonard N. Stern School of Business, NYU, January 8, 1987.

and 500 largest service companies.[3] Five hundred twelve CEOs responded to the survey anonymously, and *Fortune* compared its information with data on U.S. CEOs provided by earlier studies for 1900, 1925, and 1950, and reported in Mabel Newcomer's *The Big Business Executive* in 1955. Using the Newcomer findings as a model, *Fortune* had also done a survey of CEOs in 1976, so that its 1986 report provided data for 1900, 1925, 1950, 1976, and 1986.

The most striking trend over the eight and a half decades is the powerful push to higher education and advanced degrees by chief executives. Thus, in 1900, fully 60 percent of the CEOs were only grade school or high school graduates, while some 10 percent attended college, about 20 percent were college graduates, and under 10 percent indicated postgraduate study. In 1986, in sharp contrast, the picture was more than simply reversed. Then, fully 60 percent indicated post-graduate study, 30 percent were college graduates, about 7 percent attended college, and a minuscule 3 percent had no more than a grade school or high school diploma.[4] It is no overstatement to say that a college education, coupled with postgraduate study, is a major element today in preparing oneself for the chief executive's position.

Allen E. Murray's references to a facility with numbers and some exposure to law are also highly significant, and strongly supported by the results of the *Fortune* survey. Thus, 74.8 percent of the 512 respondent CEOs to the 1985 survey reported undergraduate majors in business (33.3 percent); engineering (24.0 percent); and economics (17.5 percent); while 71.1 percent reported graduate study in those fields (56.3 percent in business; 10.8 percent in engineering; and 4.6 percent in economics). And an imposing additional 21.4 percent reported graduate study in law.[5]

A person would be seriously misled if he or she concluded from the foregoing that formal education and higher degrees are the passports to the executive suite. After all, there are a multitude who possess those credentials and who are not chief executives. In short, *they are facilitating qualifications, not guarantees.* For actual achievement, these credentials need to be buttressed by a life-long willingness to learn from experience, as well as by possession of a critical mass of the key traits

---

[3]Maggie McComas, "Atop the Fortune 500: A Survey of the CEOs," *Fortune*, April 28, 1986, p. 26.
[4]Ibid., p. 31.
[5]Ibid.

presented earlier. And, it must never be forgotten, a person with the requisite traits and the desire to learn can overcome the liability of little formal education and still succeed in achieving executive status and power.

IS INFLUENCE IMPORTANT?

A substantial population is convinced that success comes largely from connections and influence, and only secondarily from the traits and preparation already discussed. I am neither so foolhardy nor naive as to argue that no benefit can accrue from knowing influential people and having them well disposed and willing to support one's career. But I do argue strongly that career gains based on preferential treatment unsupported by competence in performance will be of short duration.

When asked to comment on this question, Allen E. Murray said, "I had no 'connections' when I started with the company. But as I moved along in the organization, I was always able to get along with everyone. I was able to 'read' my bosses and anticipate their needs and make them look good. In that sense, a satisfied supervisor can be your best 'connection.' It was for me!"[6]

Mr. Murray makes an important point. Doing a good job won him the support of his supervisors, who were his mentors and became his sponsors for further advancement. Of course, this is not universally true. Some supervisors seek to expropriate the credit for a subordinate's good work, and even to deny the latter the advancement due. But I believe such behavior is eventually revealed and self-defeating for the perpetrator, especially in an open society with free labor markets characterized by a high degree of mobility.

This last point brings me to the present "influence" of executive search firms. They have become important movers of people in the rarified atmosphere of executive search and placement, and make it easier for disenchanted executives below the CEO level and those seeking CEOs to find each other. In a story entitled "The New Headhunters; Recruiters are now the king-makers of corporate America," *Business Week* magazine listed these ten executive search firms as the leaders in the field: Korn/Ferry International; Russell Reynolds; Spencer Stuart; Heidrick and Struggles;

[6]Allen E. Murray.

Boyden International; Peat Marwick; Paul R. Ray; Ward Howell; Jackson and Coker; and Nordeman Grimm.[7] But the first four were dominant, showing combined 1988 revenues of $319.2 million, while the remaining six showed combined revenues of $115.3 million. And, if we split the group into the top five and bottom five, by shifting Boyden International, then the top group showed $353.8 million while the bottom group showed $80.7 million, or a more than four-to-one revenue ratio in favor of the top five. *Business Week* observes: "In a day when executives are often traded as if they were baseball cards, headhunters have emerged as modern-day power brokers, the gurus of the corporate world. Executives confide in them, seek their advice, and willingly answer their queries. After all, headhunters often stand between the most coveted jobs and the people who want them. It is a business that, as one observer notes, 'helps shake and move the movers and shakers and provide the mobility to the upwardly mobile.' "

WHAT IS THE RELATIVE IMPORTANCE OF ENTREPRENEURIAL AND MANAGERIAL SKILL?

The question's answer resides in an organization's stage of development and economic environment. By definition, organizations are founded by entrepreneurs, people who are willing to take risks and enjoy the excitement and challenge of so doing. They are typically strong in their opinions and happier giving orders than taking them. They are uncomfortable under the control of others and seek the power to control their own destiny. They are also inclined to be workaholics and are often slaves to their ambitious dreams.

These traits are critical to a new enterprise, where organizational structure is yet largely unformed and interpersonal relationships casual. Technical competence in producing and selling product or service outweighs issues of long-run strategy and internal decision making. The founder entrepreneur is usually everywhere and is the key to all decisions. But as success is achieved and the organization grows, long-run strategy and internal decision making become more pressing. The entrepreneur's span of control is outgrown, and the organization needs structure of some sort

---

[7]*Business Week*, February 6, 1989, p. 67.

to preserve a sense of direction, a sense of common goals. It needs a mechanism that enables it to determine priorities, make decisions, and implement those decisions. In short, it requires management, and the skills of the manager. At that stage, the traits discussed earlier in this chapter become critical to continued success.

Unfortunately, possessors of entrepreneurial skills are often not able to make the transition to management. Perhaps the classic case is Steven Jobs, who founded and built Apple Computer. His case is unusual because he recognized his problem and undertook to solve it by recruiting John Sculley of Pepsico to manage Apple. But then, Jobs' entrepreneurial traits collided with Sculley's sense of what the organization required. And Jobs left Apple, his creation, to found a new computer firm, Next, Inc. Sculley took the leadership of Apple and led it to new heights of growth and success, at least in the half dozen or so years following Jobs' departure.

Eric G. Flamholtz, Professor of Human Resource Management and Industrial Relations at the Graduate School of Management, University of California, Los Angeles, made some perceptive observations about the problems of entrepreneur CEOs whose organizations have grown beyond one person control. Speaking of entrepreneurial characteristics, he said:[8]

> The most important of these characteristics, from the standpoint of making organizational transitions, is the entrepreneurial CEO's desire for things to be done his or her way—that is, the desire for control. . . . During the early stages of organizational growth, the typical attributes of an entrepreneurial CEO are beneficial and necessary. . . . Many consequences of an entrepreneurial CEO's desire for control, however, are less favorable during the latter stages of a company's development. Specifically, both the CEO and the organization's staff may have become used to the idea that almost every issue, whether major or not, . . . be brought to the CEO's attention for a decision or final approval. More insidiously, if the CEO has not been extremely careful, an entire organization may have inadvertently been built on people who are weaker than the CEO. . . . This means that the CEO has not been able to increase the company's capabilities beyond his or her own . . . personal skills. Such a situation puts limits on the organization's capacity to grow and develop. . . . Some CEOs . . . consciously want to retain control and therefore do not want to hire people who are better than they are at any particular task. Others are afraid that if they hire someone

---

[8]E. G. Flamholtz *How to Make the Transition from an Entrepreneurship to a Professionally Managed Firm* (San Francisco: Josey-Bass, 1986), pp. 205–6.

to perform a task that they cannot do themselves, they will become too dependent on that person.

Once he has brought the organization to maturity, the entrepreneurial CEO has four alternative possibilities according to Flamholtz: (1) do nothing; (2) sell out and start a new enterprise; (3) hire a professional manager to run the business, while he becomes chairman; or (4) change his personal behavior to accord with the skills now required to run the organization. Flamholtz believes the first alternative is an invitation to organizational ruin. The second one is viable but, in terms of my experience, not usually attractive to a founder. Instead, efforts may be made to find successors in the founder's family. When this is unavailing, then a sale or possibly a merger become more attractive. The third alternative requires a CEO who is willing to hire a strong professional manager and is then able to let him "run the show." But, as Flamholtz points out, this course cost Steve Jobs his control over Apple Computer. The fourth alternative is the most desirable one, but this means, according to Flamholtz, that the CEO will see his proper role as being "concerned with the future direction of the enterprise and its long-term objectives, to be a strategic leader and a role model for others, and finally, to focus on the culture of the enterprise. Each aspect of the CEO's new role requires the ability to think abstractly or conceptually about the business."[9]

Flamholtz's observations create the impression, perhaps inadvertently, that the mature organization no longer has need for entrepreneurial skills, a notion with which Allen E. Murray disagrees. He believes the CEO of a large organization needs both entrepreneurial and managerial skills to be successful, with one or the other set of skills being called upon by changes in the organization's environment. He puts his opinion in these words:[10]

> [m]ost senior managers in Mobil are entrepreneurs because our business of finding oil, producing it and getting it to market profitably is built on a great deal of risk. It's hard for me to name an effective manager in our organization who is not an entrepreneur and vice versa. Now, . . . does the organization require more of one than another at different stages in its development? I'd have to say that the effective senior manager seeking to be-

---

[9]Ibid., p. 8.
[10]Allen E. Murray.

come a CEO has to have the flexibility of style and intelligence to know when the organization needs more of the risk-taking, idea-generating style of the classic entrepreneur or the solid leadership mode of the classic good manager. I believe that good leaders have both.

EXECUTIVE POWER AND THE EXECUTIVE'S "HOLD" ON HIS OR HER JOB

Al Neuharth, founder of *USA Today* and former chief executive of the Gannett newspaper empire, tells of his campaign to unseat his predecessor, Paul Miller. In his autobiographical *Confessions of an SOB*, he says:[11]

> The time had come in my Gannett career to let the boss know that a new generation of leadership was ready to take over. That's not an easy job. And I didn't relish it. But that's the price of progress. Try it only if you're sure to win. Paul Miller had hired me at Gannett. Initially, he had helped me. When I became heir-apparent, he began harassing me. Now he was hounding me. For the past three years as president, I was really running the company. But as CEO Miller continued to take most of the credit. It was clear he would hang on by his fingernails as long as the Lord and the board allowed. I was determined not to be around if that happened. He was approaching sixty-seven. I was nearly forty-nine. . . . I had made several moves before 1973 to prepare Miller and me for my succeeding him as CEO. I had hoped to do it in an orderly, planned cooperative way. That would have been better for him, for me, and for the company. But each time I took a step forward, he dug in his heels and tried to push me back.

Neuharth's account encapsulates the experiences of many other CEOs and their prospective successors. A significant proportion of the former try to hang on, while the latter find "waiting in the wings" tiresome, frustrating, and eventually unbearable. A substantial degree of tension can develop between CEO and COO in such cases, especially when the COO has the title president and appears to be the heir-apparent. Of course, we are speaking here of the CEO's retirement, not of his earlier removal by the board. The problem centers in the quite common reluctance of the chief executive to surrender the power and perquisites of the position. Another

---

[11]Al Neuharth *Confessions of an SOB*, (New York: Doubleday, 1989), pp. 71–72.

aspect of the CEO's attempt to hold on is an understandable shrinking back from retirement because it means withdrawal from the most active and vital phase of one's life, with all the excitement and challenge inherent in life during those prime years, to a quieter, less demanding phase where there is too much time to contemplate one's mortality. And then there are such seemingly small matters as the loss of the staff that took care of a multitude of the CEO's personal chores, in addition to their corporate duties. I speak of such things as reconciling the CEO's personal checkbook, taking his or her car for service, making travel arrangements, handling personal correspondence, and so on. It may seem ridiculous to the uninitiated, but I know numbers of high-powered former CEOs whose most common complaint is the burdensomeness of these chores. After a couple of decades of becoming accustomed to a retinue of assistants, whether small or large, one is shocked to wake one morning and realize they are gone.

It is true that a number of corporations provide office and secretarial support for retired CEOs, especially when the former CEO continues as a member of the board. But that is not always the case, and, even when it is, the continued presence of a former chief executive can be annoying to the new chief. And, if the retired CEO doesn't recognize his new place and interferes, his successor is almost certain to feel challenged and seek his complete removal.

While Al Neuharth, when his time came to retire, acted contrary to Paul Miller and stepped down gracefully and completely,[12] other CEOs have behaved like Miller. Examples are easy to find: for example, William Paley in CBS and Harold Geneen in ITT.[13] If we shift from retirement situations to hostile takeovers, we find ourselves with other illustrations of CEOs fighting to retain power, perquisites, and prestige: for example, Ross Johnson of RJR Nabisco; Frank Lorenzo, who having swallowed Continental Airlines, Peoples Express, and Eastern Airlines, was finally undone and forced out of the airline industry as a consequence of the disastrous Eastern Airlines strike and bankruptcy; and most recently, Charles E. Exley, Jr.'s fight to keep NCR (formerly National Cash Register) from being taken over by AT & T.[14] As a matter of personal experience, I recall well the strong fight put up in 1988 by Edward (Ned)

---

[12]Ibid., p. 351.

[13]Robert J. Schoenberg, *Geneen*, (New York: W. W. Norton and Co., 1985), p. 17–18.

[14]*New York Times*, December 14, 1990, p. C5.

Evans, former CEO of Macmillan, Inc., to keep the company from being taken over by Robert Maxwell. I also recall the efforts made by Raymond Hagel, Evans' predecessor as Macmillan's chief executive, to hold off Evans' challenge in 1980. As a director and member of the board's independent committee in both situations, I personally and intensely experienced the need to place the shareholders' interest first.

In the final analysis, no matter how desperately a chief executive seeks to hold on, the board has and will eventually exercise the power to retire or remove him. Efforts may be made to obscure or sugarcoat the reality of the divorce, and there may be "rich" going-away settlements, but retired is finally retired, and out is finally out.

IS THE VIEW FROM THE TOP WORTH THE EFFORT OF THE CLIMB?

The question is probably rhetorical, especially in light of the foregoing discussion of chief executive efforts to hold on to office and power. If the view wasn't worth the effort, there wouldn't be such fighting to preserve position on the perch. In a sense, the answer resides in the traits important to winning executive office, for people possessing those traits have the ambition and drive to want power, and, having gained it, to keep it. Nor is it only a matter of power and perks, important though they are. It is also a matter of status and prestige, of social recognition and honor, and in many instances, I suspect, of feeling that one has been privileged to be of important service to both organization and community.

Allen E. Murray summed it up in these words: "I never looked for the next job. This was true for about the first 25 years of my career at Mobil. Then along about ten years ago, it became clear that I was on an ever-narrowing path. I did a lot of soul searching and asked myself if progressing higher would be worth the sacrifice to my family. After discussions with them, I concluded that I had their support, and I can tell you now that the view from the top for me has been worth the effort. It's exhilarating to head up an exciting organization like Mobil, and it's an honor to lead people of the caliber of Mobil employees."[15]

---

[15]Allen E. Murray.

I would add only that Allen Murray is a self-made man, who rode the New York subway while earning his baccalaureate at night at NYU's business school. He is plain in manner and direct in speech. He means what he says, and says what he means. So his statement about the worth of the climb to the top, because of what it means beyond power and perquisites, is meaningful. And I believe it is equally meaningful for many other chief executives. This statement does not belittle position, power, and perks. But it does put them into better perspective and balance.

CHAPTER 12

CONCLUSION

The chief executive occupies the position of organizational leader, and from it, he or she derives the authority to give orders to and direct the activities of other people. Inherent in the position is also the power to determine priorities and allocate material as well as human resources. But authority of position will not survive, especially in organizations operating in the context of a democratic society, unless it is accompanied by authority of leadership, that is, the influence granted voluntarily to one who has won the admiration, respect, allegiance, and loyalty of those thereby prepared to follow his or her lead. Successful CEOs have those core qualities of personality and character that are the necessary ingredients of leadership (intelligence, initiative, desire to lead, strength, resoluteness, foresight, and competence). These characteristics may be wedded to others, like integrity and sensitivity, so the chief executive provides leadership for ends that are ethical and good, rather than those that are unethical and bad. But it is an unfortunate fact that leadership may be exercised for ends either magnificent or mean.

A chief executive can exercise power in the context of various organizational structures, and over a spectrum of decision-making and decision-implementing styles. Organizational structures may be hierarchical and pyramidal, decentralized and horizontal, or in the form of a circular network radiating outward from a central hub. Decisional styles may range from the authoritarian, dictatorial rule of a single person to the consensual, participative mode in which an executive seeks to share power. But, whatever the structure and the style, decisional responsibility rests finally with the chief executive. This is especially true in an adverse economic climate, when hard, painful decisions are necessary. And such a climate is the ultimate testing ground of a chief executive's leadership qualities.

Further, such a climate makes it clear that the chief executive's *leadership* is indivisible, as is his or her responsibility.

In Chapter Two, I argued that a chief executive's preferences with regard to organizational structure and decisional style would reflect, to a major degree, his or her psychological maturity, or sense of inner security and confidence. A psychologically mature CEO conveys an air of calm sureness of purpose and an ability to listen to and accept the advice of other people; to weigh his or her own initial judgment alongside other judgments, and to do so objectively. I argued further that such a chief executive would be disposed to favor participative organizational structures and decisional styles over hierarchically rigid and authoritarian ones. Once again, the sharing of decisional power does not mean its abdication, for the latter carries within itself the seeds of organizational chaos, disarray, and inability to overcome the pressures of adverse conditions. In fact, if as leader, the CEO shares power through a horizontal structure and participative decisional style, then his or her qualities of leadership are more severely tested. A diffusion of authority of position demands much more of authority of leadership. And here we face a haunting question: Can authority of position change a CEO's personality and behavior? In Chapter Two, we speculated that it could, because all power is eventually corrupting and is likely to reduce its possessor's sensitivity to and tolerance of the opinions of other people. Yet authority of leadership usually reflects such sensitivity. This does not imply compassion. Saddam Hussein held sway over the hearts and minds of millions of Arabs, despite his penchant for terror and his lack of humane sensibilities. He was clearly tuned into their emotions, and that sensitivity enabled him to lead them to terrible ends.

While the CEO's responsibility for leadership is indivisible, his exercise of power is constrained not only by his degree of psychological maturity, but also by the existence of other important centers of power, both internal and external to the organization. Internally, the CEO must contend with the board of directors, who primarily represent shareholder interests, but in recent years also increasingly reflect stakeholder interests. Internal also are the other members of management and the broader mass of employees, especially when they are represented by unions. Externally, the CEO faces the various levels of government and their multitudinous regulations, as well as the pressures emanating from the media and its influence on public opinion and stock market values.

The business of being boss places on the executive basic responsibility for the ethicality of the organization's behavior and for its corporate culture. Moral qualities are critical with respect to organizational behavior vis-à-vis employees, customers, suppliers, government regulations, the admission of women into the upper echelons of management, and even the handling of takeover attempts.

In Chapter Three, I argued that the traditional view of the board of directors as a compliant tool of the chief executive was no longer accurate, even though the CEO is usually able to exercise great power over the board's decisions, and most especially so when he or she is also chairman of the board. Increased litigation and exposure to personal liability have awakened today's outside board directors from their former torpor and lethargy. Through more and increasingly active board committees, such as executive, audit, and compensation, outside directors become better informed about the organization's activities and problems and more active relative to the CEO. But the increased independence of the board does not mean that an adversarial climate between it and the CEO is healthy for the organization, for I believe the opposite to be true.

Cooperation is also the desired condition between CEO and labor. Especially today, when U.S. industry faces severe competitive pressures from abroad, it is of critical importance that labor and management recognize their fundamental mutuality of interest. They must work together to achieve a high quality of product and service at the lowest possible prices. But this is not easy to accomplish. Labor fears loss of jobs, feels insecure, and struggles to guarantee obsolete technologies and methods. Management seeks greater efficiency, resents and fights against labor's efforts to guarantee jobs. An important distinction was made in Chapter Four between guaranteeing jobs and guaranteeing employment. To recognize the distinction and benefit from it, labor must become flexible, and management must be forthcoming in striving to provide a significant measure of protection against the consequences of job losses. Above all else, management should not convey an air of implacable enmity to unionism.

The chief executive, if so disposed, can retire behind protective layers of staff into the recesses of the executive suite, and there seek to insulate himself or herself from other centers of power, and most especially external power like government and the media. But CEOs who take this stance are ill-advised and due, sooner or later, for a rude awakening under adverse circumstances. The intelligent, well-advised chief executive understands that it is ultimately his or her responsibility to deal with other power centers, and, while seeking and employing professional advice and assistance, to prepare for such encounters as time will bring. With respect to government regulation, the CEO does well to accept the basic proposition that it is a proper function of the state to act in behalf of the public welfare and to protect the polity from unscrupulous individuals and organizations who pursue profit through activities damaging to the public and dangerous to the environment. But such acceptance does not include subservience, submission to bureaucracy run wild, or acceptance of the frightened claims of fanatical perfectionists who demand of business and government a total absence of risk, which even nature does not and cannot provide. The pharmaceutical industry provided a rich example of the problems and protections residing in government regulation, and the litigation that is its frequent handmaiden.

Also vexing to the chief executive is the power of the media, which seems so often arrogant, fickle, and self-serving. Cloaked in the garb of seeker of truth and informer to the public, the media seem sensational and titillating, rather than informative. Scandal seems more suited to their taste than careful analyses of complex issues. Quick to invade the privacy of others, the media insist on their right of privacy and privileged protection of sources of information. While condemning covert activities in others, they see nothing wrong in such activity by themselves, as they seek documents and other sources of confidential information. This apparent double standard and conflict of purposes and means aggravates those who attract the attention of the media. Yet history provides a rich roster of reasons supporting the First Amendment and its protection of freedom of the press. And so chief executives are well advised to learn how best to deal with the media, even if this means taking lessons from professionals. The harsh truth is that in any confrontation between media and the CEO, the balance of power is with the former and its agents, for they control the TV camera, the questioning, and the editing of tape and published script. Above all else, the chief executive should be prepared to step forward and face the camera, interviewers (more often hostile than otherwise), and the public. Credibility, both corporate and personal, usually hangs on such an appearance, and credibility is a vital matter.

Profit-seeking corporations, both public and private, are social as well as economic organizations. Like all groups of human beings bound together in a common enterprise and by shared experiences, they develop a culture, a set of behavioral standards or norms. The traits that characterize that culture may be ethical, unethical, or even amoral. But they are usually reflective of the personality and mores of a chief executive, past or present. I have argued in this book that corporate culture is important to an organization's health, and that the CEO has the primary responsibility for influencing that culture. Further, the CEO's responsibility resides mainly in his or her own actions, rather than in words. It is what the CEO does that counts, far more than what he or she says.

I argued further that, while profits can be and often are gained by unethical actions, such behavior is reprehensible and unjustified. This is particularly true in the face of substantial feeling that there is something inherently unworthy and unethical in the pursuit of profit. Of course, profit is the key indicator for resource allocation and priorities in a market system, and attacks on it are attacks on the system itself. Given the collapse of communism and central control of economies, the superiority of capitalism, markets, and the profit motive should be clear. Yet, that is not self-evident to many people, enlarging the importance of ethical behavior by chief executives. I observed that determinations of ethicality are not always simple, that the simple-minded absolutism of fanatical purists is inferior to concepts of proportionalism in deciding good or bad, and that an ethical pragmatism is preferable to ethical absolutism. I also suggested that the widely proclaimed deterioration in ethical standards and behavior in contemporary United States may well be a matter of distorted perception, an insistence that our actual behavior conform more closely with our idealized norms than was true in the past. That perception can make us seem less ethical when, in fact, we have become more so.

Our discussion made reference to Lord Acton's famous dictum that "all power corrupts, but absolute power corrupts absolutely." Given the authority of position inherent in the chief executive's status, he or she can easily succumb to ego-flattering colleagues and surrender to the notion of being possessed of greater insight and wisdom than are the vast majority of other mortals. And the trappings of position and power are seductive, being highly attractive in and of themselves. They are not readily given up by possessor CEOs. I perceived a significant egoistic motivation in chief executives as underlying the empire building and leveraging frenzy of the '80s. Actually, the diversification drive in the decade of the '60s was an earlier manifestation of that motivation, as we observed in Chapter Nine. But it was manifested again in the excessive leveraging and divestiture drive that marked the decade of the 80s. Large egos clashed in that period as some chief executives and their investment and legal counselors sought to unseat other CEOs, while the latter fought to preserve their position and perks. The ready availability of funds from high-yield (junk) bonds made it easy in the excitement of those contests to overvalue businesses, overleverage them, and ultimately threaten them with financial ruin as they were crushed beneath unsustainable levels of debt and interest. CEO judgments of risk became distorted and contributed powerfully to this outcome. The foregoing factors were highlighted in the Fruehauf, Reliance, and RJR Nabisco cases.

Chapter 10 examined the long-term trend for ever-increasing numbers of women to enter the labor force and there seek and find compensated employment in the market economy. That trend has become a torrent, which in recent decades has begun to be reflected in significant numbers of women appearing in corporate board rooms and executive suites. Women are a rich resource in talent and energy. But their increased presence is also associated with substantial debate and some consequential problems.

The problems are found principally in differences in male-female compensation levels, and in difficulties faced mainly by women in reconciling marriage and family roles and responsibilities with the demands of a business career. The latter difficulties may be reflected somewhat in compensation differences, because career breaks and time demands, due to heavier burdens placed on women than on men in connection with household chores and nurturing of children, lessen the market value of the former. While this is inequitable, it reflects physiological fact and continuing social custom. It also appears that the issue of primacy in two-career families places more strain on wives than on husbands. In any event, where women and men are equal in career patterns, ability, and competence, there is no excuse, either economic or moral, for any difference in compensation. And no merit was found in our present review for the argument that so-called equal worth should be the basis for equal compensation.

There is a history of debate over whether women are less suited for management than men. No doubt this reflects long-standing social attitudes viewing women as a weaker, defenseless sex requiring protection by men of moral sensibility. As feminism and the numbers of women in business have advanced, however, these attitudes have been undergoing change. Our examination is skeptical about the proposition that there is an inherent genetic incapacity of women to manage, including managing in top leadership positions. There does appear to be a social conditioning that still encourages men, more than women, to seek and struggle to achieve top management positions. Yet there are managerial women just as there are managerial men, even though they are proportionately fewer in number. But times are changing, as the old cliche says, and I expect that we will find more and more women CEOs and directors in the years ahead.

In any case, today's CEOs should exert every effort to encourage this development because it will enrich our society.

Chapter 11 noted 14 traits as having significance in helping a person win and keep executive power and status. No one individual possesses all the qualities, except for a superman or superwomen. And superpeople are found only in comic strips, animated cartoons, and fantasy films. Among the roster of significant traits are, however, some that seem critical. They are leadership, courage, competence, health (physical energy), foresight, and ego. I also included psychological maturity and character, but those qualities may reflect my personal biases, my perception of the behavioral aspects of a CEO's nature that distinguish organizations possessing superior ethical elements in their corporate culture. I regard ethical CEOs and corporations as more successful than those that achieve greater financial gains through unethical and shady practices. The CEO who commands my respect and admiration is the one who achieves profitability along with organizational sensitivity to stakeholders as well as stockholders. And I do not accept the frequently found idea that influence is the key to managerial advancement. I believe what one knows and is capable of doing counts for more than whom one knows, even though the friendly support of superiors is certainly helpful. Marrying the boss's daughter may gain authority of position in the short run, but will not yield organizational leadership and success in the long run. Taking my cue from Allen Murray, CEO of Mobil Oil, I concluded that the most successful CEOs require entrepreneurial as well as managerial skills. And, finally, I concluded that the view from the executive suite was worth the effort of the climb, because otherwise so many would not make the attempt to gain that prize and then to hold on to its power and perquisites.

So it is at the end, as at the beginning, that I see leadership and the exercise of executive power as key elements in the chief executive's conduct of his business, which is the direction and management of the organization.

INDEX